STUDENT-CENTERED CLASSROOMS

STUDENT-CENTERED CLASSROOMS

Research-Driven and Inclusive Strategies for Classroom Management

EDITED BY JOANNA ALCRUZ
AND MAGGIE BLAIR

ROWMAN & LITTLEFIELD
Lanham • Boulder • New York • London

Published by Rowman & Littlefield
An imprint of The Rowman & Littlefield Publishing Group, Inc.
4501 Forbes Boulevard, Suite 200, Lanham, Maryland 20706
www.rowman.com

86-90 Paul Street, London EC2A 4NE

Copyright © 2022 by Joanna Alcruz and Maggie Blair

All rights reserved. No part of this book may be reproduced in any form or by any electronic or mechanical means, including information storage and retrieval systems, without written permission from the publisher, except by a reviewer who may quote passages in a review.

British Library Cataloguing in Publication Information Available

Library of Congress Cataloging-in-Publication Data

Names: Alcruz, Joanna, editor. | Blair, Maggie, editor.
Title: Student-centered classrooms : research-driven and inclusive strategies for classroom management / edited by Joanna Alcruz and Maggie Blair ; foreword [by] Andrea Honigsfeld.
Description: Lanham, Maryland : Rowman & Littlefield, [2022] | Includes bibliographical references and index. | Summary: "Student-Centered Classrooms presents holistic dimensions of classroom management where teachers are facilitators of learning who aim to foster and support students rather than manage classrooms"— Provided by publisher.
Identifiers: LCCN 2022019307 | ISBN 9781475847642 (Cloth) | ISBN 9781475847659 (Paperback) | ISBN 9781475847666 (epub)
Subjects: LCSH: Classroom management. | Teaching. | Learning. Classification: LCC LB3013 .S87 2022 | DDC 371.102/4—dc23/eng/20220719 LC record available at https://lccn.loc.gov/2022019307

To Joseph, Janek, Julianka, and Karolinka,
who keep me anchored on what matters most.
—Joanna

To my daughter, Alexandra Elizabeth,
who took me on a long, unplanned professional journey.
I am grateful to have had her in my life.
—Maggie

Contents

List of Tables ix

List of Figures xi

Foreword ANDREA HONIGSFELD xiii

Acknowledgments xvii

INTRODUCTION:

Introduction to Student-Centered Classrooms: Research-Driven and Inclusive Strategies for Classroom Management 1
MAGGIE BLAIR AND JOANNA ALCRUZ

CHAPTER 1

Proactive Strategies for Student-Centered Classrooms 9
VICKY GIOUROUKAKIS, FRANCINE WISNEWSKI, AND MATINA STERGIOPOULOS

CHAPTER 2

Whether, When, and How Teachers Can Intervene 47
AUDRA CERRUTO AND RICKEY MORONEY

CHAPTER 3

Applications of Applied Behavioral Analysis to Classroom Management 71
KATHLEEN QUINN, SARAH FARSIJANY, AND JILL SNYDER

CHAPTER 4

Understanding the Role of Emotions in the Classroom   99
TYCE NADRICH, CANDICE R. CRAWFORD, DAVID JULIUS FORD,
HEATHER C. ROBERTSON, AND AMY WEINSTOCK

CHAPTER 5

Integrating Gender Equity into Positive Classroom Culture   135
DONNA CEMPA-DANZIGER, TRICIA KRESS, AND MAUREEN T. WALSH

CHAPTER 6

Technology as a Classroom Management Asset   153
MADELINE CRAIG AND LINDA KRAEMER

Index   179

About the Authors   189

List of Tables

TABLE 1.1:	Teachers' Transitions for Class Activities	14
TABLE 2.1:	The Four Teacher Types	49
TABLE 2.2:	Relationship-Building Activities	53
TABLE 2.3:	Technology Resources to Promote Self-Monitoring Skills	57
TABLE 2.4:	De-Escalation Techniques	60
TABLE 2.5:	Using Technology to Intervene	65
TABLE 3.1:	Antecedent, Behavior, Consequence Overview	76
TABLE 3.2:	Antecedent, Behavior, Consequence, Anecdotal	78
TABLE 3.3:	Interval Recording	79
TABLE 3.4:	Antecedent and Consequent Manipulations	80
TABLE 3.5:	Behavior and Operational Definitions	81
TABLE 3.6:	Examples of Positive Reinforcement	84
TABLE 3.7:	Examples of Punishment and Reinforcement	85
TABLE 3.8:	Types of Prompts	86
TABLE 3.9:	Examples of Replacement Behavior Statements	90
TABLE 3.10:	Classroom Management—Dos and Don'ts	95
TABLE 5.1:	Summary of Terminology Related to Gender and Sexual Orientation	137
TABLE 5.2:	Teacher Suggestions for Promoting Classroom Positivity	148

TABLE 6.1:	Classroom Environment Technology Tools	155
TABLE 6.2:	Home–School Connection Technology Tools	160
TABLE 6.3:	Student-Centered Instructional Technology Tools	166
TABLE 6.4:	Learning Management System (LMS) Tools	171

List of Figures

FIGURE 2.1:   Morning Greetings   52
FIGURE 2.2:   Emotional Thermometer   63
FIGURE 3.1:   The Rug Rules   88

Foreword
Student-Centered Classrooms: Research-Driven and Inclusive Strategies for Classroom Management

ANDREA HONIGSFELD

> *Falling into a pedagogy of compliance that values orderliness over the messiness of complex work means we miss the opportunity to ignite engagement naturally.*
>
> ZARETTA HAMMOND (2021, PARA 4).

WE CANNOT EXPECT CHILDREN to become excited about learning if we are not excited about teaching and learning. That is a simple fact. Let's change the way we interact with our students. Let's excite them. Let's inspire them beyond their imaginations (Peters, 2007, p. 98).

Learning is messy! Classrooms that have high levels of engagement are noisy! Active participation is lively with lots of authentic questions, meaningful conversations, "aha" moments and affirmations, and even interruptions. Compliance, control, and rigid classroom rules—even when co-created with students—are far from being the hallmarks of successful classroom management. It is time to reimagine what shared expectations for authentic learning may look like, sound like, and feel like in our K–12 classrooms! This volume will ignite your imagination and help establish a novel approach in your context.

It has been well established that successful classroom management is invariably tied to student engagement and empowerment. A decade ago, Denti (2012) noted that student empowerment begins with "recognition and encouragement from proactive educators" (p. 8). There is ample empirical and experiential evidence that successful educators are intentional about polishing their craft, establishing a thriving classroom culture, and focusing on students' interest and natural curiosity to learn and grow.

More currently, there is a growing emphasis on creating learning opportunities that honor student ownership, autonomy, and agency (see, for example, Honigsfeld et al., 2021). Thus, deeply understanding students' complex identities and experiences, building meaningful relationships with them, and responding to their academic, social, and linguistic needs must be at the core of any classroom management approach.

The chapters in this volume are well-aligned to this contemporary vision of student engagement. The contributing authors masterfully present a diverse range of approaches to classroom management integrating cutting-edge research and theoretical frameworks with practical applications for the diverse, contemporary classroom. The forthcoming chapters support both novice and experienced educators to further enhance their practice by learning—among many other evidence-based strategies—how to:

- create a student-centered learning environment
- mitigate disruptions or prevent them before they even emerge
- embrace culturally responsive and sustaining teaching practices
- cultivate a collaborative classroom culture that builds on sincere interpersonal relationships
- develop self-monitoring and foster a range of essential social-emotional skills
- integrate technology and other current tools and techniques that ensure high levels of student participation
- implement applied behavior analysis
- connect with families and the larger school community

And there is more—much, much more! The book you are about to read will not only further your understanding of current educational trends but it will also invite you to implement the must-use strategies that unfold on the forthcoming pages. You won't want to miss anything this comprehensive resource has to offer!

References

Denti, L. (2012). *Proactive Classroom Management K–8: A practical guide to empower students and teachers*. Corwin Press.

Hammond, Z. (2015). *Culturally responsive teaching and the brain*. Corwin Press.

Honigsfeld, A., Dove, M. G., Cohan, A., & McDermott Goldman, C. (2022). *From equity insights to action: Critical strategies for teaching multilingual learners.* Corwin Press.

Peters, S. (2007). Capture, inspire, teach! Reflections on high expectations for every learner. In A. M. Blankstein, R. W. Cole, & P. D. Houston (Eds.), *Engaging every learner* (pp. 83–99). Corwin Press.

Acknowledgments

Joanna

I, FIRST AND FOREMOST, thank my husband, Joseph, for his endless support in all my academic endeavors. I thank my children, Janek, Julianka, and Karolinka, who peeked over my shoulder multiple times during this project and motivated me to continue. My sincere appreciation goes also to my co-editor, Maggie Blair, who in the midst of the COVID-19 pandemic kept us focused with her boundless energy and humor. I thank all my colleagues who contributed to this volume for sharing their knowledge and expertise, which came from the heart of loving what they do best—uplifting others through teaching.

Maggie

I begin my acknowledgments with my life partner of almost fifty years: my husband, Tommy, without whom my life would never have been the same. I am grateful to my own boys, T and Timmy, and their special life partners, Tasha and Nathalie, who have given me Lachlan, Sawyer, and Camille—my beautiful grandchildren who continue to teach me to look at the world through fresh eyes. Thank you to my very special co-editor, Dr. Joanna Alcruz, whose calm and focused approach to this project brought it to fruition. And finally, to all those whom I have met, worked with, and learned from over the years, thank you all! I am most grateful to have had each and every one of you in my life!

Introduction
Student-Centered Classrooms: Research-Driven and Inclusive Strategies for Classroom Management

MAGGIE BLAIR AND JOANNA ALCRUZ

WE ARE DELIGHTED TO SHARE with you the second volume in our two-book series on classroom management, *Student-Centered Classrooms: Research-Driven and Inclusive Strategies for Classroom Management.* This book is primarily intended for teachers who have some experience working in the classroom but are ready to revisit classroom management through the lens of current, research-based approaches.

If you have had an opportunity to explore *Engaging Diverse Learners: Enhanced Approaches to Classroom Management,* you will know that the two books came about as a product of extensive collaboration among educators, fieldwork experts, social workers, and mental health counselors connected to the Molloy University School of Education and Human Services in Rockville Centre, New York.

Initially, our plan was for one volume, but as we explored the current complexities of "managing" twenty-first-century classrooms and spoke with colleagues from a variety of disciplines, we realized that one volume would limit our ability to appropriately address the myriad of topics and the rich discussions we had shared with our colleagues.

Through data extracted from alumni surveys, we identified several common areas of need for current educators, and classroom management was a consistently recurrent theme. This need, along with the recent pause in traditional learning delivery that resulted from the COVID-19 pandemic, called for a reassessment of how and why students engage and learn, with the ultimate goal of revisiting and reimagining outdated instructional and management practices.

Before embarking on the journey to produce an updated look at classroom management, we discussed what *classroom management* meant to us.

Neither one of us liked the term because it was both linear and limited when used to describe the complexities of managing teaching and learning in twenty-first-century schools. We realized that any new publications on this topic required a multidimensional approach to effectively address current classroom needs.

As we pulled through the layers of topics to be included, we realized that the focus of our books had to be on student diversity and recent breakthroughs in current research. Therefore, our books place a greater emphasis on an awareness of students' strengths and challenges and the positive impact of current, research-based learning approaches.

Therefore, one book became two books. In each book, we purposefully navigated away from the traditional view of classroom management as behavior management. Rather, we focused our attention on teachers and their ability to rethink the way they view students; to recalibrate their expectations for all students; and to facilitate interactive, respectful learning in which all students are both supported and held responsible for meeting personal learning goals.

Throughout both books, we consistently echo the sentiments of Dr. Alfie Kohn (1996, 2021), who emphasized the need to steer away from the "managing" aspect of the classroom to focus on engaging and responding to student needs. This final, two-book product is a culmination of all of our rich collaboration and circled back to why teachers are in the classroom in the first place, which is to create and facilitate a positive, interactive, and student-centered learning environment.

While a more systemic change needs to occur in the classroom to rethink curriculum and pedagogical approaches, our work—presented in both *Engaging Diverse Learners: Enhanced Approaches to Classroom Management* (Alcruz & Blair, 2022) and this book—focuses primarily on strategies and solutions supporting diverse learners from the perspective of growth mindset, self-regulation, mindfulness, and social-emotional learning.

This volume serves as an introductory text to current best practices in classroom management, which aims to identify, highlight, and discuss proactive strategies that are often embraced by master practitioners. Therefore, while this book was primarily intended for seasoned educators, it will also benefit novice teachers who are ready to take a deeper look into strategies that can help them further enrich teaching and learning environments and experiences for themselves and their students.

In a recent research article, Rebekka Stahnke and Sigrid Blömeke (2021) discussed the different ways that novice and expert teachers approach classroom management. They found that expert teachers have a broader perspective on classroom management and attend more to the whole picture rather than to individual incidents of behavior. Furthermore, expert teachers are more focused on understanding the causes of misbehavior or, in other more behavioral language, understanding the function of the behavior. Their approach is more holistic, situational, and interconnected. As a result of this type of approach, the more seasoned teachers will seek proactive strategies to modify classroom behavior, rather than reactive strategies that focus only on the issue(s) at hand.

Expert teachers show greater control over their own behavior in the classroom, exhibiting enthusiasm and being cool under pressure. With such confidence, they allow students more autonomy in choices and are less concerned with exhibiting teacher authority. They use adaptive strategies to address classroom behavior that are tailored to the student as well as to the context.

Keeping these findings in mind, we organized our *Student-Centered Classrooms* book to address holistically different dimensions of classroom management that would focus more on *proactive* strategies for student engagement and less on *reactive* managing of behavior.

This book includes six intertwined chapters which discuss different dimensions of what it means to run a classroom like an expert teacher.

Chapter 1, Proactive Strategies for Student-Centered Classrooms opens this publication with a full chapter dedicated to proactive strategies for student-centered classrooms. This chapter sets the focus and tone of this book: an emphasis on proactive strategies to create student-centered learning environments. Two of the authors have successfully collaborated in the past to publish nationally recognized, content-based textbooks.

The authors begin by presenting their mutually agreed upon goals: (1) to suggest techniques that might reduce the potential for disruptions inherent in certain instructional methods, (2) to offer effective procedures for establishing rules and helping students comply with them, and (3) to include ways to gain insight into how a teacher's approach to establishing procedures can influence the ways disruptive situations are managed. The authors accomplish their goals by introducing examples of potentially disruptive K–12 classroom situations and providing techniques for effectively handling each of the proposed situations. The authors also successfully provide ways to adapt classroom management techniques to students' stages of moral development.

Finally, this chapter continues to discusses how culturally responsive pedagogy can be used to instruct and manage a classroom more effectively based on students' diverse backgrounds and experiences. The approach recognizes the importance of taking into consideration learners' diversity and cultural referents when using intervention techniques.

Chapter 2, Whether, When, and How Teachers Can Intervene looks at classroom management as a dynamic process between the classroom teacher and the students. This chapter examines the impact that both teachers' and students' self-efficacy and personal dispositions have on their interpersonal relationships and their collective classroom culture. The authors have worked together on several community projects linking Molloy University to local school districts, and they discuss the importance of looking at and evaluating several factors when determining whether, when, and how to intervene in a nonoptimal classroom situation.

In this chapter, they discuss the importance of looking at each student and each situation encountered as unique. The authors emphasize the importance of initially analyzing and interpreting the function of any behavior and then looking at that behavior through the lens of established classroom rules and procedures. While the process may seem tedious, this process ensures dignity for all and heightens the importance of respecting individual differences.

In addition, the authors introduce, discuss, and offer specific techniques and strategies to build classroom relationships, to promote self-monitoring skills, to de-escalate volatile situations, and—when necessary—to intervene. Several of their techniques and strategies include the effective utilization of technology in the classroom. Readers will notice strong interconnections between this and chapters three and five later in this book.

Chapter 3, Applications of Applied Behavioral Analysis to Classroom Management presents the possibility of seamlessly integrating applied behavior analysis practices into the classroom and provides classroom teachers with research-based practices to effectively analyze and determine the function of a behavior so they can design, successfully implement, and monitor a behavior plan. It also provides classroom teachers with the language and tools they need to work collaboratively with behavioral consultants who may be assigned to work with specific students in their classrooms as well as to empower classroom teachers to become active members of a behavior intervention team.

In this chapter, the authors identify and define the language of applied behavior analysis. Using scenarios, they then encourage the reader to manipulate information and apply the language identified, defined, and explained to complete an activity related to completing a functional behavior assessment and/or effectively implementing and monitoring a behavior intervention plan. After each activity, the authors provide readers opportunities to self-evaluate skills.

One of the authors of this chapter is a licensed board-certified behavior analyst (BCBA), providing consultant services to school districts and currently teaching classes for BCBA certification. The other is a faculty member in a college-based transitional program for young adults diagnosed with autism spectrum disorder and other developmental disabilities. Through their rich experiences working directly with behaviorally challenged individuals, these authors successfully provide their readers with a deeper understanding of the expansive possibilities of applied behavior analysis across settings.

Chapter 4, Understanding the Role of Emotions in the Classroom focuses on how emotions can facilitate learning and behavior in the classroom. The authors offer their expertise and unique perspective from the field of clinical mental health counseling. Highlighting the importance of recognizing the affective dimension of students, the authors offer a framework for understanding emotions and how they impact the interpersonal and classroom dynamics through the lens of culture and power.

Using theories of basics emotions or Bronfenbrenner's ecological systems, the authors shed light on how emotions develop, shape the identity of students, and connect to what can transpire in the classroom. The strategies for navigating students' emotions in the classroom offer reflective insights that can promote the emotional well-being of all.

Chapter 5, Integrating Gender Equity into Positive Classroom Culture focuses on incorporating a gender equity lens into a positive classroom culture. A doctoral candidate along with an expert in critical approaches in education and a retired higher education administrator provide an innovative and critical perspective of classroom management through the lens of gender equality. The authors introduce key terminology related to gender as not only a biological but also a social construct. They also discuss how gender bias and stereotyping undermine student potential to learn and succeed academically and their impact on educational settings.

Using the strategies to promote positivity in gender-diverse classrooms, the authors offer key approaches to help make students feel accepted by their teachers and peers. They also expand teachers' understanding beyond the heteronormative mindset and position them as agents of change who advocate for all students.

Chapter 6, Technology as a Classroom Management Asset is an insightful overview of the positive impacts of classroom technology on classroom instruction and classroom management, effectively linking all the chapters in this book and the *Engaging Diverse Learners* book together. The authors of this chapter skillfully blend research-based information on current instructional technologies and pragmatic applications for these technologies in the classroom throughout their chapter. Connections to chapters in both books are easily identified; this chapter is pivotal in bringing this project to a sustainable conclusion.

The authors of this chapter have previously collaborated successfully on instructional initiatives, both with students at Molloy University and through publications. Their chapter organization, selection of topics addressed, and style of writing easily engage readers. The content is summarized into tables, which are interspersed throughout this chapter by topic and are current, user friendly, and can provide pragmatic support for classroom teachers in their journey to effectively instruct and manage diverse student populations.

The ever-changing make-up of twenty-first-century classrooms includes students who bring their diverse perspectives, experiences, and backgrounds, as well as their unique strengths and challenges to the forefront of who they are as individuals. While this diversity provides rich opportunities for teachers to engage students with one another in the learning process, it also brings new and often different challenges for classroom teachers to effectively meet the needs of their students both individually and collectively.

Our focus in *Student-Centered Classrooms: Research-Driven and Inclusive Strategies for Classroom Management* was to provide experienced (and not-so-experienced) teachers with a more in-depth look at current, instructional, behavioral, and social-emotional approaches to support their diverse student populations. Through our colleagues' various backgrounds and experiences, we were able to successfully expand on topics introduced in our *Engaging Diverse Learners: Enhanced Approaches to Classroom Management* volume.

We hope our readers will find both books to be rich resources as they consistently move forward to meet the needs of all students.

References

Alcruz, J., & Blair, M. A. (Eds.) (2022). *Classroom management for diverse learners: Essential approaches*. Rowman & Littlefield.

Kohn, A. (1996). *Beyond discipline: From compliance to community*. Association for Supervision & Curriculum Development.

Kohn, A. (2021). The classroom-management field can't stop chasing the wrong goal: When will we stop trying to "manage" children? *Education Week*, September 17. https://www.edweek.org/teaching-learning/opinion-the-classroom-management-field-cant-stop-chasing-the-wrong-goal/2021/09.

Stahnke, R., & Blömeke, S. (2021). Novice and expert teachers' situation-specific skills regarding classroom management: What do they perceive, interpret, and suggest? *Teaching and Teacher Education, 98*. https://doi.org/10.1016/j.tate.2020.103243.

Proactive Strategies for Student-Centered Classrooms

1

VICKY GIOUROUKAKIS, FRANCINE WISNEWSKI, AND
MATINA STERGIOPOULOS

THERE ARE SEVERAL EFFECTIVE TECHNIQUES for handling potentially disruptive K–12 classroom situations in ways that can avoid behavior problems. This chapter aims to accomplish three goals: (a) suggest techniques that could be used to reduce the potential for disruptions inherent in certain instructional methods; (b) offer effective proactive procedures for establishing rules and helping students comply with them; and (c) include ways to gain insight into how a teacher's approach to establishing procedures can influence the way disruptive situations are managed.

If a situation is not handled well, this could tempt generally well-behaved students to misbehave. Here are some examples of potentially disruptive situations:

- beginning class at the start of the day, after recess, or after lunch
- transitioning between activities
- having students wait to request permission for certain activities
- having students enter and leave class for different reasons
- informing students about what was covered and the homework missed
- facing unanticipated schedule changes
- participating in fire drills or lockdowns

The following section outlines practical strategies that teachers can use to eliminate disruptive behaviors and promote equitable learning environments for all learners.

Potentially Disruptive Situations

Managing disruptive situations can be challenging for all teachers, from novices to veterans. However, "maintaining a positive and organized classroom setting free from disruption is critical to providing an instructional environment conducive to teaching and learning" (Skiba, Ormiston, Martinez, & Cummings, 2016, p. 120). Since each new group of students brings its own set of joys and obstacles, teachers must be equipped with a set of research-based strategies to anticipate and address potential disruptive situations. In considering these strategies, teachers should be responsive to students' cultural, academic, or social needs, and establish a learning environment grounded in respect and rapport.

START-UPS

At the elementary or intermediate levels, the first few minutes of class as the day begins, right after recess, or following lunch can be a waiting time for students who arrive early. It would be beneficial to keep them busy until everyone is ready by having optional work on the board for them to do. These options may include new vocabulary words, map research for social studies, an interesting puzzle, or a special "stumper problem." The teacher can also let students work on their journals, get a head start in silent reading, complete an upcoming assignment on their tablets, or select a learning center to work at for the first few minutes.

TRANSITIONS

When students are finishing one activity and starting another one, they are usually not actively engaged in productive work. Disruptive behavior problems are more likely to occur when transitions are not smooth—when students are waiting to be told what to do, are confused about what to do next, do not have enough time to end one activity and prepare for the next, and have teachers who are distributing or putting away items rather than attending to the students in the class (Christofferson & Sullivan, 2015).

Transitions can be especially disruptive if they occur without any warning or when the bell for recess, lunch, or dismissal sounds while the students are still working. At such times, students are ready and eager to leave and reluctant to delay their departure to put things away, to hear what the homework assignment is, and so on.

When transitions are smooth, however, students switch from one activity to another quickly and without disruptions. They also have more time for learning. Paying attention to transitions is part of good classroom management skills.

TIMING

Determining when to end an activity and begin another one is just as important as determining how to make the transition between two activities. Because attention spans differ, students are not all capable of working efficiently and cooperatively for the same amount of time. Thus, whether students are working individually at their seats or in small or large groups, it is important to end the activity before they are no longer able to cooperate and start misbehaving.

One way to determine when students "have had it" with an activity is to identify a few students with the shortest attention span and monitor them. Another way is to monitor the group as a whole for signs that some of them are losing interest. Some indicative signs are fidgeting, looking around, combing hair, talking to others, using phones, and writing or exchanging notes.

It is just as important to give the fast-working students self-directed activities to engage in while they wait for peers who may require more time to complete assignments. Students who are unable to complete classwork in the allotted time may be more willing to proceed to the next activity without resisting if given an opportunity to complete their assignments at a later, more convenient time. Providing appropriate differentiation to a lesson by including scaffolds for struggling learners and enrichment for advanced learners may assist in maintaining students' attention, thereby deterring negative behaviors.

Using a timer and chronicling the start and end time on the board may be useful when attempting to maintain students' attention (Fallon, Collier-Meek, & Kurtz, 2019). Frequently referencing the time remaining may support students in completing the task in a timely manner, thereby avoiding restlessness. Using a brisk pace in instruction may decrease downtime and opportunity for student misbehavior (Cooper et al., 2018).

When the whole group requires more time to work on an activity but risks becoming restless, the teacher might try boosting their interest. Helpful comments include, "I know you can do this! We only have a few more minutes on this activity" or "We're almost done—let's try to finish up before we quit." If this doesn't help, the teacher can give the group an opportunity to practice mindfulness or meditation-based techniques and then return to the activity if the schedule permits (Long, Renshaw, & Camarota, 2018).

Four Common Mistakes during Transitions

Kounin (1970) identified four common mistakes teachers make during transitions, which he called thrusts, dangles, flip-flops, and fragmentations.

THRUSTS

These occur when the teacher suddenly interrupts an activity with no warning: "Time's up," "Everyone stop working," "Close your books," or "It's recess time." When teachers end activities without warning, students in the middle of their work may interfere with the transition by expressing their reluctance to end what they were busy doing. In some instances, they may continue working on the earlier activity and not hear the directions that they will need to do the next activity well.

The teacher can avoid such situations by giving students advance notice that an activity will end soon. Simple ways of avoiding thrusts include telling students that they will have to stop in five minutes or advising them not to start another problem if they won't be able to finish it in the next few minutes.

DANGLES

Educators leave students "dangling" when they get too involved in setting up materials, reviewing lesson plans, conversing with a student who needs extra attention, or making students wait too long for the next activity. The students are ready, but they have nothing to do except wait patiently or "get into trouble."

Teachers can sidestep having students dangle during transitions by having the needed materials readily available. Instead of having students wait for the teacher to write things on the board, other tools can be used such as a SmartBoard, chart paper, or handouts. It is also good to establish automatic routines with students for putting things away, collecting and distributing materials, and doing other classroom activities to reduce their waiting time during transitions.

Another option is to assign two or three monitors to help if the students are old enough to assume that kind of responsibility. Establishing automatic routines using students' assistance will reduce waiting time and free the teacher to attend to students rather than do housekeeping chores.

Another strategy is to avoid bottlenecks during transitions by putting materials in an easy-to-reach spot and by having more than one distribution point where students can pick up or check out what they need. The furniture and equipment can be arranged in the classroom so it doesn't block traffic when students have to move from one place to another.

Stainback, Stainback, and Froyen (1987) suggest testing out the traffic pattern:

> Teachers can identify major traffic routes by "walking through" the activities that are likely to occur during the course of a school day. They may find that furniture and equipment placed in close proximity to storage areas, the cloakroom, or the classroom door must be relocated to allow for smooth, unobstructed travel. Likewise, traffic pattern testing may suggest a classroom plan or rule that can eliminate some congestion or disruption, for example, "No more than three students are allowed in the cloakroom at one time," "Enter the cloakroom from the left and exit from the right." (p. 13)

With younger students, the teacher can arrange their cubbies, coat hangers, lockers, and other access areas so that large groups can get to these areas at the same time without having to wait too long for turns. The teacher can help kindergartners and students in early elementary grades by identifying storage locations with color codes or pictures.

FLIP-FLOPS

Flip-flops occur when educators direct their students' attention back to a previous activity after they have started a new one. Examples of flip-flops include stopping a science lesson to return to math homework or interrupting a lesson to answer questions from students who were not paying attention while the class was being prepared for the activities. Such flip-flops interfere with the momentum of the lesson and make it difficult to get the class back on track.

To avoid flip-flops, the teacher can make sure to complete all aspects of one activity before moving to the next one. The teacher should check that all students are paying attention while preparing them for the next activity and double-check that all of them know what they are supposed to do. Whenever the teacher discovers having omitted something after changing activities, it is good to ask if it really needs to be dealt with at the moment or if it can wait for a less disruptive time.

FRAGMENTATIONS

Fragmentation refers to moving the group along piecemeal instead of together. Educators can fragment a group by having the class start a new activity one row at a time or by preparing one group for the reading assignment while having the other group wait a turn to be told what to do. Again, when students are waiting with nothing to do, they may be

Table 1.1. Teachers' Transitions for Class Activities

Effective Management Techniques	Ineffective Management Techniques
Warning students that an activity will end shortly (e.g., five-minute warning)	Ending an activity abruptly without warning
Shortening the transition time by preparing materials in advance, such as special paper, crayons, iPads, etc.	Poor housekeeping procedures, such as stopping to write things on the board or distributing materials
Using several distributors and distribution points	Bottlenecks caused by students waiting to receive materials
Arranging the room to facilitate student movement, providing easy access to cubicles or lockers, color-coding storage areas	Traffic jams in the classroom
Checking for students' understanding using a systematic approach or protocol confusion	Letting students continue to work without checking progress, which leads to misconceptions and confusion
Completing all aspects of an activity before beginning a new one; making sure everyone is paying attention before giving directions or initiating an activity	Interrupting one activity to return to an earlier one
Preparing all students for an activity simultaneously; assigning self-directed activities if students have to wait	Moving the group along piecemeal
Monitoring students' attention span	Requiring students to continue an activity they can't concentrate on
Providing self-directed activities for students who finish early	Requiring faster students to wait idly
Providing students who are unable to complete their work on time with other chances to complete their work	Penalizing students who are unable to complete their work on time with an incomplete grade or extra homework

tempted to pass the time doing things that they wouldn't ordinarily do if they were actively engaged in learning activities.

The teacher can avoid fragmentations by preparing the whole class simultaneously for a new activity. If the teacher needs to work with different groups separately before starting the activity, one group can engage in a self-directed activity while the other group can receive their instructions and/or materials. Table 1.1 lays out effective management techniques versus ineffective management techniques that teachers can use to promote smooth and successful transitions.

Obtaining Permission

When teachers are busily involved with helping a student, working with a group of students, or doing work at their desk, they may not notice that a student is waiting to ask permission to sharpen a pencil, get a drink, go to the bathroom, and the like. Young students with low frustration tolerances or strong needs (to use the bathroom) may not be able to wait very long before interrupting their teachers or expressing their frustration in disruptive ways.

One way to handle such situations is to allow students to attend to certain needs without obtaining permission. This will cut down on students' waiting time and the potential for associated disruptions.

However, because some students may abuse the freedom to move around the room without consulting the teacher, it might be good to have students obtain permission in these situations. In that case, it is important to establish routines that enable students to gain the teacher's attention as quickly and unobtrusively as possible. This will cut down on students' waiting time and maintain some control over their movements. Routines can also be established to minimize the need for students to leave their seats by handing out sharpened pencils at the beginning of the class and meeting other anticipated needs before they arise.

There are three approaches to handling student disruptions, and the ideal choice depends in part on the teacher's personal preferences.

1. A conscious choice should be made ahead of time about how to handle each disruptive scenario. Teachers may decide to allow students to get up without permission to do certain things (but not others) or they may allow students to move around the room freely, but not leave the room without permission.
2. Whatever choice is made, the classroom environment should be organized to minimize disruptions. For example, teachers can select pencil sharpeners that do not make a lot of noise and locate several of these at a place where students can reach them easily. This same principle applies to movable storage cabinets, wastepaper baskets, and so on.
3. A good balance is created by maximizing activities in which students can be self-directed and minimizing those for which students must obtain permission. This gives the teacher more time for important things and fosters students' personal growth.
4. The students' maturity level should be carefully considered for granting the privilege of doing some things without asking permission. Younger children may be able to use the pencil sharpener without any problem, but allowing them to get materials from storage cabinets could cause difficulties. It is essential to

monitor students closely, especially at the beginning of the school year, to make sure they can handle the privilege and not abuse it.

In general, students should not be permitted to disturb others while moving around; nor should they be allowed to be absent from the classroom with repeated trips or long visits to the water fountain or bathroom. One way of supervising when, how often, and how long students leave the room is to locate one or two larger passes for the drinking fountain and the bathroom in a place that is easy to monitor. Another way to supervise them is to include a sign-in and sign-out sheet.

As noted in the previous sections, it is possible to avoid many potentially disruptive problems by establishing procedures for doing such things as starting activities, distributing materials, moving from place to place, and obtaining permission. However, just telling students about certain procedures is not enough. With older students, teachers can collaboratively develop and negotiate the classroom procedures with their students, thereby establishing a sense of shared decision-making (Samanci, 2010). With younger students, the teacher may need to explicitly teach the procedures and give students opportunities to practice these procedures.

Typical procedures include where students line up for a fire drill, how materials are distributed, and what students do when they come late. The best time to teach such procedures is during the first few days of the school year. It may seem that having students practice the desired procedures uses up time at the beginning of the year and is more tedious than other activities, but doing this can make the class more trouble-free for the rest of the year.

Young children are not the only students who may have to be taught procedures. Any students who are not familiar with school routines may need to learn them. This may apply to itinerant, immigrant, and refugee students—especially those who have never attended school. Students who move from rural to urban areas and other students who are not used to the procedures in their new schools may also have to learn them.

The techniques for assisting students to follow rules are discussed in more detail later in this chapter under "Establishing Rules."

Potentially Disruptive Situations during Three Instructional Approaches

Each of the methods teachers use for instruction has certain inherent characteristics that may stimulate behavior problems if not handled properly.

Three of the most common approaches educators use to instruct students are assigning students classwork to be done individually, lecturing students interspersed with question-and-answer periods (direct instruction), and stimulating student interaction through group work and discussions.

The following discussion is designed to help the teacher use these instructional strategies in ways that maximize their effectiveness while minimizing their potential for disruptiveness.

Classwork

Students may not always wait patiently for the teacher to notice and attend to them. Possible reasons for not continuing to work on their own are because they need help with a particularly difficult problem, are missing a step in a process, or need to have their work checked before going on to another activity. The following suggestions can help the teacher avoid any associated problems:

1. Established routines should enable students to gain the teacher's attention as quickly as possible (Rawlings-Lester, Bolton-Allanson, & Notar, 2017).
2. Instead of requiring students to keep their hands raised while waiting to be noticed, the teacher can establish an alternative signal, such as a small cardboard stand they can place on their desk. If it is likely for a number of students to require the teacher's assistance with a particular project or assignment, methods can include a take-a-number system or names listed in a prominent place so they can be attended to in order.

    Alternatively, with older students, a formative assessment strategy may be used to restructure groups, thereby affording the teacher the opportunity to provide strategic support. For example, students can hold up a green notecard indicating that they are ready to move on to the next activity, a yellow notecard if they understand the task but need more time, and a red notecard if they cannot continue because they are struggling with the task. The teacher may then restructure groups to provide the greatest support to students who held up the red notecards.
3. It may be educationally sound to check students' work before permitting them to go on—to determine if they have mastered a particular skill and can move ahead. The downsides to this approach are that it uses up a lot of class time and students have

to wait if the teacher can't respond to them immediately. As an alternative, the teacher can allow them to place completed work in a to-be-checked folder to review at a more convenient time.

To handle fast-working students who may get into trouble if they have nothing to do but wait, the teacher can instruct students to proceed to the next group of problems or questions when they finish. If that is not feasible, they can select an acceptable activity at their desks or at a learning center of their choice. The latter can create more problems than it solves if it motivates students to be more interested in finishing fast to gain free time than in doing their work well. To avoid this possibility, it is important to monitor the quality of the fast-working students' work.

Students who work at a slower pace than their peers might benefit from a little extra time to finish. The teacher might also allow these students to complete some of their work at home or modify the task to include fewer problems, while maintaining the same expectations. In particular, students who struggle to read may require a head start if they are going to finish something that the whole group will be discussing.

Direct Instruction

During direct instruction, most behavior problems occur when the teacher is lecturing or other students are reciting. Instead of listening to what is being said, students can begin daydreaming, scribbling, engaging in side conversations, writing, passing notes, and so forth.

The following techniques can help maintain the students' attention during direct instruction:

- Select topics and materials that are interesting and relevant to the students.
- Adjust the method of presentation to match the students' developmental levels (Therrien, Benson, Hughes, & Morris, 2017).
- Use proper pacing and timing.
- Actively involve students in the learning process by encouraging them to react to the presentation, directing them to query when they are confused or in doubt, and asking questions periodically to evaluate the effectiveness of the presentation.
- Instruct students to take notes so they may actively engage in direct instruction (Ilter, 2017).

The following techniques can help maintain the group's attention during question-and-answer periods. Teachers using these techniques must be sensitive and maintain an awareness of students' participation preferences.

- Vary the procedure to increase student participation. The teacher can ask for volunteers at times and call on students randomly at other times. The latter approach of random selection can maintain their attention, as they will not know if they will be asked to respond. This also keeps them actively thinking because they can't just sit back and passively wait to hear what the volunteers have to say.

    This technique is not appropriate for all students since some may be extremely uncomfortable about talking in class if they have not volunteered. Students with emotional problems may feel threatened by having to answer questions when they are not ready to do so.
- Ask the question first, give students a few moments to think about it, and then call on someone. This will maintain students' attention better than calling on an individual because the students won't know whether they will be called on.
- Call on students in order only when a question has many possible answers, as in naming the five most recent presidents, the "ten reasons why," and so on. Then ask students not to repeat any of the answers given by other students.
- Intersperse group recitation with individual recitations. Have every student in class express his or her opinions or vote on a decision by a show of hands. This technique is culturally inappropriate for some students. Students from some cultural backgrounds may be reluctant to express their opinions if they differ from those expressed by their peers. They may also resist voting on decisions if they are accustomed to arriving at group decisions through consensus building.

Group Work and Discussions

Probably the most challenging instructional strategy for classroom management is having students work together, but this is also the most engaging for students. The following techniques can assist in maintaining the group's attention when students are interacting with one another in a whole-group discussion:

- Teach students to talk to the rest of the class, not only to the teacher.
- Make sure everyone is paying attention before beginning ("one, two, three, eyes on me").
- Check to see whether everyone can hear and whether they understand what their peers have said. Students have no reason to pay attention when their peers recite if they can't hear or understand them.
- Have students engage in academic discourse by commenting on what the other students have said. This technique should be used on a voluntary basis because many students are uncomfortable commenting about their peers' contributions, especially if their comments may seem critical.

It is also important for students to learn to engage effectively in group work. The following techniques will assist in teaching important communication and collaboration skills, which will foster a successful classroom environment:

- Assign specific roles that suit each individual student best so that every group member has a responsibility to complete the task successfully.
- Ensure that students are focused and carrying out their assigned roles to the best of their abilities.
- Provide a lot of guidance before students begin the task so that they are clear on what is expected of them; this avoids students asking too many questions about what to do during the activity, which can become disruptive.
- Create a set of guidelines with students on how to work together successfully to accomplish the task at hand. Monitor and make sure that students are following these guidelines. Have students rely on one another and less on the teacher for guidance.
- Provide students with scaffolds to help them learn to speak to one another in respectful and effective ways. Use response starters that students can practice so they know how to take turns speaking and responding, listening, and giving feedback.
- Model and provide opportunities for students to practice working in groups so that they can learn to collaborate more independently as well as to self-regulate.

Establishing Rules

Like procedures, rules are expectations for how students should behave. But procedures describe routines that students should follow in carrying out certain tasks that are basically functional and that may vary considerably from school to school and teacher to teacher. Rules, on the other hand, describe appropriate behavior. For example, students should wait their turn, work independently during tests, and respect the property of others. Rules typically describe how students should relate to one another and to their teachers or how they should behave in certain situations. Cangelosi (2013) suggests that classroom rules serve four purposes:

a. To maximize on-task behavior and minimize off-task behavior in the classroom.
b. To provide students with a safe and comfortable learning environment.
c. To prevent students from disturbing others.
d. To maintain acceptable standards of decorum.

Necessary Rules

Rules will help the classroom run smoothly. Students can know what is expected of them and teachers can focus on academics rather than on managing off-task behaviors. Education experts agree that rules are necessary (Koran & Koran, 2018; see also Pas, Cash, O'Brennan, Debnam, & Bradshaw, 2015; Skiba et al., 2016). Without rules, students would not know how to behave appropriately because expectations of acceptable behavior inside and outside of school can differ (Garwood, Harris, & Tomick, 2017).

Outside of school, it may be completely appropriate for students to move around and take breaks whenever they want to while doing their homework, for more than one person to speak at a time, or for students to express themselves in four-letter words. But in school, these behaviors are likely to be unacceptable.

While rules are necessary, some are more necessary than others. Sometimes teachers establish rules that reflect their particular preferences and desires rather than what is necessary for classrooms and groups to function effectively. These kinds of rules may seem arbitrary and unnecessary to students and cause them to feel resentful—particularly at the high school level. Therefore, if a teacher decides to establish a rule that is somewhat unique to the class, it would be helpful, if not imperative, to explain the reasons to the students and encourage them to discuss their thoughts and feelings about it.

Reasonable Rules

Rules are reasonable if they are necessary and not arbitrary. For example, it is necessary for students to be silent during fire drills, to keep their hands off of other students during class, and to respect the property of others. But is it reasonable to prohibit students from chewing gum, from wearing clothes in class that may make teachers uncomfortable, or from swearing? Educators disagree about the rationale of such prohibitions.

EFFECTIVE RULES

Many empirical studies have shown that creating a few rules that are observable and stated positively are effective at managing behaviors in the classroom (Alter & Haydon, 2017; see also Johnson, Stoner, & Green, 1996; Simonsen et al., 2015). Creating effective rules will help to establish a positive classroom environment from the beginning of the school year.

OBSERVABLE RULES

Some educators believe that certain rules—for example, that students should be polite, respectful, responsible, and the like—are difficult for students to conform to because ideas about what polite, respectful, and responsible mean vary widely across cultures (Mercado & Trumbull, 2018; see also Tjosvold, 1980). For example, students from different backgrounds bring with them their own cultural norms, which may differ from the norms of the school they are in at the moment.

Because students may be confused about exactly what to do and not to do when they are told to be polite, responsible, and so on, rules should be observable (Rahman, 2013). Närhi, Kiiski, and Savolainen (2017) show that when teachers create clear and observable expectations for their students, the behavioral climate of the classroom is enhanced. It is also important to note that these expectations should be set at the start of the year and followed consistently as the year progresses (Whitaker, 2013).

Examples of observable rules are "Walk, don't run, in the hallways" and "Do your own work on tests." Emmer and Evertson (2017) suggest creating general rules and then leading students in a discussion of what behaviors are appropriate for each rule. Talking about concrete examples of each rule can help students understand what the rules mean and how to properly follow them. It is preferable to create general rules such as "Keep the classroom neat" and "Treat others with courtesy and respect" because these guidelines are applicable to many situations and the teacher can avoid preparing a long and unnecessary list of specific things to do and not to do.

POSITIVELY STATED RULES

To the extent possible, rules should state what students are to do rather than what they should not do. The value of this approach is that it will provide students with guidelines on how to behave correctly. For example, "Raise your hand and wait to be called on" is preferable to "Don't call out!" because it teaches a procedure. In certain cases, though, negative statements are necessary (e.g., "Don't spit!" versus "Keep your saliva in your mouth").

FEW RULES

Most experts suggest that a few good rules are better than many detailed rules (Emmer & Evertson, 2017; see also Marzano, 2017). First, students may experience a long list of rules as oppressive. Also, they may not be able to remember and follow them, especially in the primary grades. Too many rules could hinder execution. Marzano (2017) suggests restricting the number of rules to between five and eight. This is a reasonable number of rules that the teacher can easily refer to during class and the students can remember.

Who Should Establish Rules?

Some educational theorists suggest that students should participate in developing classroom rules (Emmer & Evertson, 2017; see also Marzano, 2017; Parkay, 2016). To support their approach, these authors typically cite one or more of the following reasons. Participating in the development of rules teaches students how to function in a democratic society. Such participation also helps students understand why specific rules are necessary, which in turn makes them more willing to abide by them. And students, like all people, are more willing to accept rules they help formulate. In fact, teacher-formulated rules can engender hostility and rebellion in some students who have difficulty obeying authority.

Other educational theorists believe that teachers should formulate rules on their own and explain them to their students because of the belief that educators cannot achieve educational goals unless they possess the power to maintain classroom environments that suit them as individuals (Borich, 2014; see also Whitaker, Whitaker, & Whitaker, 2016). Thus, educators have the right to establish the conditions necessary for them to succeed. At the middle school and high school levels, students have many teachers during the day, and this can lead to confusion.

If teachers in a school can agree on a few schoolwide rules, then students will know what is expected of them throughout the day as they change classes (Närhi et al., 2017). In addition, these theorists believe that teachers, not students, know what behaviors and standards have to be enforced so that students can learn.

They also suggest that teachers, not students, are responsible for the classroom, as allowing students to help set standards of behavior abrogates the teacher's responsibility. Whitaker et al. (2016) explain that classroom rules reflect the philosophy of the teacher and to set the intended tone, the teacher should establish his or her own rules. And finally, students in a democratic society have to learn to abide by rules that are formulated by others.

Theorists also point out that by the time students have been attending school for a while, they realize that a schoolwide set of norms exists for almost all aspects of behavior (Myles & Simpson, 2001; see also Rahman, 2013). There are some very basic rules that students learn early on in their educational careers. In general, students know that they should sit in their seats and wait for directions from the teacher; if they want to participate in a discussion or ask a question, they should raise their hands. These are the aspects of the hidden curriculum that are learned by simply attending school and hearing the same messages over and over again.

Although there are conflicting opinions on who should create classroom rules, Emmer and Evertson (2017) posit that if reasonable rules are established, explained well, and enforced consistently, most students will be willing to follow them.

When to Establish Rules

Most theorists suggest that classroom rules should be established and taught as early as possible in the school year (Capizzi, 2009; see also Emmer & Evertson, 2017; Evertson & Emmer, 1982). Four reasons are typically cited for establishing classroom rules early. The first is that establishing rules early could avoid some misbehavior that occurs simply because students do not know what is expected of them. Second, the sooner students know the rules, the sooner they will start following them. Third, students are more receptive to learning rules at the beginning of the year. And finally, correcting students' behavior before they have been told what is expected of them is unfair.

In contrast to this approach, Jones and Jones (2016) explain the following idea:

> While it will be necessary to teach several key procedures that will facilitate the smooth flow of classroom or schoolwide activities, the creation of general classroom behavior standards can usually wait several days or even until there is some indication these need to be discussed and established. (p. 172)

For middle school and high school students who attend many different classes on the first day of school, reviewing basic classroom rules in each of those classes will not be necessary. Most of these students have been in school for many years and know the basics of how to behave.

TEACHING RULES

Alter and Haydon (2017) found that teaching classroom rules was a behavior of more effective classroom managers across the board, though the way the rules were taught differed depending on the grade level of the students.

Experts in the education field agree that students, especially in the primary grades, need to be taught how to abide by class rules (Alter & Haydon, 2017; see also Emmer & Evertson, 2017; Koops, 2018). Merely telling them the rules is insufficient. Here are some suggestions for teaching rules to students in the lower grades:

- Describe and demonstrate the desired behavior. Do not tell students to "be good" or to "behave themselves." Using interactive modeling will help the teacher effectively demonstrate appropriate behaviors. Interactive modeling consists of several steps:

    a. The teacher explains the behavior that will be modeled and then models the behavior with the students watching.
    b. There is a debriefing session.
    c. Students model the behavior.
    d. Another debriefing session follows.
    e. The class practices the behavior and the teacher provides immediate feedback (Responsive Classroom, 2017).

- Provide students with opportunities to practice the desired behaviors. Have them go through activities in which the rules come into play or role-play interpersonal situations in which they

apply. This will help them learn how to behave appropriately and enable the teacher to determine when they have learned to do so.
- Give students feedback about how they are doing and correct their mistakes.
- Wait until students know the rules and can comply with them before beginning to enforce them by means of consequences.
- Post the rules for students who may be too young to remember them. Provide students with their own copy of the rules if you think it would be helpful.

Such procedures are usually unnecessary with older students, who have been exposed to a wide variety of school rules for many years. If these procedures are used with high school students, they may perceive the teacher, with some justification, as talking down to them. This doesn't mean that the teacher should not inform them of expectations. They need to know which of the many rules that they have learned during their school careers they will be expected to follow in the class.

Teachers of high school students should review their rules at the beginning of the school year. Some teachers choose to have students write the rules in their notebooks, or they provide students with a handout listing the behavior expectations for the class. Whether rules are posted in the class, distributed on a handout, or written by the students themselves, they must be reviewed at the beginning of the school year, reinforced, and consistently followed each day. Unless a new and somewhat unique rule is instituted, older students will not need to learn how to follow them.

SCHOOLWIDE RULES

Schoolwide rules that are consistently enforced by all faculty and staff are more likely to be accepted and followed by students. Rules that are not schoolwide can seem arbitrary to students, and teachers who establish and enforce them may seem strict and unfair. On the other hand, teachers who ignore schoolwide rules may be surprised that sometimes their students perceive them as weak and overly lenient. This may be true, even if the rules make students unhappy—as long as students believe that the rules are necessary and fair.

Therefore, all things being equal, the classroom rules will be more effective if they conform to those established and enforced by colleagues. In addition, teachers will appear to be doing the job they are supposed to do if schoolwide rules are enforced to the same extent as colleagues.

Teachers may not always agree with all the schoolwide rules they are expected to enforce (e.g., too permissive or too restrictive). They have a number of options when there is disagreement on a particular schoolwide rule: (a) decide to enforce it, (b) attempt to avoid situations in which it is likely to apply, and (c) attempt to get the rule changed. The choice should be based on thoughtful consideration of the alternatives.

ENFORCING RULES

Classroom management is about preventing misbehaviors with specially designed rules or expectations of acceptable behavior. For rules to be effective, teachers have to clearly communicate their rules and enforce them consistently (Borich, 2014). Consistency is the key to the success of any classroom management system. If the teacher does not fairly and consistently enforce the rules, the students will lose respect for his or her authority and question the importance of the rules (Borich, 2014; see also Capizzi, 2009; Skiba et al., 2016).

Not all students will require the same amount of enforcement to bring them into compliance. Certain students have to expect that they will be caught if they break the rules and will also have to pay consequences for their transgressions. But many other students will obey school rules without close supervision simply because they are motivated to do so—unless there are extenuating circumstances.

Teachers who believe that most students can be encouraged to want to behave appropriately emphasize techniques that motivate students toward appropriate behavior and de-emphasize enforcement. Teachers who perceive students as less than willing to abide by the school rules stress the expectation that the rules will be enforced. The point of view espoused in this chapter is that enforcement (extrinsic motivation) plays an essential role in classroom management, but increasing students' motivation to want to behave (intrinsic motivation) should take precedence as essential preparation for life in a democratic society.

Rule enforcement involves two steps: monitoring students' behavior and intervening when they misbehave. The sections that follow discuss these two key aspects of rule enforcement.

Monitoring Behavior

Teachers should constantly monitor students to ensure they are on task and following class rules. By planning effective instruction to keep students engaged during a lesson, students are more likely to stay on task and to be following the rules (Nagro, Fraser, & Hooks, 2019). When something starts to go wrong, teachers should intervene immediately before things get out of hand (Evertson & Emmer, 1982, 2017; see also Sieberer-Nagler, 2016). The following seven suggestions are aimed at helping the teacher effectively monitor students by convincing them of the two important points that (a) the teacher is always watching them, and (b) the teacher will intervene quickly if they are not on task:

1. Arrange the classroom furniture and the teacher's desk to see and hear what is going on.
2. Maintain eye contact with students and move around the room, using physical presence as a way of discouraging misbehavior. The teacher should positively interact with students while moving around the room (Collier-Meek, Johnson, & Farrell, 2017).
3. Keep eyes and ears open; in addition, periodically scan the entire classroom while working with individuals or small groups (Simonsen et al., 2015).
4. Be on the lookout for signs of impending trouble, such as scowls and frowns, students looking around the room, or a small flurry of energy, and intervene before anything actually happens.
5. As soon as a disruptive incident occurs, intervene before it becomes serious or spreads to other students.
6. When intervening, the teacher's attention should be focused on the initiator of the problem, not on an innocent student if there is one. Specifically, intervene with the student who actually passed the note, asked to see someone's answers during an exam, or made a remark about a student's mother. It's important to not address the unwitting recipient of the attack, such as the student who responds, "Do your own work," or says, "Don't say anything about my mother or else."
7. When two disruptive events occur simultaneously—a student on his or her phone in one part of the room and two students teasing a third elsewhere—attend to the more serious misbehavior first.

Intervening with and without Consequences

There are many different strategies to reinforce good behavior and provide consequences for inappropriate behavior (Whitaker et al., 2016). According to Wolfgang and Glickman (1986), there are three major perspectives on discipline that teachers follow: the "noninterventionist," the "interventionist," and the "interactionist."

The noninterventionist teacher does not intervene but instead emphasizes classroom and behavior management techniques that help students understand what the right thing is and why rules are necessary. They provide students with the skills that enable and empower them to make right decisions and control their own behavior. Ritter and Hancock (2007) believe the teacher must allow the students to exert significant influence in the classroom and the teacher should be less involved in adjusting student behaviors.

On the other hand, the interventionist believes that the teacher should be in complete control and should address misbehavior as it happens. Interventionists see themselves as providers of information, direction, and control. They believe that students follow rules best when they are given a lot of supervision. They maintain that the teacher is the best judge of what is appropriate behavior and what are appropriate consequences for following and not following rules. They stress the importance of extrinsic consequences and requiring students to do the right thing.

Here are two representative examples of the point of view that teachers should intervene with consequences in order to encourage students to follow rules and expectations:

1. The teacher must give the consequences any time a student breaks one of the rules. If students see that consequences are not consistently enforced, then the classroom rules will quickly become meaningless and potentially become more harmful than good (Whitaker et al., 2016, p. 27).
2. The teacher asks an offending student to go to a designated place (inside or outside the classroom) until the student is ready to resume regular classroom activities. The teacher might use a graduated three-step process for sending a student to time out:

    a. warning
    b. time-out inside the classroom, where the student can attend to the academic activities that are occurring
    c. time-out outside the classroom (Marzano, 2017, p. 104)

And still another group of teachers promote interaction and the shared responsibility for classroom situations with their students. Djigic and Stojiljkovic (2011) studied the classroom management style of eight elementary schools in Serbia. They found the interactionalist classroom management style significantly contributed to overall effective teaching.

Examples of their philosophy are found below:

> The teacher encourages interaction and cooperation into the classroom, respects students' personalities, appreciates initiatives, interests and needs of students, uses teaching methods and materials that obtain full activity of the whole class during the lessons, designs activities well focused to learning goals, implements procedures to build positive discipline based on self-control and responsibility of students. (Djigic & Stojiljkovic, 2011, p. 827)

> Faced with a lack of discipline in the classroom, the teacher reacts by checking what is going on and trying to find a suitable solution together with students and again draws students' attention to the lesson. (Djigic & Stojiljkovic, 2011, p. 823)

Keeping in mind that the goal of any intervention is to decrease the probability that misbehavior will occur, teachers should select intervention techniques that are appropriate for the causes of their students' problems and their developmental levels (Borich, 2014). Teachers often fail to do this. Research suggests that most teachers—particularly those who teach secondary school—are interventionists, which is developmentally unsound since older students are better able to control their impulses, make reasoned choices and decisions, and thus manage their own behavior (Kwok, 2018; see also Pas et al., 2015; Roache & Lewis, 2011).

Sometimes, even with older students, the application of immediate, routine, and consistent consequences is a useful and necessary technique for students who need to be discouraged from misbehaving because they have not yet acquired the intrinsic motivation necessary to abide by rules. But it is equally, if not more, important to motivate these students to want to behave, even in the absence of consequences.

Most teachers do a good job with whatever approach they utilize. However, some noninterventionists are too lenient and laissez-faire. They lose control of their classes, and students suffer the distracting and disruptive results of too many student conversations, arguments, and so on. When nonintervention is done properly, students are more motivated, more willing to do class assignments, and less bored (Moghtadaie & Haveida, 2015).

On the other hand, some interventionists are too authoritarian, insisting that students always follow many inflexible rules and procedures immediately and to the letter. They deprive students of any experience of freedom and self-actualization in their classrooms and increase their students' boredom and resentment.

As teachers gain more experience teaching, they will find the style that works best for them in their classrooms.

Students' Moral Development

The importance of adapting classroom management techniques to students' motivational development levels was discussed in this book's introduction. This section covers how to adapt classroom management techniques to students' stages of moral development.

The Three Stages

Numerous factors affect the pace and final form of an individual's moral development. Despite these individual and group differences, however, it is possible to identify various stages that typify the moral development of most people.

Piaget (1965), Kohlberg (1984), and others (Scarlett, 2015; see also Staub, 1979) have researched and thus describe the stages children go through in relation to the reasons for their conforming to societal expectations. Although these authors disagree on certain points, in general, their work indicates that children's moral development includes at least three stages. (Keep in mind, though, that just as children learn to walk and talk at different times, the ages at which they pass through these stages also vary for each individual.)

First Stage: Extrinsic Consequences

Children are in the first stage of moral development until the age of seven or eight. Able to see the world from their own perspective only, they cannot control their behavior by empathizing with others (putting themselves in the other person's shoes) or by accepting the idea that others also have rights. Their level of morality, called moral realism, is based primarily, but not exclusively, on the question of what the adults will do to them if they take a certain action.

At this stage, children do what is expected of them because adults have authority over them; positive consequences follow "good" behavior and negative consequences follow "bad" behavior. According to the theory of mind, children as early as three to five years old develop the ability to understand the desires, intentions, and beliefs of others (Baron-Cohen, Leslie, & Frith, 1986). However, it is not until they get older that they are better able to identify underlying motives of human action and develop more sophisticated moral reasoning (Loureiro & Souza, 2013).

TODDLERS

Even this preliminary kind of morality takes years to develop in children. Infants do whatever they want, but by the toddler age, youngsters have to submit to authority. Toddlers control themselves for three basic reasons. First and perhaps foremost, adults force their will on them. By taking things out of their hands, putting things beyond their reach, dressing them in certain clothing, holding onto them firmly in public buildings, and so on, adults teach toddlers that they can both keep them from doing things and force them to do things.

When children realize this, they are less likely to engage in power struggles that they know they cannot win. Second, adults teach toddlers that when they do what they are told, they get positive reinforcements such as smiles, hugs, praise, sweets, and the like. But when they don't do as they are told, they are scolded, deprived of their toys, or given "time out" away from the others. Finally, adults model the way they want toddlers to behave and give them enough attention, nurturance, and love to motivate them to want to copy adults.

PRESCHOOL STUDENTS

Teachers use the same three techniques with preschoolers. They teach children to submit to authority by means of positive and negative consequences; they model the behavior they want the students to copy and motivate them to want to copy it. Although preschoolers have a greater capacity to control themselves, the type of self-control they are capable of is still very much like the self-control of toddlers. That is, when they are told not to do something—especially if they are told repeatedly—they generally respond appropriately. But they still cannot be relied on to exercise self-control without others there to tell them what to do and what not to do.

The words that adults use with toddlers are almost invariably a command like "Don't," "Stop," or "No." Preschoolers are ready for more advanced types of commands, such as "Wait," "Just a minute," "Later," and "Do it," "Pick it up," or "You do it." Thus toddlers can begin to learn that they can't do everything they want, but preschoolers can also learn to wait and to do things for themselves or to at least help out a little.

PRIMARY-GRADE CHILDREN

When students are in kindergarten and first grade, typical self-control issues they struggle with include waiting to be called on, taking turns, not interrupting others, listening when other students are reciting, and sharing materials. Fortunately, by this time, they can remember the consequences of their previous behavior. As a result, teachers have a fourth method they can use to teach these students to behave appropriately: they can remind them what happened the last time they did the wrong thing or did not wait.

Primary-grade students can also understand, although at a basic level, the ideas that people can't all fit through one door at the same time and no one can be heard if everyone talks at once. This gives teachers a fifth technique: they can explain the reasons why certain rules and procedures are necessary.

Lacking experience and maturity, these youngsters have only a limited capacity to understand and recall the reasons their teachers give them for certain behaviors. But explaining the whys and wherefores to them in a way they can understand may still be helpful. Such explanations can help them progress to the next stage, since submitting to authority is only the beginning in a democratic society that calls for citizens with a higher level of moral development.

Second Stage: Natural Consequences

Students between the ages of seven and eleven are usually in the second stage of moral development sometimes referred to as the cooperative, reciprocal, or constructive stage. At this stage, students are much more able to understand why rules are necessary. They can readily see that they have to be quiet so their classmates can hear the speaker or that they must put things back where they belong so they can find the items the next time. But once students can appreciate why some rules are necessary, they may question the necessity for other rules that seem arbitrary to them.

For example, they may want to know why they can't chew gum in class or dress the way they want since these actions do not hurt or interfere with anyone else. During this stage, they want to be told why they should or should not do certain things, and they are less willing to do things just because their teachers say so. Teachers who rely too often on power to control students who have progressed beyond moral realism may find that their techniques spark dissatisfaction or outright rebellion in students who want to be treated more maturely.

Because students at this stage can appreciate why rules are necessary, they are able to distinguish between necessary and arbitrary rules and can see other people's points of view and empathize with their feelings. They can also understand concepts of justice, fair play, and so on, and so they are able to participate in making classroom rules and determining the consequences when students don't abide by them.

Third Stage: Intrinsic Consequences

When students enter the third stage of moral development (usually when they enter junior high school), they begin to behave appropriately because it is the "right" or "good" thing to do. Instead of conforming just because of what teachers will do to them and what other students will think about them, they begin to exercise self-control and behave appropriately, even if no one will know what they do or no one rewards or punishes them.

As a result, at this stage, educators can place greater emphasis on rational discussion and appeals to social responsibility instead of positive and negative consequences when attempting to motivate their students. They can now encourage their students to behave appropriately for the good of the class or because it is the "right" way to behave.

A democratic society cannot function properly unless its citizens have reached this stage of development, and so one goal of education should be to help students attain this level of morality. Overreliance on extrinsic consequences and failure to provide students with the opportunity to exercise the third stage of moral self-control may stunt their development. Class discussions about moral issues and taking part in projects that right injustices and reduce inequality—such as helping the homeless and confronting prejudice—can foster students' moral development.

Since the turn of the twenty-first century, moral psychology has become broader and includes theories that moral behavior is a function of many factors and not just developmental stages. Moral judgment, reasoning, and emotion can be attributes of moral behavior.

Adapting to Students' Moral Development

Students in the first stage of moral development—preschool and primary-grade students—respond to consequences. Rewarding them for behaving appropriately and applying negative consequences when they misbehave help teach them about the real world. Thus, although consequences should not be the teacher's main approach to classroom management, they do play an important role with young students.

Older students who have not been exposed to life's lessons at home or elsewhere and come to school believing they can "get away with" doing whatever they please also need to learn that, at least in school, they have to abide by rules. But such students are only a small fraction of the school population. These students also need to develop intrinsic motivation so they will not want to get away with things.

Knowing that there will be consequences if one misbehaves is also needed to keep many well-behaved students on track—just as knowing that the IRS may audit one's taxes or the parking meter attendant may ticket one's car helps citizens abide by the laws. In general, however, negative consequences should play an extremely minor, insignificant, and primarily deterrent role with upper elementary and secondary school students.

Teachers who rely heavily on the threat of punishment for control risk making students resentful and rebellious about being treated like "babies" or "criminals." These teachers also neglect their responsibility to help students develop the intrinsic motivation needed to function as true citizens in a democratic society.

Because upper elementary and secondary students can understand why it is necessary to behave appropriately, follow rules, and be good group members, they should be approached—at least in part—as rational people capable of managing their own behavior once they know how they should behave and why it is necessary for them to behave that way.

Secondary school teachers in particular should foster their students' intrinsic motivation. This is not meant to imply that secondary school teachers and administrators can dispense with consequences. Consequences are a fact of life. What it means, once again, is that after the primary grades, consequences should play a minor, deterrent role.

Building a community of learning and establishing positive relations with students should be the focus of the teacher so that classroom management can work successfully. When students and teachers work together to discuss and establish classroom goals, they become partners in the educational process. Rewards and punishment may not be necessary because students value and appreciate the learning community and derive satisfaction from the intrinsic benefits of collaboration, such as trust, respect, and care (Scarlett, 2015).

Students come to school with their own particular learning, behavioral, and motivational styles, which are influenced by their cultural and ethnic backgrounds, the contextual factors in their lives, their gender, socioeconomic situation, and so on. By the time they begin school, they have also become accustomed to the management and disciplinary styles used by the adults who have been responsible for caring for them. Sometimes, teachers' styles conflict with students' ethnicities, cultures, genders, and socioeconomic statuses, and teachers must reflect on and use approaches that are culturally appropriate, relevant, and responsive to students' diverse needs.

Racial, Ethnic, Gender, and Class Differences

Historically, racial and ethnic minority students have received exclusionary discipline actions, such as suspensions and referrals to special education (Bradshaw, Mitchell, O'Brennan, & Leaf, 2010; see also Losen & Gillespie, 2012). African American male students are more likely to get suspended or referred for special education evaluations than Caucasian students, and males are at a higher risk (Porowski, O'Conner, & Passa, 2014; Wallace, Goodkind, Wallace, & Bachman, 2008). First, teachers may not understand the cultures of students in terms of how they impact behavior; and second, they may not be equipped to bridge the gap between culturally diverse students' home cultures and that of the school.

According to research, students of color are often disciplined for "inappropriate behaviors" that are not intended to be disruptive when seen through a critical lens (Monroe & Obidah, 2004). Teachers can misinterpret students' behaviors and discipline students unnecessarily. Also, they may not know how to deal with cultural conflicts or how to reach students who are racially and ethnically diverse because of a lack of understanding or training.

In terms of gender, male students receive suspensions and expulsions at higher rates than female students (Bradshaw et al., 2010). Students with disabilities as well as lesbian, gay, bisexual, transgender, and queer students are at risk for disproportionate disciplinary actions (Himmelstein & Brückner, 2011; see also Poteat, Scheer, & Chong, 2016).

Research shows that teacher and student interactions are often biased (Beaman, Wheldall, & Kemp, 2006). Female students have typically received more positive feedback than male students in recent years (Stevens, 2015), whereas male students tend to get in more trouble than females for misbehaving and receive more negative attention (Sadker & Sadker, 1986). Consuegra and Engels (2016) find that females who receive very high levels of positive feedback at the beginning of the year are more likely to maintain their favored status and show more positive behaviors.

Two theories may account for the biased teacher–student interactions. One is that different expectations of female and male students may contribute to teachers' differential treatment. Another theory is that male students' misbehavior could be provoking teachers' criticism. Consuegra, Struyven, and Engels (2014) found that teachers criticize both male and female students alike, but that female students get away with calling out and male students tend to call out more.

However, teachers were found to be unaware of their differential treatments based on gender (Garrahy, 2001). Howe (1997) finds that studying the proportion of positive to negative interactions rather than separate occurrences may lead to more significant findings in terms of how this deferential treatment affects students. Most research indicates that educators' gender also influences their instructional and classroom management styles in many ways (Glock, 2016).

Male teachers are generally more direct with their students and are more inclined to pick up verbal cues, while female teachers are more indirect and more inclined to pick up nonverbal cues. Also, female teachers create more student-centered learning environments and use more cooperative learning than males, who are more likely to lecture and use competitive learning (Organisation for Economic Co-operation and Development, 2009). Female teachers are more likely to provide interventions to correct student behavior when dealing with male students than female students (Glock, 2016).

Perception bias extends to socioeconomic status. Teachers tend to have higher expectations for students of high socioeconomic status and lower expectations for students from disadvantaged backgrounds (Mizala, Martinez, & Martinez, 2015). The teachers' own socioeconomic class backgrounds also influence their classroom and behavior management styles. Teachers tend to expect students to behave like they did and do, and they use classroom management approaches that resemble the disciplinary approaches they learned at home.

Heath (1983) reveals that children from working-class families were used to directives and had difficulty following the indirect requests that many teachers have used because they did not sound like explicit rules or directives to them. "Delpit explained that when urban students ignore commands that sound more like questions than directives, teachers may perceive students as uncooperative and insubordinate whereas students innocently fail to understand what is expected and why they are being disciplined" (Delpit, 1985, as cited in Brown, 2004, p. 270).

Differences in race, ethnicity, gender, and social class necessitate an approach that helps teachers create an effective learning environment for all learners.

Culturally Responsive Approach to Classroom Management

Culturally responsive pedagogy is an approach used to teach and manage a classroom more effectively based on students' diverse backgrounds and experiences. It combines the research of "culturally responsive teaching" by Gay (2010) and the empirical research of "culturally relevant pedagogy" by Gloria Ladson-Billings (1994, 1995, 2000). Culturally responsive pedagogy focuses on how teachers do the following:

- use culture as a capital to teach students
- establish and enforce classroom rules and expectations that are fair and culturally consistent
- build caring relationships with students, thereby fostering positive engagement and participation
- establish positive ties and maintain communication with students' parents, families, and communities (Bal, 2018; see also Brown, 2004; Vincent, Randall, Cartledge, Tobin, & Swain-Bradway, 2011; Weinstein, Curran, & Tomlinson-Clarke, 2003; Weinstein, Tomlinson-Clarke, & Curran, 2004)

The literature suggests that improving teachers' use of culturally responsive classroom management strategies may reduce the disproportionate number of racial and ethnic minority students who receive exclusionary discipline actions. On the other hand, culturally responsive classroom management strategies that affirm students' identity can facilitate a more inclusive and equitable learning environment, leading to fewer tensions (Gay, 2006). Such approaches to classroom management reflect sociocultural participation-centered techniques (Hickey & Schafer, 2006), which require teachers to assume the identities and backgrounds of their students to encourage participation in classroom processes and enhance the learning environment.

Understanding the relationship between culture and classroom behavior may assist teachers in making informed judgments on inappropriate and appropriate classroom behavior. These practices include making the curriculum more relevant to students (e.g., connecting it to real-world examples and incorporating cultural artifacts), varying how students engage in and display understanding (e.g., encouraging discussion and opportunities to share different perspectives and ways of knowing), and varying how teachers communicate (e.g., using humor).

Determining whether the use of such strategies is associated with a reduction in disparities in exclusionary discipline actions between Black students and White students remains an important next step in this line of research (Bottiani, Larson, Debnam, Bischoff, & Bradshaw, 2017). When teachers and students share the same culture, there is a better chance that the teacher will appraise the student's classroom behavior and performance more fairly than teachers who lack the cultural understanding.

As a result, teachers are more apt to offer opportunities and services to students to enhance their educational experience. For example, when dealing with behavior problems, Latinx teachers prefer to provide flexibility, accommodate to individual differences, and provide students with alternatives (Monzo & Rueda, 2001). They are more likely to use consequences to convince students to modify their behavior. They are also more concerned about preventing future problems. These approaches are more in line with Latinx parents' interactional patterns with their children.

Research indicates that Black teachers also have preferred ways of functioning that support Black students' experiences (Simpson & Erickson, 1983). Compared to other racial groups, they use more authoritarian disciplinary techniques and are more sensitive to and concerned about the feelings of others. McCray, Sindelar, Kilgore, and Neal (2002) show that many Black teachers are strict and demanding in terms of classroom management, have high student expectations, and believe that teacher reprimands are necessary to establish a climate of success and caring for their students. When dealing with classroom management problems, Black teachers favor explaining the reasons that students should or should not behave in a particular way and helping them understand the effects of their behavior on others.

These practices are in contrast to the racial stereotyping that students experience in schools on a daily basis. For example, Okonofua and Eberhardt (2015) show that teachers' negative racial stereotypes of Black students resulted in elevated disciplinary infractions as opposed to White students, even when the students behaved similarly. These findings suggest that matching teacher assignments with students of the same race or ethnicity may yield subjective ratings of students' behavior and academic ability and can have a positive impact on classroom management in general.

Although any teacher can adopt a culturally responsive pedagogy, teachers of color often have a greater awareness of the "cultural referents" that can assist in teaching. Black and Latinx students are rated as being less frequently disruptive in class when assigned to a Black or Latinx teacher, respectively, although the evidence base is strongest for Black students with Black teachers.

Evidence also indicates that Black and Latinx students' academic abilities are rated more positively when assigned to a teacher of the same race and ethnicity (and less positively when assigned to a teacher of another race and ethnicity [Redding, 2019]). Although this pattern is found in both primary and secondary grades, the evidence is more consistent in the higher grades.

The culturally responsive approach to classroom management does not imply partiality but rather inclusive pedagogical methods. Connecting with students requires valuing each child's importance and working to develop commonalities (Ladson-Billings, 1994, 1995, 2000). Thus, teachers need to ensure that they are using culturally responsive techniques to address each student's unique needs.

Conclusion

By properly handling potentially disruptive situations involved in starting up class, transitioning to different activities, and through students obtaining permission, teachers can sidestep many classroom behavior problems. Establishing procedures and rules can also help to eliminate problems. To ensure that students will comply with established procedures and rules, it is necessary to monitor the students' behavior and intervene when they misbehave. Such intervention techniques should be suited to students' level of moral development and their racial, ethnic, gender, and class differences.

The culturally responsive approach to classroom management recognizes the importance of taking into consideration students' diversity and cultural referents when using intervention techniques. It is also helpful to be aware of and modify, if necessary, personal preferences regarding classroom management techniques.

Application Activities

I. List some activities you could assign students at the beginning of the school day, after recess, or after lunch that would help avoid potential problems during start-ups.

II. Review the arguments for and against each of the following controversial practices.

Formulate your opinion and state the reasons for your perspective:

- including versus not including students in developing classroom rules
- establishing rules at the beginning of the school year versus later in the term
- intervening immediately, automatically, and consistently when students misbehave versus taking the causes of students' misbehavior into consideration

References

Alter, P., & Haydon, T. (2017). Characteristics of effective classroom rules: A review of the literature. *Teacher Education and Special Education, 40*(2), 114–27. doi: 10.117/0888406417700962.

Bal, A. (2018). Culturally responsive positive behavioral interventions and supports: A process-oriented framework for systemic transformation. *Review of Education, Pedagogy, and Cultural Studies, 40*(2), 144–74. https://doi.org/10.1080/10714413.2017.1417579.

Baron-Cohen, S., Leslie, A., & Frith, U. (1986). Mechanical, behavioural, and intentional understanding of picture stories in autistic children. *British Journal of Developmental Psychololgy, 4*(2), 113–25. doi: 10.1111/j.2044-835X.1986.tb01003.x.

Beaman, R., Wheldall, K., & Kemp, C. (2006). Differential teacher attention to boys and girls in the classroom. *Educational Review, 58*(3), 339–66.

Borich, G. D. (2014). *Effective teaching methods: Research-based practice* (8th ed.). Pearson.

Bottiani, J. H., Larson, K. E., Debnam, K. J., Bischoff, C. M., & Bradshaw, C. P. (2017). Promoting educators' use of culturally responsive practices: A systematic review of in-service interventions. *Journal of Teacher Education, 69*(4). doi:10.1177/0022487117722553.

Bradshaw, C. P., Mitchell, M. M., O'Brennan, L. M., & Leaf, P. J. (2010). Multilevel exploration of factors contributing to the overrepresentation of black students in office disciplinary referrals. *Journal of Educational Psychology, 102*(2), 508–20. https://doi.org/10.1037/a0018450.

Brown, D. F. (2004). Urban teachers' professed classroom management strategies: Reflections of culturally responsive teaching. *Urban Education, 39*(3), 266–89. https://doi.org/10.1177/0042085904263258.

Cangelosi, J. S. (2013). *Classroom management strategies: gaining and maintaining students' cooperation* (7th ed.). John Wiley & Sons.

Capizzi, A. M. (2009). Start the year off right: Designing and evaluating a supportive classroom management plan. *Focus on Exceptional Children, 42*(3), 1–12.

Christofferson, M., & Sullivan, A. (2015). Preservice teachers' classroom management training: A survey of self-reported training experiences, content coverage, and preparedness. *Psychology in the Schools, 52*(3), 248-264. doi:10.1002/pits.21819.

Collier-Meek, M. A., Johnson, A. H., & Farrell, A. F. (2017). Development and initial evaluation of the measure of active supervision and interaction. *Assessment for Effective Intervention, 43*(4). doi:10.1177/1534508417737516.

Consuegra, E., & Engels, N. (2016). Effects of professional development on teachers' gendered feedback patterns, students' misbehaviour and students' sense of equity: Results from a one-year quasi-experimental study. *British Educational Research Journal, 42*(5), 802–25.

Consuegra, E., Struyven, K., & Engels, N. (2014). Beginning teachers' experience of the workplace learning environment in alternative teacher certification programs: A mixed methods approach. *Teaching and Teacher Education, 42*(7), 79–88.

Cooper, J., Gage, N., Alter P., LaPolla, S., MacSuga-Gage, A., & Scott, T. (2018). Educators' self-reported training, use, and perceived effectiveness of evidence-based classroom management practices. *Preventing School Failure, 62*(1), 13–24. doi:10.1080/1045988X.2017.1298562.

Djigic, G., & Stojiljkovic, S. (2011). Classroom management styles, classroom climate and school achievement. *Procedia-Social and Behavioral Sciences, 29*, 819–28.

Emmer, E. T., & Evertson, C. M. (2017). *Classroom management for middle and high school teachers* (10th ed.). Pearson Education.

Evertson, C. M., & Emmer, E. T. (1982). Effective management at the beginning of the school year in junior high classes. *Journal of Educational Psychology, 74*(4), 485–98.

Fallon, L., Collier-Meek, M., & Kurtz, K. (2019). Feasible coaching supports to promote teachers' classroom management in high-need settings: An experimental single case design study. *School Psychology Review, 48*(1), 3–17. doi:10.17105/SPR-2017-0135.V48-1.

Garrahy, D. A. (2001). Three third-grade teachers' gender-related beliefs and behaviour. *Elementary School Journal, 102*(1), 81–94.

Garwood, J. D., Harris, A. H., & Tomick, J. K. (2017). Starting at the beginning: An intuitive choice for classroom management. *Teacher Education and Practice, 30*(1). Retrieved from: https://www.researchgate.net/publication/316982528_Starting_at_the_Beginning_An_Intuitive_Choice_for_Classroom_Management.

Gay, G. (2006). Connections between classroom management and culturally responsive teaching. In C. M. Evertson, & C. S. Weinstein (Eds.), *Handbook of classroom management: Research, practice, and contemporary issues* (pp. 343–70). Routledge.

Gay, G. (2010). *Culturally responsive teaching: Theory, research, and practice* (2nd ed.). Teachers College Press.

Glock, S. (2016). Stop talking out of turn: The influence of students' gender and ethnicity on preservice teachers' intervention strategies for student misbehavior. *Teaching and Teacher Education, 56,* 106–14. https://doi.org/10.1016/j.tate.2016.02.012.

Heath, S. B. (1983). *Ways with words: Language, life and work in communities and classrooms.* Cambridge University Press.

Hickey, D. T., & Schafer, N. J. (2006). Sociocultural, knowledge-centered views of classroom management. *Handbook of classroom management: Research, practice, & contemporary issues.* Simon & Schuster Macmillan.

Himmelstein, K. E. W., & Brückner, H. (2011). Criminal-justice and school sanctions against nonheterosexual youth: A national longitudinal study. *Pediatrics, 127*(1), 49–57. http://doi.org/10.1542/peds.2009-2306.

Howe, C. (1997). *Gender and classroom interaction: A research review.* Scottish Council for Research in Education.

Ilter, I. (2017). Notetaking skills instruction for development of middle school students' notetaking performance. *Psychology in the Schools, 54*(6), 596–611. doi: 10.1002/pits.22021.

Johnson, T. C., Stoner, G., & Green, S. K. (1996). Demonstrating the experimenting society model with classwide behavior management interventions. *School Psychology Review, 25*(2), 199–214.

Jones, V., & Jones, L. (2016). *Comprehensive classroom management: Creating communities of support and solving problems* (11th ed.). Pearson.

Kohlberg, L. (1984). *The psychology of moral development.* Harper & Row.

Koops, L. H. (2018). Classroom management for early childhood music settings. *General Music Today, 31*(3), 82–86.

Koran, S., & Koran, E. (2018). Classroom management and school science labs: A review of literature on classroom management strategies. *International Journal of School Sciences & Educational Studies, 5*(2), 64–72.

Kounin, J. (1970). *Discipline and group management in classrooms.* Holt, Rinehart & Winston.

Kwok, A. (2018). Classroom management actions of beginning urban teachers. *Urban Education, 54*(3), 339–67. doi: 10.1177/0042085918795017.

Ladson-Billings, G. (1994). *The dreamkeepers.* Jossey-Bass.

Ladson-Billings, G. (1995). Toward a theory of culturally relevant pedagogy. *American Educational Research Journal, 32*(3), 465–91.

Ladson-Billings, G. (2000). Fighting for our lives: Preparing teachers to teach African American students. *Journal of Teacher Education, 51*(3), 206–14. https://doi.org/10.1177/0022487100051003008.

Long, A., Renshaw, T., & Camarota, D. (2018). Classroom management in an urban, alternative school: A comparison of mindfulness and behavioral approaches. *Contemporary School Psychology, 22*(3), 233–48. doi: 10.1007/s40688-018-0177-y.

Losen, D. J., & Gillespie, J. (2012). *Opportunities suspended: The disparate impact of disciplinary exclusion from school.* Retrieved from: http://civilrightsproject.ucla.edu/

resources/projects/cen-ter-for-civil-rights-remedies/school-to-prison-folder/federal-reports/upcoming-ccrr-research/.

Loureiro, C. P., & Souza, D. D. (2013). The relationship between theory of mind and moral development in preschool children. *Paideia, 23*(54). https://doi.org/10.1590/1982-43272354201311.

Marzano, R. J. (2017). *The new art and science of teaching.* Solution Tree Press.

McCray, A. D., Sindelar, P. T., Kilgore, K. K., & Neal, L. I. (2002). African-American women's decisions to become teachers: Sociocultural perspectives. *International Journal of Qualitative Studies in Education, 15*(3), 269–90. https://doi.org/10.1080/09518390210122845.

Mercado, G., & Trumbull, E. (2018). Mentoring beginning immigrant teachers: How culture may impact the message. *International Journal of Psychology, 53*(S2), 44–53. doi: 10.1002/ijop.12555.

Mizala, A., Martinez, F., & Martinez, S. (2015). Pre-service elementary school teachers' expectations about student performance: How their beliefs are affected by their mathematics anxiety and their student's gender. *Teaching and Teacher Education, 50,* 70–78.

Moghtadaie, L., & Haveida, R. (2015). Relationship between academic optimism and classroom management styles of teachers-case study: Elementary school teachers in Isfahan. *International Education Studies, 8*(11), 184–92.

Monroe, C. R., & Obidah, J. E. (2004). The influence of cultural synchronization on a teacher's perceptions of disruption: A case study of an African American middle-school classroom. *Journal of Teacher Education, 55,* 256–68. doi:10.1177/0022487104263977.

Monzo, L. D., & Rueda, R. S. (2001). *Sociocultural factors in social relationships: Examining Latino teachers' and paraeducators' interactions with Latino students* (Research Report 9). Center for Research on Education, Diversity and Excellence (ERIC ED 451 724).

Myles, B. S., & Simpson, R. L. (2001). Understanding the hidden curriculum: An essential social skill for children and youth with Asperger syndrome. *Intervention in School and Clinic, 36*(5), 279–86.

Nagro, S. A., Fraser, D. W., & Hooks, S. D. (2019). Lesson planning with engagement in mind: Proactive classroom management strategies for curriculum instruction. *Intervention in School and Clinic, 45*(3), 131–40.

Närhi, V., Kiiski, T., & Savolainen, H. (2017). Reducing disruptive behaviours and improving classroom behavioural climate with class-wide positive behavior support. *British Educational Research Journal, 43*(6), 1186–205. doi: 10.1002/berj.3305.

Okonofua, J. A., & Eberhardt, J. A. (2015). Two strikes: Race and the disciplining of young students: *Psychological Science, 26,* 617–24.

Organisation for Economic Co-operation and Development. (2009). *Creating effective teaching and learning environments: First results from TALIS.* Retrieved from

http://www.oecd.org/education/school/creatingeffectiveteachingandlearning environmentsfirstresultsfromtalis.htm.
Parkay, F. W. (2016). *Becoming a teacher* (10th ed.). Pearson Education.
Pas, E. T., Cash, A. H., O'Brennan, L., Debnam, K. J., & Bradshaw, C. P. (2015). Profiles of classroom behavior in high schools: Associations with teacher behavior management strategies and classroom composition. *Journal of School Psychology, 53*, 137–48.
Piaget, J. (1965). *The moral judgment of the child*. Free Press.
Porowski, A., O'Conner, R., & Passa, A. (2014). *Disproportionality in school discipline: An assessment of trends in Maryland, 2009–12* (Report #REL 2014-017). Washington, DC: U.S. Department of Education, Institute of Education Sciences. Retrieved from http://ies.ed.gov /ncee/edlabs.
Poteat, V. P., Scheer, J. R., & Chong, E. S. K. (2016). Sexual orientation-based disparities in school and juvenile justice discipline: A multiple group comparison of contributing factors. *Journal of Educational Psychology, 108*(2), 229–41. doi .org/10.1037/edu0000058.
Rahman, K. (2013). Belonging and learning to belong in school: The implications of the hidden curriculum for indigenous students. *Discourse: Studies in Cultural Politics of Education, 34*(5), 660–72.
Rawlings-Lester, R., Bolton-Allanson, P., & Notar, C. (2017). Routines are the foundation of classroom management. *Education, 137*(4), 398–412.
Redding, C. (2019). A teacher like me: A review of the effect of student–teacher racial/ethnic matching on teacher perceptions of students and student academic and behavioral outcomes. *Review of Educational Research, 89*(4), 499–535.
Responsive Classroom. (2017, August 17). *Starting the year off with joy*. Retrieved from: https://www.responsiveclassroom.org/starting-the-year-off-with-joy/.
Ritter, J. T., & Hancock, D. R. (2007). Exploring the relationships between certification sources, experience levels, and classroom management orientations of classroom teachers. *Teaching and Teacher Education, 23*(7), 1206–16. https://doi .org/10.1016/j.tate.2006.04.013.
Roache, J. & Lewis, R. (2011). Teachers' views on the impact of classroom management on student responsibility. *Australian Journal of Education, 55*(2), 132–46. doi:10.1177/000494441105500204.
Sadker, M., & Sadker, D. (1986). Sexism in the classroom: From grade school to graduate school. *The Phi Delta Kappan, 67*(7), 512–15.
Samanci, O. (2010). Democracy education in elementary schools. *The Social Studies, 101*, 30–33. doi: 10.1080/00377990903285499.
Scarlett, G. (2015). *The Sage encyclopedia of classroom management*. Sage.
Sieberer-Nagler, K. (2016). Effective classroom-management and positive teaching. *English Language Teaching, 9*(1), 163–72.
Simonsen, B., Freeman, J., Goodman, S., Mitchell, B., Swain-Bradway, J., Flannery, B., Sugai, G., George, H., and Putnam, B. (2015). *Supporting and responding to student behavior: Evidence-based classroom strategies for teachers* (OSEP

Technical Assistance Brief). Retrieved from: https://osepideasthatwork.org/sites/default/files/ClassroomPBIS_508.pdf.

Simpson, A., & Erickson, M. (1983). Teachers' verbal and nonverbal communication patterns as a function of teacher race, student gender, and student race. *American Educational Research Journal, 20*, 183–98.

Skiba, R., Ormiston, H., Martinez, S., & Cummings, J. (2016). Teaching the social curriculum: Classroom management as behavioral instruction. *Theory into Practice, 55*(2), 120–28. doi:10.1080/00405841.2016.1148990.

Stainback, W., Stainback, S., & Froyen, L. (1987). Structuring class to prevent disruptive behaviors. *Teaching Exceptional Children, 19*(4), 12–16.

Staub, E. (1979). *Positive social behavior and morality*. Academic Press.

Stevens, K. (2015). Gender bias in teacher interactions with students. *Master of Education Program Theses, 90*. https://digitalcollections.dordt.edu/med_theses/90.

Therrien, W., Benson, S., Hughes, C., & Morris, J. (2017). Explicit instruction and next generation science standards aligned classrooms: A fit or a split? *Learning Disabilities Research and Practice, 32*(3), 149–54.

Tjosvold, D. (1980). Control, conflict, and collaboration in the classroom. *The Educational Forum, 44*(2), 195-203.

Vincent, C. G., Randall, C., Cartledge, G., Tobin, T. J., & Swain-Bradway, J. (2011). Toward a conceptual integration of cultural responsiveness and schoolwide positive behavior support. *Journal of Positive Behavior Interventions, 13*(4), 219–29. https://doi.org/10.1177/1098300711399765.

Wallace, J. M., Goodkind, S., Wallace, C. M., & Bachman, J. G. (2008). Racial, ethnic, and gender differences in school discipline among U.S. high school students: 1991–2005. *The Negro Educational Review, 59*(1–2), 47–62.

Weinstein, C. S., Curran, M., & Tomlinson-Clarke, S. (2003). Culturally responsive classroom management: Awareness into action. *Theory into Practice, 42*(4), 269–76.

Weinstein, C. S., Tomlinson-Clarke, S., & Curran, M. (2004). Toward a conception of culturally responsive classroom management. *Journal of Teacher Education, 55*(1), 25–38. https://doi.org/10.1177/0022487103259812.

Whitaker, T. (2013). *What great teachers do differently: 17 things that matter most* (2nd ed.). Routledge.

Whitaker, T., Whitaker, M., & Whitaker, K. (2016). *Your first year: How to survive and thrive as a new teacher*. Routledge.

Wolfgang, C. H., & Glickman, C. D. (1986). *Solving discipline problems: Strategies for classroom teachers* (2nd ed.). Allyn & Bacon.

Whether, When, and How Teachers Can Intervene

2

AUDRA CERRUTO AND RICKEY MORONEY

CLASSROOM MANAGEMENT IS A DYNAMIC PROCESS between the classroom teacher and students. Teachers may vary their classroom management style and approach to be effective with different classes and/or individual students. As a diverse group of teachers and learners comprise each classroom, the classroom management techniques should be responsive to the needs of the situation. Ultimately, self-efficacy and individual dispositions impact the relationship between teacher and students, which in turn cultivates the classroom climate. To determine whether, when, and how teachers can intervene in a challenging classroom situation, many elements must be considered.

The circumstances surrounding a behavior can be interpreted by exploring the function of student behavior, the established rules and procedures of the classroom, and the implementation of self-monitoring skills. While this is a great deal of work to engage in thoughtful reflection prior to intervening in a less-than-desirable situation, it ensures the promotion of dignity for all. Teachers and students should strive to respect individual differences, to expect successful teaching and learning experiences, and to value the opportunities to meet the individual needs of classroom members.

Self-Efficacy

Self-efficacy is "the belief in one's capabilities to organize and execute the courses of action required to manage prospective situations" (Bandura, 1995, p. 2). To paraphrase, self-efficacy is believing in yourself to take action. Albert Bandura originated the theory of self-efficacy, which he defined as the belief in one's effectiveness to perform specific tasks.

His theory maintains that people are likely to participate in activities to the extent that they perceive themselves to be proficient. There are four sources of self-efficacy, according to Bandura's theory:

a. Performance Accomplishments (based on an individual's accomplishments; previous successes raise mastery expectations, while repeated failures lower them).
b. Vicarious Experience (gained by observing others perform the activities successfully; often referred to as modeling, observers can improve their performance via observations).
c. Social Persuasion (people believe they can cope successfully with specific tasks through strategies such as coaching and giving evaluative feedback on performance).
d. Physiological and Emotional States (individuals' physiological or emotional state influence their self-efficacy judgments concerning specific tasks and their emotional reaction to their ability to complete the tasks [Bandura, 2017]).

Teacher Self-Efficacy

Teacher self-efficacy is a teacher's attitude toward the profession of teaching. A teacher's disposition toward students and colleagues, motivation, and belief in their impact on student learning contribute to a sense of self-efficacy. This perspective influences how they view their effectiveness in the classroom, level of effort necessary to meet the needs of students, attitude toward students, degree of persistence and resilience in the face of challenges, and levels of aspiration. The teachers' perspective of their self-efficacy impacts the classroom management style of the teachers, which in turn impacts student behavior (Bandura, 1993; see also Cayci, 2011; Fallon, 2007; Tschannen-Moran & Hoy, 2001).

A teacher's self-efficacy influences the classroom climate in multiple ways. Aside from instructional effectiveness, it can guide students' sense of responsibility for their actions and the level of respect held for their teacher. Lewis, Romi, and Roche (2012) indicate that based on certain teacher behaviors, students' level of ownership of their behaviors is impacted.

Australian students participated in a study that addressed expulsion from the classroom. When teachers took the time to warn, explain, and discuss the nature of the behavior and the impact it was having on the classroom climate, students readily took responsibility for their actions. However, if a teacher did not engage in a dialogue with the students, the students were more likely to blame the teacher for their behavior. In these situations, the students felt their behavior was the result of their teacher's disposition rather than their own.

Okonofua, Paunesku, and Walton (2016) explore students' respect for teachers based on teachers' mindsets about discipline. Their research suggests that teachers who discipline with a punitive mindset—rather than an empathetic mindset—lost their students' respect. The use of an empathetic dialogue between teachers and students decreased suspension rates. In addition, studies on the impact of zero-tolerance policies reveal an increase in students' disrespect for authority figures based on the punitive approach to behavioral problems (Gonzalez, 2012; see also Teasley, 2014). The establishment of positive teacher/student relationships impacts more than teaching and learning; it shapes the classroom climate.

Purkey and Stanley (1991) offer descriptions of four teacher types and the impact of teacher-type attributes on classroom climate and the establishment of relationships (see table 2.1). Based on the four teacher types—(a) intentionally uninviting, (b) intentionally inviting, (c) unintentionally uninviting, and (d) unintentionally inviting—there can either be a classroom climate of mutual respect, trust, and positive mindset, or a classroom climate of negative, dismissive, and pessimistic attitudes.

Table 2.1. The Four Teacher Types

Teacher Type	Samples of Behaviors
Intentionally Uninviting	Deliberately demean, discourage, defeat, and dissuade students. They never smile.
Intentionally Inviting	Possess a professional attitude, conscientious, strive to be more effective, put into practice a sound philosophy of education, and can analyze the process of student learning. They are inviting and use proper emotions at appropriate times.
Unintentionally Uninviting	Oblivious to the fact that they are negative, feel they are well meaning, but not seen that way by others who see them as patronizing, thoughtless, and condescending. They keep their arms folded when interacting with students.
Unintentionally Inviting	"Natural-born teachers" are generally well-liked and effective but unaware that they are effective, affable, sincere, and enthusiastic. They want to be friends with students, but the students may not be learning to their fullest potential.

Student Self-Efficacy

When students are confident in their self-efficacy, they can successfully negotiate academic, emotional, and social situations. Their self-efficacy comes from direct and explicit experience, encouragement, and appropriate emotional responses (Bandura, 1986). This knowledge and supported development of skills often facilitate appropriate responses or behaviors. Students will act accordingly only if they have the confidence to respond suitably.

Student self-efficacy can play a role in regulating social behavior as well as having a positive approach to life events and choosing a positive method of solving conflicts. Chung and Elias (1996) find that students' positive social self-efficacy aids their recognition of normative peer standards that reduces or lessens problem behavior; positive social self-efficacy helps to form friendships and results in more effective communication skills. Self-control and self-efficacy also bolster students' conflict resolution skills.

Teachers and school counselors can use skill-building interventions to improve nonaggressive student behavior and students' sense of personal control (Bandura, 1991). Some effective techniques and strategies suggested by Vera, Shin, Montgomery, Mildner, and Speight (2004) include (a) direct experiences, such as role playing; and (b) vicarious experiences, including role modeling. The national model of the American School Counseling Association (2003) supports these same techniques, emphasizing respect for the self and others and developing skills to interact with others.

This model provides a framework for all stakeholders in the school community and outlines the elements of a school program that are essential to the school's mission to have a meaningful, constructive impact on student achievement, attendance, and discipline. It guides school programs to create a developmentally appropriate curriculum focused on the attitudes and behaviors of all students for their success, close the achievement and opportunity gaps, and eventually result in improved student achievement, attendance, and discipline.

Teacher and student self-efficacy, or collective efficacy, highlights the importance of the personal relationship between teachers and their students. Evans and Tribble (1986) purport that problems such as classroom discipline can be mitigated by the establishment of meaningful teacher/student relationships with a positive sense of efficacy. A collective efficacy in which all participants demonstrate a sense of competency, enthusiasm, commitment, and motivation facilitates an environment of mutual respect and dignity for all. As such, classroom behavior can be positively impacted by a positive sense of collective efficacy. In other words, the personal relationships among members of the classroom community have the power to impact behavior.

Relationships

To determine whether, when, and how teachers can intervene in a classroom setting, student behaviors should be interpreted through the lens of the classroom climate, which includes understanding the teaching and learning environment established by the teacher and embraced by the classroom community. According to Smith, Fisher, and Frey (2015), there are two elements of effective learning environment relationships and high-quality instruction.

The old adage of "students don't care what you know until they know you care" is a powerful statement (Smith et al., 2015, p. 2). The restorative perspectives view misbehavior as an act against relationships and as such, seek accountability for actions in the spirit of empathy and repairing of harm. In this way, restorative justice approaches support the critical connection between the teacher and student when creating an effective teaching and learning environment that can, in turn, foster a high-quality education.

Through restorative practices, teachers can create a positive teaching and learning environment by establishing relationships with their students. Smith et al. (2015) highlight several strategies that teachers can implement to develop and maintain relationships with their students. Simple suggestions to creative a positive classroom climate include knowing and using students' names; spending time learning about each student's interests, passions, and personal and academic goals; exploring students' families' and parents' expectations about school and behaviors; and identifying students' expectations about school and behaviors. Collecting data about students can take the form of surveys, interviews, informal conversations with the student and/or the parents, and projects.

Examples of Creating a Positive Teaching and Learning Environment

VIGNETTE 1

As Mrs. Judy greets her kindergarten students each day at the classroom door, each student may tap on one of the wall signs (see figure 2.1; see also The Core Coaches, 2020) that describes how they want to be greeted that day (Judy, 2018). This teacher provides the students with an opportunity to communicate their needs and wants and is responsive to those requests, thereby creating a positive classroom climate.

Good Morning or Good Bye

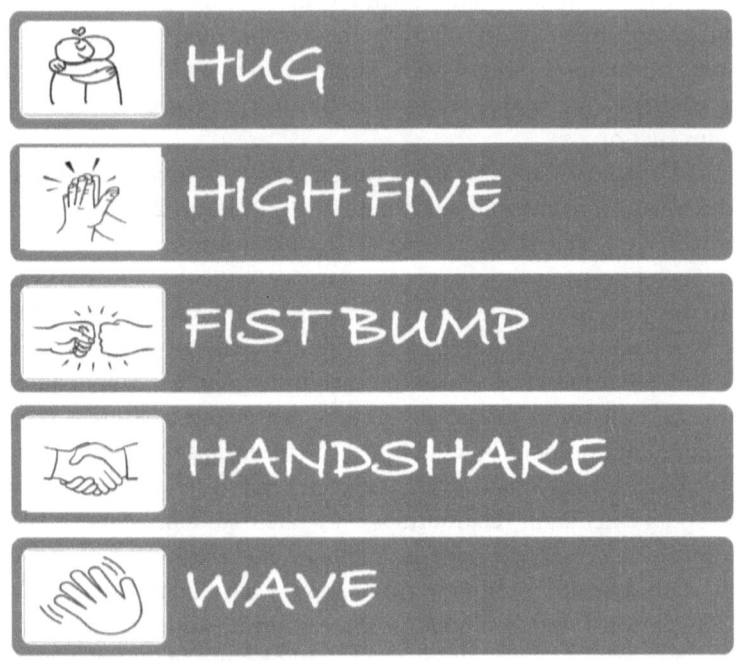

Figure 2.1. Morning Greetings
Source: Adapted from Core Coaches, 2020

VIGNETTE 2
Another teacher, Mr. White, has developed a unique handshake with each of his fifth-grade students. Every morning, he welcomes each student to his classroom with this action (WCNC, 2017). Incorporating students' interests and passions into lessons is an intentional way to demonstrate that the teacher values the unique attributes of the student body.

Relationship-Building Activities

There are many fun activities to welcome students into the classroom, to facilitate building relationships, to promote familiarity, and to engage students in the learning process. The activities in table 2.2 offer some ways to engage students in this process.

Table 2.2. **Relationship-Building Activities**

Activity	Description
Silent Interview (Deardorff, 2003)	Students pair up and interview one another by communicating nonverbally, using gestures, and guessing answers to personal descriptive questions. After an allotted amount of time, they share the answers to those questions verbally. Students get to know one another and establish relationships based on common interests.
Who Could It Bee? (Moroney, 2019)	Students write three little-known facts about themselves, put their name at the top of the paper, and fold it over. The teacher reads the first student's three facts, then the student who guesses the person's identity reads the next three facts, and the game continues until each student's facts are revealed. This gives the teacher and students an opportunity to get to know each other more deeply.
Cross the Line (Tullis, 2004)	All the students line up on one side of a rope, and when a statement is read that applies to them, they cross the line (e.g., "If you're wearing blue, cross the line"). Students begin to see all of the things they have in common. Teachers also learn about students' likes, dislikes, their families, what they do outside of school time, etc.
Find Someone Like You (Algebra That Functions, 2006)	The objective is to find someone who has the same interests. A questionnaire is distributed to each student with questions such as, "Locate a person who has a pet in their home." Each student would find another person who has a pet and writes down the type of pet and the other person's name. Teachers can help facilitate student connections. Students discover common interests and begin to talk about their commonalities.
Classroom Circles (Costello, Wachtel, & Wachtel, 2010)	Classroom circles serve as a way to build relationships and resolve conflicts in classroom communities. Moderated by the teacher or a trained professional, these formal and informal dialogue circles help students understand their own role in and take responsibility for creating and maintaining a happy and peaceful classroom.

Smith et al. (2015) posits that teachers should maintain a positive attitude to facilitate creating a positive classroom climate. Although it is a reasonable suggestion, there are a variety of pressures faced by teachers every day that can make it a challenge to be consistently uplifting. Teachers are under pressure to address

a. established learning standards;
b. preparing students for high-stakes assessments;
c. collecting, interpreting, and applying data; and

d. creating a safe, engaging, and stimulating environment for their students.

The stress of these pressures can lead to job dissatisfaction, ineffective teaching, inconsistent and poor classroom management, and ultimately teacher burnout. Therefore, the development of a positive sense of self-efficacy and meaningful relationships is essential to addressing these issues and can help educators respond to individual variability, address adversity, and support resilience, enabling both teachers and students to find positive pathways to school success.

Whether to Intervene

Function of Behavior

It is important to determine a student's purpose for his or her behavior to ascertain whether a teacher should intervene. Different behaviors have different purposes based on the individual needs of the student. As a result, each behavior may require a different intervention.

Facilitating dignity for all in the classroom setting is paramount for teachers. As a result, teachers need to consider that each child is different, has unique needs, and may engage in a behavior for different purposes and outcomes. Without minimizing the importance of the individual needs of students, it is helpful to explore the common reasons for student behavior. Generally speaking, student behavior can be interpreted as attention seeking, avoiding or escaping, tangible power/control, or fulfilling a sensory need (Smith et al., 2015; see also Teaching Tolerance, 2016).

Teaching Tolerance utilizes the acronym EATS to highlight four of the most common needs that drive student behavior. EATS (escape, attention, tangible gains, and sensory needs) can facilitate the interpretation of the behavior's purpose and determine whether an intervention is needed. For example, "avoidance" or "escape" behaviors reveal a need for the student to disengage from a situation that is aversive—possibly in a physical, emotional, and/or cognitive manner.

Attention-seeking behavior—to gain the attention of others—may be used to gain positive or negative input or feedback. Some behaviors are designed to acquire something preferred, whether that might be an object or activity for tangible gain. A student may engage in a behavior to satisfy a sensory or internal need for self-regulatory or self-soothing purposes. Finally, a student may engage in a behavior to gain power or control. Each behavior communicates to the teacher the student's needs and should be interpreted accordingly (Smith et al., 2015).

In addition, it is critical for teachers to consider the developmental level of each student, accounting for cognitive and social-emotional functioning, in order to interpret a behavior. A sixth grader, who may function at a third-grade level, may engage in a particular behavior with a different purpose than a sixth grader functioning at grade level.

For example, a student may be disruptive during a reading task that is above his or her reading level with the purpose of escaping the activity that is too difficult to engage in, whereas a student functioning at grade level may be disruptive to gain the attention of his or her peers (Korpershoek, Harms, de Boer, van Kuijk, & Doolaard, 2016). Sensitivity and awareness of the potential function of student behavior is useful to determine the need to intervene in a situation.

Rules and Procedures

Another criterion to determine if teacher intervention is needed is to consider whether the behavior violated the rules and procedures of the classroom. However, research neither supports nor negates whether it is more effective for students to co-create classroom rules with the teacher or for the teacher to generate rules. Research clearly supports that rules and procedures need to be explicitly taught to the students and reviewed and practiced on a regular basis to ensure that the students understand class expectations (Alberto & Troutman, 2013; see also Alter & Haydon, 2017; Mitchell, Hirn, & Lewis, 2017).

Scott, Anderson, and Alter (2011) as well as Kerr and Nelson (2010) report that teachers should teach classroom rules in the same manner as academic material and should provide a rationale, examples, and opportunities to practice through role play. Alter and Haydon's (2017) research supports the optimal use of four rules written in a positive tone. In terms of whether or not to intervene, teachers must carefully analyze whether a behavior, interpreted through its function, is violating a class rule or procedure.

Self-Monitoring

There is another critical element that needs to be in place and taken into consideration prior to deciding whether to intervene: has the student been given feedback on his or her behavior and the opportunity to self-correct prior to an intervention? There are many technology tools available to track, monitor, and impact behavior in the classroom. These tools provide feedback and can redirect a student to change the behavior prior to teacher intervention.

Some apps are often able to make a positive difference for both students and teachers, as is suggested by a study of middle school students conducted by Cetin and Cetin (2018), as well as another study conducted with elementary students by Dillon, Radley, Tingstrom, and Barry (2019). Both studies used ClassDojo, which is an app that reports and tracks behaviors in real time. Cetin and Cetin (2018) focus on individual motivation and the ability to recognize and modify behavior through feedback with ClassDojo, while Dillon et al. (2019) focuses on positive peer behavior to motivate behavioral change.

There are a few reasons why ClassDojo and other tracking and monitoring strategies applications are effective in creating opportunities for students to self-correct. As students' social skills develop, young learners may not immediately be able to identify their negative behaviors. Students may develop self-monitoring skills through these applications to identify when unwanted behaviors occur. They then might receive tangible feedback about the unwanted behaviors, which promotes self-regulation. Instead of feeling unable to control or impact the behaviors, students develop a sense of control. Weber, Bockenholt, Hilton, & Wallace (1993) state the goals for self-monitoring:

- focusing on the task or assignment (on-task)
- making positive statements to peers
- completing work
- complying with the teacher's requests

Using ClassDojo, both students and teachers can simultaneously track data. The monitoring portion of the app can be set for a pre-selected duration, and when the timer goes off (e.g., every five minutes), both the teacher and the student can mark whether the student is on-task or off-task. Using joint monitoring, the student can develop the ability to determine if, in fact, the behavior was off task. This identification can lead to the implementation of new strategies and interventions to promote on-task behaviors, and the data can be collected over time and can even be shared with parents daily via email. Table 2.3 presents additional technology-based resources to promote self-monitoring skills among students.

Table 2.3. Technology Resources to Promote Self-Monitoring Skills

Tool	Function	Description
ClassDojo	Develop self-monitoring skills and increase positive classroom behaviors.	• Awards students points for positive classroom behaviors. • Great for homeschool communication. • Parents view their child's points in real time. • Automatically generates weekly behavior reports sent to parents. • Students customize monster avatars to display running point totals. • Teachers view class points to create some friendly competition.
Too Noisy	Can encourage students to self-monitor the volume in the classroom and make changes accordingly.	• Teachers can set this noise-level meter to an agreed-upon volume for the current classroom activity. • If the volume exceeds an acceptable level, graphics simulate a cracking screen and an alarm is sounded.
Stop Go!	Transitioning between activities in an educational setting frequently causes disruptive behaviors. Stop Go! can make classroom transitions run more smoothly.	• A traffic light app paired with a timer can be set to clearly signal to students that it is time to finish an activity and go to the next one. • As the light changes, a bell chimes, signaling students with both auditory and visual cues.
The Great Behavior Game	Teachers monitor student progress, generate and print reports, and send home weekly progress reports. Student scores are displayed so students can monitor their progress throughout the day.	• In this "game," teachers award students bonus points for good behavior and staying on task during instructional time and assign penalties for poor behavior. • Can also penalize particularly disruptive students with "timeouts" and "freezes," during which they're temporarily unable to earn points or advance to the next level. • The leaderboard allows teachers to encourage friendly competition and rewards high-performing students throughout the day (Lynch, 2017).
Teacher's Assistant	Helps teachers track student behavior, notice trends, communicate with parents, and manage their students.	• Teachers can easily document student behavior. • Can create categories to monitor recurring behaviors like talking, bullying, etc. • App also allows teachers to log positive behavior. • Teachers manage student behavior and reinforce positive behavior using real-time data. • Can note and use data in cases of negative behavior trends to work with students on behavior management plans to improve and identify negative behavior.

When to Intervene

The teacher can determine whether to intervene based on several factors such as the classroom climate, teacher-student relationships, the function of the student's behavior interpreted through the lens of established classroom rules and procedures, and prior student's opportunities to self-monitor and adjust behavior. Relevant information needs to be synthesized and analyzed by the teacher to determine an appropriate intervention.

Knowing the students is critical to decide as to when and how to intervene in a timely manner. First, the teacher will determine if an immediate, delayed, or deferred intervention should occur. If the behavior is harmful, distracting to others, ignites undesirable behaviors in other students, or challenges the established system, it is appropriate to intervene.

However, there is a caveat; if the student or teacher is not in a frame of mind to be open to a dialogue, the intervention should be delayed until another time. For example, if a student is agitated, the priority should be to calm the student and to create a safe space. In this case, having a conversation may escalate the emotions of the individuals involved. Smith et al. (2015) suggested several restorative justice techniques to de-escalate a situation: speak in a low and soft tone, recognize and identify the student's feelings, do not interpret the student's behaviors as a personal attack, do not shame the student because of the behavior, and engage in a nonjudgmental manner.

When teachers model a calm aura through their tone, facial expression, and posture, students react less defensively. Teachers should (a) listen to discover what might be behind the student's behavior; (b) concentrate on the student's emotions, thoughts, and reactions; and (c) create time and space for reflection for both parties. Teachers must also practice techniques to calm their own reactions by taking deep breaths, allocating time to calm down, stretching, and modeling these actions for the student. It may also help to redirect the student by asking them to get a drink of water or to take deep breaths before any discussion takes place (Desautels, 2019).

Educators can support self-regulation skills in students by implementing co-regulation techniques in the classroom (see the section on co-regulation below). Teachers must first look for cues signaling stress or anxiety in a student. These cues may include (a) inappropriate behavior; (b) outbursts; (c) negative remarks; (d) refusal to work; (e) whining; and (f) indications of anxiety such as fidgeting, leg shaking, or fist clenching. How can teachers guide the students to a self-regulating mindset? Teachers can teach self-calming skills using de-escalation techniques, according to Vollrath (2020). Teaching these underdeveloped, self-calming skills to their students will be essential to students' school success.

How to Intervene

The following section introduces the concept of *co-regulation* and corresponding strategies that can facilitate monitoring and regulating students' behavior in the classroom. The overarching goal is to guide participants to become self-regulating individuals who make appropriate and positive decisions according to the environmental needs and demands.

Co-Regulation

According to Desautels (2019), *co-regulation* is the process of aiding a student who has made a poor choice of behavior to recover their equanimity while beginning to increase the teacher's awareness of how that student is feeling. This process also regulates the teacher's own responses as they address student interactions. Co-regulation is a key component in discipline and can be a key strategy in maintaining a positive classroom climate.

Today's students come to school with a variety of adverse childhood experiences manifesting as anxiety, adversity, and trauma. While a school's social-emotional programs may address some of these problems, rethinking discipline policies and procedures can help to develop desirable behavioral qualities. Traditional discipline is effective for students who need it least and often does not work for those who need it most.

The success of co-regulation depends on building a trusting relationship between the student and the teacher. As the teacher remains calm to co-regulate the student, he or she is ensuring a safe environment and a personal connection through which a poor choice of behavior can be handled. A trusting relationship can take many forms but will always have mutual respect as the cornerstone.

To be clear, the creation of a calm and trusting environment does not necessarily lead to a lack of consequences for poor behavior choices. Rather, it helps students to regulate their emotions and effect change in future behavior. Students' buy-in and commitment are critical and can be best developed in a calm and trusting environment. Mutual respect and commitment can help the teacher to understand the core reason (function of behavior) and the pattern of the behavior, as well as the student's feelings and actions.

De-Escalation Strategies

Co-regulation strategies to promote a calm and safe environment take various forms and will vary according to the unique needs of teachers and students. A few strategies that help prevent and de-escalate volatile situations may be implemented to promote positive interventions (see table 2.4).

Table 2.4. De-Escalation Techniques

Activity	De-Escalation Techniques	
	How	When
Older Children (middle school through high school)		
Breathing techniques to regain calmness	Teacher says, "I notice you're really upset. Let's work together on breathing slowly for one minute in order to manage your impulses."	After behavior occurs to provide time and a technique for the student to calm down
Invite and encourage the student to be aware of thoughts and feelings	Teacher says, "What's going on in your brain and body right now? Tell me how you feel and what you're thinking, and if you're ready to focus on moving forward to become calmer."	When the behavior is occurring
Encourage the student to redirect their thoughts	Teacher says, "Take a minute, close your eyes, breathe slowly, and think about something that makes you happy."	As the behavior is occurring or immediately after
Give positive feedback to calm the student	Teacher says after asking the student to close eyes, "Now open your eyes. How are you feeling? Let me know if you need more time to settle down. You should feel happy and excited about getting to this point in your work."	Right after the behavior occurs
Give student time to refocus	Teacher says, "Take another minute and do something for yourself. Go for a walk, get some air, tell me about a recent pleasant experience."	Right after the behavior occurs
Ask the student to prepare a reflection to use in the future	Teacher says, "The next time you're feeling this way and I'm not with you, what can you say to yourself to take charge of your thinking and behavior, and regulate or calm yourself down?"	When the student's agitation or anger has begun to subside
Younger Children (early childhood through elementary)		
Create a safe classroom environment for children to form trusting relationships with adults	Teacher encourages children to form a trusting relationship with them as the teacher becomes a caregiver in the classroom setting.	At all times
Meet children's needs to build trust	Teacher provides responsive, consistent, nurturing care to form trust with children so that they feel comfortable and happy.	At all times
Promote positive thoughts and feeling in children	Teacher nurtures children to feel positive, supported, and confident to help them develop strong self-regulation skills.	At all times
Model self-regulation	Teacher promotes the process of co-regulation so that students learn healthy ways to manage their feelings.	At all times

FRIEND-IN-NEED SYSTEM

This strategy (Desautels, 2019) encourages the student to choose a buddy—either a peer or a trusted adult—to go to when feeling anxious or irritated. The student can take a break, remove himself or herself from the environment, and talk through behavioral challenges with the buddy. This technique is an example of a preventative discipline approach and allows student choices when negative feelings arise.

VALIDATION

This is another strategy to calm students who are angry or agitated (Desautels, 2019). Teachers can begin conversations using phrases such as:

- "That must be awful."
- "You seem really angry."
- "You seem really frustrated."
- "What a difficult situation you're in."

These validation phrases can reduce anxiety and engage students in a dialogue with their teacher. The technique of validation can open student–teacher discussions using choices, consequences, and creation of a behavior action plan for the future. The teacher's model of behavior using the techniques and strategies can be compelling for students to begin to act in the same ways.

TEACHING AND PRACTICING SELF-CALMING SKILLS AND DE-ESCALATION TECHNIQUES

These skills and techniques can aid both the student and the teacher to decrease negative impulses and emotions (Vollrath, 2020). They require rapport and a trusting relationship between the teacher and the student. According to Vollrath (2020), the de-escalation process should be centered on the student, should only take four to six minutes, and can begin with any number of the following techniques:

- Provide time for the student to regain calmness by saying something like, "I notice you're really upset. Let's work together on breathing slowly for one minute in order to manage your impulses."
- Invite and encourage the student to be aware of his or her thoughts and feelings by saying, "What's going on in your brain and body right now? Tell me how you feel and what you're thinking, and if you're ready to focus on moving forward to become calmer."

- Ask the student to redirect his or her thoughts by saying, "Take a minute, close your eyes, breathe slowly, and think about something that makes you happy." Give an example of a happy experience that the student may have shared with you, or if you are working with the whole class, ask students to focus on a happy experience.
- Give the student more time to refocus by saying, "Take another minute and do something for yourself. Go for a walk, get some air, tell me about a recent pleasant experience."
- Lead the student to engage in a "six-second pause activity" (Goalbook Toolkit, 2020). This activity involves shifting attention to a cognitively challenging task, such as asking the student to spell his or her name backward, listing pizza toppings, or listing states that begin with a vowel. Refocusing attention allows the brain a chance to calm down.
- Ask the student to project a reflection to use for the future and say, "The next time you're feeling this way and I'm not with you, what can you say to yourself to take charge of your thinking and behavior, and regulate or calm yourself down?"

These co-regulating techniques will work with very young children, according to Gillespie (2015):

- Teachers should create an environment where children can form a trusting relationship with you, the teacher, as a caregiver.
- Teachers must provide responsive, consistent, nurturing care and let the children know that their needs matter. Consistency exhibits and builds trust with children. When you nurture, you form a relationship with the child. Children learn to trust and feel comfortable and happy.
- Teachers can promote thoughts and feeling in children where they gain a level of comfort and feel positive, supported, and confident, which can help them develop strong self-regulation skills (McClelland & Tominey, 2018).
- Teachers should model self-regulation. This will promote the process of co-regulation. Learning healthy ways to manage emotions like being angry, overwhelmed, or burned out will help to promote a calm and supportive classroom environment for young children.

Teaching Self-Calming Skills

Many students do not know how to calm down, according to Minahan and Rappaport (2012). These three simple steps will help children to identify and address stress in their classroom environment:

1. Teach the student to identify emotions. Students who seem to get angry quickly typically grow angry or frustrated more gradually, but both the teacher and the student do not notice the buildup. Teaching students to recognize this escalation is essential to successfully catch their emotions before they burst. By showing the student an image called an "Emotional Thermometer" (see figure 2.2; Minahan & Rappaport, 2012), the teacher can explain how emotions grow over time from calm, to frustrated, to angry. Ask them to pay attention to their emotions at different times of the day and check in as needed to discuss what they are noticing over several weeks.

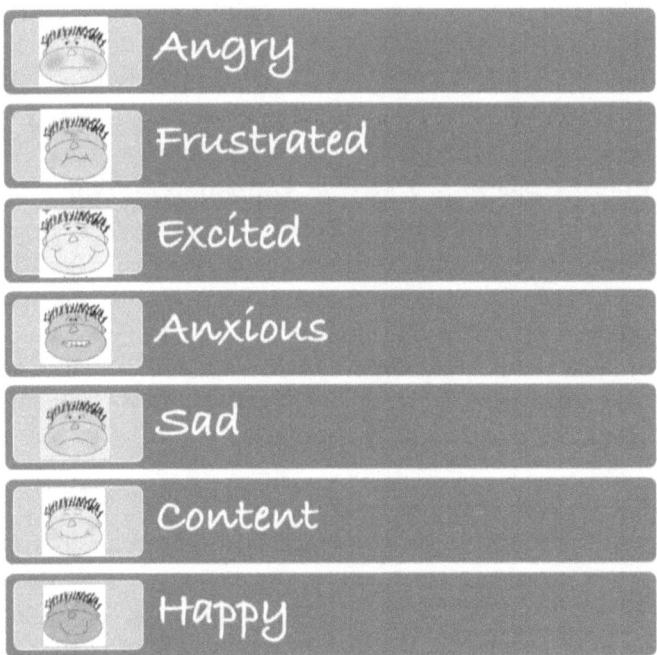

Figure 2.2. Emotional Thermometer
Source: Adapted from Minahan & Rappaport, 2012, p. 79.

2. Teach the student self-calming strategies. Once the student can identify the moment of frustration or anger, he or she can make use of a calming strategy. Teachers may need to take some time and try a variety of strategies for each student. The student may need frequent, gentle reminders to utilize the chosen strategy at first. Here are a few suggestions:

- reading a book
- deep breathing
- listening to music
- drawing
- doing yoga stretches

3. Practice with the student. Each day when students are calm, ask them to role-play what they look like when they are anxious, angry, or frustrated, and then ask them to practice their self-calming strategy.

Some students learn these skills quickly and others may need continued support. This training only takes a few minutes each day, but focusing on it daily is important until students have a grasp of the techniques. It is an essential skill for school success, as well as one that students will use at home and in all social settings.

Technology to Promote Positive Student Behavior

Tracking and monitoring student behavior helps students to recognize negative behavior at the time it occurs, to develop self-regulation skills, and to learn to keep the behavior in check. Incorporating technology into the self-monitoring process can motivate students to stay on-task (Bielefeld, 2016). The technologies listed in tables 2.3 and 2.5 can support and enhance co-regulation, self-calming skills, de-escalation techniques, and positive student behavior in the classroom.

STAYING ON-TASK

Students and teachers can simultaneously track off-task behavior and collect data using ClassDojo. Setting the monitoring piece of the app at a pre-selected interval, such as every five minutes, both the teacher and student can indicate whether the student was on-task or off-task. This can help students recognize their ability to determine their attention to tasks

Table 2.5. Using Technology to Intervene

Technology	Purpose	Outcome
ClassDojo	Staying on task.	Helps students recognize their ability to determine their attention to tasks and open a dialogue between the teacher and the student as they look at the collected data over time
Video	Positive peer interaction.	Shows other students how to behave; students who created a video also deepened their understanding of behavioral expectations
Timer	Work completion.	Keeping track of the data will help students pace themselves through tasks and aid their ability to focus
Doing-What-You-Are-Told	Students complete tasks on time.	Using data to self-monitor can raise students' awareness of both positive and negative behavior and help students focus and see their growth over time

and can open a dialogue between the teacher and the student as they look at the collected data over time.

POSITIVE PEER INTERACTION

A good example of this, according to Bielefeld (2016), was when a teacher asked a student to create a video about behavioral expectations throughout the school building, such as in the cafeteria or in the library. The objective of the video was to show other students how to behave in the cafeteria by illustrating how to go through the line, ask for help, and clean up when they were finished. The students who created the video also deepened their understanding of behavioral expectations.

WORK COMPLETION

Using a timer so students can complete tasks on time and keeping track of the data will help students pace themselves through tasks and aid their ability to focus. For example, in Doing-What-You-Are-Told, the self-monitoring approach can raise students' awareness of both positive and negative behavior.

Students can ask themselves, "Am I making good choices?" and be asked by their teacher, "What happened?" and "What was supposed to happen?" Teachers can use counter apps to tally the times students are focused during a finite duration, such as thirty minutes. Collecting that data on a chart can help students focus and see their growth over time. All data should be confidential to protect the student's identity, and conversations with students should be private.

Using technology effectively can change classroom dynamics. Creating opportunities for students to use technology in the classroom helps to identify positive and negative behavior and to monitor self-calming activities. It is critical to empower students to take charge of both their academic learning and their social-emotional learning. By systematically engaging in the deliberate practice of co-regulation techniques and self-calming skills, students can become resourceful decision makers.

Conclusion

This chapter helps educators to recognize whether, when, and how to intervene effectively to address student behavior that defies the established norms of the classroom environment. Aspects of exploration include the many factors contributing to an individual student's behavior and the dynamics of the relationships between the students, their peers, and the teacher.

Strategies to identify and resolve situational conflicts in the classroom, either personal or interpersonal, were discussed. The chapter specifically addresses approaches to classroom interventions, including recognizing students' behaviors and teachers' management styles, the importance of self-efficacy and self-monitoring skills, and techniques and strategies to successfully resolve disputes.

Effective classroom management is a process between the teacher and the students and will vary according to the teacher's style and approach, as well as the makeup of the class and the individual students. It is complex and considers both teacher and student self-efficacy and their dispositions, the impacts of their relationship, the circumstances and function of the student's behavior, and the ability to self-monitor. Each student and each unique behavior require a thoughtful, reflective process involving all parties before intervention can take place to ensure dignity for all and respect for individual differences.

Teachers' self-efficacy, their attitudes and dispositions toward students and colleagues, their motivation, and their awareness of their impact on student learning contribute to their classroom effectiveness. An empathetic mindset, mutual respect, trust, and the commitment to take the time to warn, explain, and discuss behavior often result in a positive classroom environment.

Encouraging and supporting student self-efficacy—a sense of confidence to address academic, social, and emotional situations—is critical. Teachers can encourage students' positive self-efficacy through direct experiences, role playing, and modeling. By building personal relationships and fostering collective efficacy, classrooms will become a place of mutual learning—academically, socially, and emotionally.

Educators must consider the individual needs of each student. Different students will require different interventions. The reasons for students' behavior should be interpreted as attention seeking, avoiding or escaping, tangible power/control, or fulfilling a sensory need. Considering these factors will determine the need for intervention in a situation.

Various factors play into when and how teachers should intervene: the classroom climate, the teacher-student relationship, the function of the behavior as established by the rules and procedures of the classroom, opportunities to monitor and adjust behavior, and the teacher's determination of whether or not to intervene. Intervention choices can be immediate, delayed, or deferred. Analysis and reflection are necessary to weigh all factors and determine when and how to intervene.

Considerations should include the type and severity of the behavior and the parties' frames of mind. Can a dialogue take place? Can the situation be de-escalated? Can both the teacher's and student's feelings be taken into account? Can the teacher engage in a nonjudgmental path to intervention?

Teachers should model calmness through tone, facial expression, and posture. They must listen to the student to find out what is behind the behavior, concentrating on the student's emotions, thoughts, and reaction(s). Teachers must exhibit, encourage, and teach self-calming skills, de-escalation techniques, self-regulation, and co-regulation. Using the suggestions, ideas, techniques, and strategies put forth in this chapter, educators can recognize and evaluate student behavior and facilitate positive outcomes in challenging situations.

References

Alberto, P. A., & Troutman, A. C. (2013). *Applied behavior analysis for teachers* (9th ed.). Pearson.

Algebra That Functions. (2006). *Find someone like you*. Retrieved from: https://www.teacherspayteachers.com/Product/Back-to-School-Activity-Find-Someone-Like-You-2544814.

Alter, P., & Haydon, T. (2017). Characteristics of effective classroom rules: A review of the literature. *Teacher Education and Special Education, 40*(2), 114–27.

American School Counseling Association. (2003). *The ASAC national model: A framework for school counseling programs*. Author.

Bandura, A. (1986). *Social foundations of thought and action: A social-cognitive theory*. Prentice-Hall.

Bandura, A. (1991). Social cognitive theory of self-regulation. *Organizational Behavior and Human Decision Process, 50,* 248–87.
Bandura, A. (1993). Perceived self-efficacy in cognitive development and functioning. *Educational Psychologist, 28*(2), 117–48.
Bandura, A. (1995). *Self-efficacy in changing societies.* Cambridge University Press. https://doi.org/10.1017/CBO9780511527692.
Bandura, A. (2017). Self-efficacy: Towards a unifying theory of behavioral change. *Psychological Review, 84,* 191–215.
Bielefeld, K. (2016). *Promote positive student behavior through technology.* Retrieved from: https://blog.mimio.com/promote-positive-student-behavior-through-technology.
Cayci, B. (2011). The relationship between the elementary teacher candidates' teacher efficacy and their attitudes towards the profession of teaching. *Education, 132*(2), 402–18.
Cetin, H., & Cetin, I. (2018). Views of middle school students about ClassDojo education technology. *Acta Didoctica Nopocenia, 11*(34), 89–97.
Chung, H., & Elias, M. (1996). Patterns of adolescent involvement in problem behavior: Relationship to self-efficacy, social competence, and life events. *American Journal of Community Psychology, 24,* 771–84.
The Core Coaches. (2020). *Morning greetings: Hug, handshake, high-five, or fist-bump.* Retrieved from: https://thecorecoaches.com/2015/06/http-thecorecoaches-com-2015-06-when-i-was-classroom-teacher-i-moved/.
Costello, B., Wachtel, J., & Wachtel, T. (2010). *Restorative circles in schools: Building community and enhancing learning.* International Institute of Restorative Practices.
Deardorff, D. K. (2003). *Cross-cultural communication activity: Silent interview.* Retrieved from: http://www.ufic.ufl.edu/pd/downloads/ici-Activities/silent.pdf.
Desautels, L. (2019). *The role of co-regulation in discipline.* Retrieved from: https://www.edutopia.org/article/role-emotion-co-regulation-discipline.
Dillon, M. B. M, Radley, K. C., Tingstrom, D. H., & Barry, C. T. (2019). The effects of tootling via ClassDojo on student behavior in elementary classrooms. *School Psychology Review, 48*(1), 18–30.
Evans, E. D., & Tribble, M. (1986). Perceived teacher problems, self-efficacy, and commitment to teaching among preservice teachers. *Journal of Educational Research, 80*(2), 81–5.
Fallon, P. D. (2007). Nexus aliquis: In pursuit of efficacy, resilience, and full potential. *Adolescence, 42*(165), 73–101.
Gillespie, L. (2015). It takes two: The role of co-regulation in building self-regulation skills. *Young Children, 70*(3), 94–6.
Goalbook Toolkit. (2020). *6 second pause strategy.* Retrieved from: https://goalbookapp.com/toolkit/v/strategy/6-second-pause.

Gonzalez, T. (2012). Keeping kids in schools: Restorative justice, punitive discipline and the school to prison pipeline. *Journal of Law and Education, 41*(2), 281–335.

Judy, Jonathan. (2018). *Mrs. Judy greets her class!* Retrieved from: https://youtu.be/TQAKOarAxss.

Kerr, M. M., & Nelson, C. M. (2010). *Strategies for addressing behavior problems in the classroom* (6th ed.). Pearson.

Korpershoek, H., Harms, T., de Boer, H., van Kuijk, M., & Doolaard, S. (2016). A meta-analysis of the effects of classroom management strategies and classroom management programs on students' academic, behavioral, emotional, and motivational outcomes. *Review of Educational Research, 86*(3), 643–80. https://doi.org/10.3102/0034654315626799.

Lewis, R., Romi, S., & Roche, J. (2012). Excluding students from classroom: Teacher techniques that promote student responsibility. *Teaching and Teacher Education: An International Journal of Research and Studies, 28*(6), 870–78.

Lynch, M. (2017). *5 must have behavior apps, tools, and resources.* Retrieved from: https://www.thetechedvocate.org/5-must-behavior-apps-tools-resources/.

McClelland, M. M., & Tominey, S. L. (2018). *Self-regulation and early school success.* Routledge.

Minahan, J. (2013). *Teaching self-calming skills.* Retrieved from: https://www.responsiveclassroom.org/teaching-self-calming-skills/.

Minahan, J., & Rappaport, N. (2012). *The behavior code: A practical guide to understanding and teaching the most challenging students.* Harvard Education Press.

Mitchell, B. S., Hirn, R. G., & Lewis, T. J. (2017). Enhancing effective classroom management in schools: Structures for changing teacher behavior. *Teacher Education and Special Education: The Journal of the Teacher Education Division of the Council for Exceptional Children, 40*(2), 140–53. https://doi.org/10.1177/0888406417700961.

Moroney, R. G. (2019). *Who can it bee?* [Unpublished paper].

Okonofua, J. A., Paunesku, D., & Walton, G. M. (2016). Brief intervention to encourage empathic discipline cuts suspension rates in half among adolescents. *Proceedings of the National Academy of Science of the United States of America, 113*(19), 5221–26.

Purkey, W. W., & Stanley, P. H. (1991). *Invitational teaching, learning, and living: Analysis and action series.* National Education Association.

Scott, T. M., Anderson, C. M., & Alter, P. J. (2011). *Managing classroom behavior using positive behavior supports.* Pearson.

Smith, D., Fisher, D., & Frey, N. (2015). *Better than carrots or sticks: Restorative practices for positive classroom management.* ASCD.

Teaching Tolerance. (2016). *Reframing classroom management: A toolkit for educators.* https://www.learningforjustice.org/sites/default/files/general/TT_Reframing_Classroom_Managment_Handouts.pdf.

Teasley, M. (2014). Shifting from zero tolerance to restorative justice in schools. *Children & Schools*, *36*(3), 131–33.

Tschannen-Moran, M., & Hoy, A. W. (2001). Teacher efficacy: Capturing an elusive construct. *Teaching and Teacher Education*, *17*, 783–805.

Tullis, T. (2004). Beyond P.C.: Let's understand each other. Northwest Association of College & University Housing Officers.

Vera, E. M., Shin, R. Q., Montgomery, G. P., Mildner, C., & Speight, S. L. (2004). Conflict resolution styles, self-efficacy, self-control, and future orientation of urban adolescents. *Professional School Counseling*, *8*(1), 73–80.

Vollrath, D. (2020). *A de-escalation exercise for upset students*. Retrieved from https://www.edutopia.org/article/de-escalation-excercise-upset-students.

WCNC. (2017). *Charlotte teacher connects to students with handshakes*. Retrieved from https://youtu.be/QC3Vsv6OjgA.

Weber, E. U., Bockenholt, U., Hilton, D. J., & Wallace, B. (1993). Determinants of diagnostic hypothesis generation: Effects of information, base rates, and experience. *Journal of Experimental Psychology: Learning, Memory, and Cognition*, *19*(5), 1151–64.

Applications of Applied Behavior Analysis to Classroom Management 3

KATHLEEN QUINN, SARAH FARSIJANY, AND JILL SNYDER

THIS CHAPTER EXPLORES THE USE of applied behavior analysis (ABA) principles and strategies for day-to-day management of a classroom. Since ABA-based strategies are evidence-based, proactive, and promote an inclusive learning environment, they can be effectively implemented by classroom teachers to manage, reduce, and improve problem behaviors for all students.

When appropriately used, ABA strategies enable classroom teachers to gain an understanding of behavioral cause and the relationships between environmental factors and students' behaviors. This awareness ultimately supports faculty and staff to make informed decisions when adjusting the classroom environment for specific students as well as when designing either individual or whole-class-based behavioral interventions. ABA-based principles fit the needs of all students and support proactive classroom management.

Impact of ABA on Classroom Management

Although ABA principles and strategies can be used beyond the classroom to address a broad variety of behaviors across multiple settings, this chapter centers on the day-to-day management of the K–12 classroom. In the classroom, teachers might use ABA principles and strategies not only to reduce a problem behavior or increase a desirable behavior but also to teach and maintain new skills as well as generalize behavior to perform such skills under different conditions exhibited over time.

ABA has evolved over the past four decades. Despite its evolution, several common misconceptions about ABA interventions remain; one such misconception is that ABA strategies are only suitable for students on the autism spectrum. However, it is important to note that ABA principles can be applied across age and ability levels in a variety of social, functional, and academic contexts (Briesch & Briesch, 2016). ABA can be used with all students, regardless of ability, allowing educators to break the barriers of segregation and foster inclusive settings to maximize each student's success in the least restrictive environment.

Bloh and Axelrod (2008) affirm the idea that ABA has the empirical ability to address behaviors in the classroom, thereby positively impacting instruction and classroom management. When the Individuals with Disabilities Education Act was reauthorized in 2004, US Congress specified that behavioral support domains are vital for students to be successful in the classroom.

These domains included positive behavior supports, behavioral interventions, and effective student and classroom management practices. With these policy revisions in place and the availability of resources and technology advancements, ABA has the power to enhance both instruction and classroom management practices.

What Is Applied Behavior Analysis?

Does ABA ring a "bell"? In Pavlov's (1927) experiment, a dog salivated every time a bowl of food was provided because Ivan Pavlov simultaneously rang a bell while providing the food. One day, Ivan rang the bell but did not provide the food, and the dog still salivated. With that, Pavlov discovered that the bell, now associated with food, was a conditioner and could elicit the dog's salivation on its own.

Our behavior is learned and controlled by previous experiences in the environment. For example, we respond to a fire alarm because we've been taught that the alarm indicates potential danger and, therefore, we must evacuate. When our phone vibrates, we know that we have received a call or a message and therefore our immediate impulse is to check for the call, the text message, email, or a social media message. These are two examples of how our behavior has been conditioned by auditory input from our environment, and this is the core of ABA.

This chapter explores ABA strategies to improve students' behavior as well as to promote new skills within the classroom. The purpose of this chapter is to connect the principles of ABA to positive behavior changes in classrooms. We discuss different models and procedures that teach more appropriate ways to behave in the classroom while supporting teachers in maintaining a positive classroom environment.

As teachers, we have all had students who present with behavioral challenges. Consider this common classroom scenario:

> Billy is a fourth-grade student who continuously calls out throughout the school day. Ms. Miller has tried having a conversation with him to address how his behavior impacts the class. She has had numerous phone discussions with his parents and has even taken away his recess time. A colleague suggested that Ms. Miller place a visual of a raised hand on Billy's desk. Any time Billy would call out, Ms. Miller would simply point to the visual and call on him any time he raised his hand appropriately. Eventually, Billy stopped calling out and began to raise his hand independently in class.

The above scenario focuses on one specific behavior that requires a replacement behavior. In this instance, the behavior being decreased is "calling out" throughout the day. Through the implementation of an appropriate behavior intervention, Billy learned that if he uses the alternative behavior of "raising his hand appropriately," recess will not be taken away and the teacher is more open to his participation. This serves as an overview of how behavioral theory can be used to change students' classroom behavior. Applying the dimensions and characteristics of ABA can be used to modify behavior for students in any classroom setting.

According to Cooper, Heron, and Heward (2007), ABA is a scientific approach focused on influencing socially significant behavior by objectively defining the cause of the behavior and developing behavior change procedures. In other words, the principles of ABA take targeted behaviors and change them through a system of rewards and consequences.

More specifically, ABA is a scientific approach used to identify environmental factors surrounding behavior in order to increase socially appropriate behavior and decrease inappropriate behavior within the environment. It is important to note that socially significant behavior can include academics, communication skills, and adaptive living skills. Therefore, *socially significant behavior* is any behavior that can have immediate or long-term benefits for the student within the classroom.

One way to determine socially significant behaviors for students is to consider creating a hierarchy of skills based on students' chronological age, developmental levels, and anticipated classroom challenges, and then prioritizing—for individual students in each domain—those behaviors that will have the greatest immediate and long-term impact on that student's classroom integration. Consider the case of Rebecca:

Rebecca is a kindergarten student who is **profiled with and was assessed for** the following socially significant behaviors:
1) Toilet training (Adaptive Living Skill)
2) Identifying symbol/sound relationships of letters (Academic Skill)

Rationale for social skill selection:
1) Since Rebecca is not potty trained, teaching her how to use the toilet independently as an Adaptive Living Skill would be more socially significant than teaching her how to tie her shoes because using the toilet independently has the greater immediate impact on her classroom integration at this time.
2) Since Rebecca is currently exploring pre-reading skills, it would be more socially significant to first teach her symbol/sound connections (Academic Skill) than to focus on decoding/encoding words because sound/symbol relationships have the greater immediate impact on her classroom integration at this time.

This example illustrates the importance of ranking *socially* significant behavior to the needs of specific students in the classroom.

What Is Behavior?

A *behavior* is an observable, recordable, and measurable act performed by an individual. Behaviors are neither good nor bad—just simply observable actions. In ABA, a "target behavior" is considered a specific behavior selected by a therapist for change or improvement. A selected target behavior must first be operationally defined by a working description of the observable actions identified and described in observable, behavioral terms.

An example of a target behavior in a classroom context might be noncompliance, but this can be characterized by a variety of observable actions that are off task or meant to defy specific rules or expectations. Noncompliance can look different from one student to another. As illustrated in our previous scenario, Billy calls out to gain his teacher's attention rather than follow the classroom rule to "raise his hand" for recognition. Therefore, Billy's noncompliance can be defined and described by his observable action of "calling out."

In summary, the actions of raising a hand or calling out in class are both behaviors. They are both observable, recordable, and measurable. Neither action is positive nor negative; they are both simply actions. Other examples of behaviors include simple actions such a sitting at a desk, ripping a paper, shaking hands, running in the hall, screaming in the playground, talking to a friend, listening to a story, writing a letter, reading a sign, or crying in a corner. A behavior is always an observable, recordable, and measurable action. In fact, behavioral observation may involve more than just sight; observation may also be accomplished through sound, touch, and even smell.

Defining Functions of Behavior

To engage in effective ABA therapy, it is critical to first identify why a given behavior occurs, which is defined as the function of behavior. Ultimately, the function of the behavior provides behavioral practitioners with relevant information to determine corrective actions if the behavior is problematic.

Behavior can be impacted by antecedent variables and consequence variables. Antecedent variables are stimuli or events that trigger a behavior. Consequence variables are stimuli or events that either continue the behavior or end the behavior. When the function of a problem behavior is identified, interventions can be designed to alter and/or to teach alternative behaviors (Cooper et al., 2007).

There are four functions of behavior: Escape, Attention, Tangible, Sensory (EATS) (Hanley, Iwata, & McCord, 2003):

- **E**—Escape (Escape/Avoidance)—The student engages in a behavior that would lead to removal of unwanted activities (classwork), interactions (small-group work), and situations (physical education class).
- **A**—Attention—The student engages in a behavior to gain attention (calling out or raising a hand for the teacher's attention).
- **T**—Tangible—The student engages in a behavior to gain access to a preferred activity (completing an assignment for screen time) or an item (fighting with another child for a toy).
- **S**—Sensory—The student engages in a physical, stimulating behavior to create a favorable outcome without involving another person. For example, this physical stimulation can offer comfort or pleasure (holding a favorite blanket) or remove something that feels bad (rocking one's body if the noise level becomes too loud).

Functional Behavior Assessments

Data is key to making informed decisions. Data drives the identification of a behavior, provides the information needed to analyze the function of the behavior, and drives the selection and evaluation of intervention strategies and programs. In addition, data provides requisite baseline information and ongoing information to accurately monitor the success of the intervention plan. By using data to guide the process, decisions about the intervention can be made based on the evidence of what is working and what is not working (DuPaul, Stoner, & O'Reilly, 2002).

Data-Collection Strategies for Educators

Accurate data collection is imperative to the success of any intervention. The key elements of accurate data collection protocols are consistency and organization. There are several different, usable protocols to effectively collect data. The first and most commonly used protocol is the A-B-C Recording Chart.

The A-B-C Recording Chart

The A-B-C Recording Chart (see table 3.1) is an assessment tool used to gather information regarding environmental events that surround a target behavior (Alberto & Troutman, 1999; see also Bijou, Peterson, & Ault, 1968). Environmental events that impact "**B** = behavior" on this assessment tool are "**A** = antecedent" and "**C** = consequence." The A-B-C

Table 3.1. Antecedent, Behavior, Consequence Overview

Antecedent	Behavior	Consequence
Erica was in math class. The teacher was handing back graded projects. Erica's project was placed at the bottom of the pile.	Erica started yelling, "I want my project back right now!"	The teacher told Erica that if she wants to get her project back, she needs to lower her voice.
Meredith was waiting in line at the school cafeteria. It was very crowded and students were being very loud.	Meredith covered her ears and began to engage in vocal stereotypy.	The teaching assistant went over to Meredith and said, "It's okay. You can have lunch in the classroom."
Kim walked into the classroom and sat at her desk. The teacher handed out a worksheet.	Kim shoved the worksheet back. The teacher prompted Kim to do her work. She immediately screamed, "NO!"	The teacher continued to provide redirection to Kim.

chart provides a narrative of the environmental events that occurred prior to the behavior (A) and a narrative of the specific actions taken as a result of the occurrence of the behavior (C). This recording tool requires a written account of all observable antecedent and consequential events.

The A-B-C Recording Chart is used to examine a student's behavior to determine the function of the behavior based on environmental events.

Antecedent: What happened before the behavior? An antecedent helps to describe the events leading up to the behavior. This can include any pertinent information, including what was happening in the classroom, who was there, and what was said.

Antecedents answer the following questions: Who? What? Where? When? and Why?

Behavior: What did the behavior look like? A description of the behavior needs to be recorded on the chart in observable and measurable terms. The behavior must be specifically defined, described, and recorded exactly as observed.

Consequence: What happened directly after the behavior occurred? A consequence includes a description of the actions taken: what occurred and what was said immediately after the behavior took place. Although most people think of a consequence as a time-out or the removal of a reward, an immediate consequence could simply be teacher attention.

Immediate consequences have the greatest effect in behavior change: "Behavior is most sensitive to stimulus changes that occur immediately after, or within a few seconds of, the responses" (Cooper et al., 2007, p. 34). When a positive behavior is immediately reinforced, a connection is made between the behavior and the reinforcing consequence. If there is a temporal delay, the behavior may not be reinforced and thus not increase the future frequency of that behavior. In other cases, a behavior that was not intended for reinforcement may be reinforced based on initial responses within the immediate environment.

Example: Brian, a student, completes a task as directed by his teacher. The teacher walks over to another student, Kevin, to help him complete the task. Brian begins to draw on his desk with a pen. The teacher walks over to check Brian's work and provides verbal praise, "Great job, Brian!" Inadvertently, the teacher has now positively reinforced Brian's drawing on the desk rather than his completed assignment.

Here is an opportunity to apply the A-B-C recording chart strategy. After reading this scenario, list the antecedent, the behavior, and the consequence in the appropriate column in table 3.2.

> **Scenario:**
> Johnny is a fourth-grade student in a general education classroom. He sits next to two of his friends from football. The teacher hands a test to each student and reminds them they have one hour to complete the assessment. The teacher starts the timer. Johnny immediately puts his head and pencil down. When the teacher walks over to his desk, Johnny climbs under his desk. The school psychologist is called to the room and Johnny is taken to her office. He starts the test when he is in the psychologist's office. Once finished, he returns to the classroom.

Table 3.2. Antecedent, Behavior, Consequence, Anecdotal

Time/Setting	Antecedent	Behavior	Consequence	Anecdotal Notes
1/16/2020 12:15 p.m.				Johnny completed the test successfully in the psychologist's office.

Answer Key: Antecedent, Behavior, and Consequence Chart:

Time/Setting	Antecedent	Behavior	Consequence	Anecdotal Notes
1/16/2020 12:15 p.m.	Teacher hands out the test and begins the timer.	Johnny puts his head and pencil down—then climbs under the desk.	Johnny is taken to the school psychologist's office to complete the test.	Johnny completed the test successfully in the psychologist's office.

Types of Data Collection

Whether you want to increase positive behaviors or decrease problem behaviors, some forms of data collection allow for a specific behavior to be assessed for its frequency of occurrence and for the duration of each behavioral episode.

> **Frequency data** is a simple count of how many times the behavior occurs and is recorded in a set period of time.
> Example of an actual chart notation: *Hitting: 5x in 30 minutes*
>
> **Duration data** is the length of time the behavior occurs during each behavioral episode. The duration of a behavior has a specific beginning and ending.
> Example of an actual chart notation: *Screaming, 2min 35s*

This information is critical both before and after interventions are in place. Data collection on frequency and duration can be used to determine if there are any patterns to the behavior being measured. Upon analysis of this type of data, specific patterns can be identified, such as which days of the week or which times of the day the behavior becomes more frequent or lasts longer than others.

The data can also support a better understanding of which settings or what individuals can trigger more frequent or more intense behaviors. In addition, this type of data collection also allows for the creation of a clear, visual representation or graph. There are many ways to record this data.

Table 3.3 includes an example of an interval recording data sheet. Option A uses +/- symbols to indicate the observation of the behavior. Option B uses Y/N to indicate the observation of the behavior. Note that the form has a preset time at equal time intervals.

Option A: + (occurrence of behavior)
- (nonoccurrence of behavior)
Option B: Y (occurrence of behavior)
N (nonoccurrence of behavior)

Table 3.3. Interval Recording

	9:00	9:10	9:20	9:30	9:40	9:50	10:00	10:10	10:20	10:30
Option A	+	–	+	+	–	+	+	–	–	+
Option B	Y	N	Y	Y	N	Y	Y	N	N	Y

Data-Collection Steps

STEP 1: IDENTIFY THE BEHAVIOR(S) AND ESTABLISH THE IMPORTANCE OF AN INTERVENTION

Based on accurate data collected with fidelity, teams of professionals can successfully identify recurring, impactful behaviors exhibited by individual students across settings and within specific time periods over the course of a school day. Oftentimes, several behavioral patterns emerge concurrently. Therefore, the team needs to prioritize behaviors requiring immediate interventions based on the following questions:

1. Is the behavior posing a danger to the student or others?
2. Does the behavior hinder academic engagement for the student or others?
3. Is the behavior limiting access to other environments for the student?
4. Do typical peers of the same age engage in similar behavior?
5. Does the child engage in this behavior consistently?

In addition to collecting and analyzing data that reflects observable behavioral challenges, we must also consider other deficits in a student's repertoire of academic and social skills. Collaboration among educators, related service providers, and families is critical to accurately identify and prioritize academic and social behaviors that need to increase.

Table 3.4 provides several examples of academic and social behaviors that might need to increase in a classroom setting to proactively enhance students' behavior.

Table 3.4. Antecedent and Consequent Manipulations

Academic	Social	Emotional	Study Skills	Activities of Daily Living
—Listening and responding in class —Following directions —Completing in-class assignments —Arriving to class on time —Answering questions —Raising the hand	—Initiating conversations —Responding to a peer's question —Taking turns —Respecting the personal space of others —Showing an interest in a peer's hobby	—Utilizing coping strategies —Thinking flexibly —Honoring a growth mindset —Listening to others speaking	—Managing time —Using organizational skills —Asking questions —Using test-taking strategies	—Zippering a jacket —Buttoning a shirt —Tying shoes —Washing hands —Brushing teeth —Toileting

STEP 2: DEFINE THE BEHAVIOR

When defining a behavior, it is important to include an operational definition of what the behavior looks like, ensuring that the description is observable, measurable, and repeatable (Cooper et al., 2007). Table 3.5 includes some examples of operational definitions. Note that each example clearly states a specific action that is observational, measurable, and repeatable.

Table 3.5. Behavior and Operational Definitions

Behavior	Operational Definition
Attending	Anytime a student —**participates** in the classroom, including active listening —**exhibits** an open posture toward the speaker —**maintains** eye contact with the speaker —**raises** a hand —**follows** directions. —**looks** at the teacher when he/she presents visual material Attending does not include looking at the teaching assistant preparing work in the back of the room.
Tantrum "Meltdown"	Anytime a student —**throws** self on the floor —**yells** or **screams** —**throws** objects —**slams** fist on the table or floor —**kicks, hits,** or **bites** This behavior does not include chanting with other students or lying in the field during recess.
Disruptive Behaviors	Anytime a student —**gets out** of the seat without permission —**calls out** without permission —randomly **engages** peers in conversations during academic tasks —repetitively **taps** items on a desk or chair —**takes** items off peers' desks

STEP 3: ANALYZE THE DATA COLLECTED FOR ENVIRONMENTAL ADJUSTMENTS

Before implementing a positive reinforcement plan, patterns in the collected data should be recorded and analyzed. Always begin by looking for environmental patterns in the data collected that might possibly be contributing factors for any behavioral changes. For example, if a behavior consistently occurs while the student is sitting on the carpet, then perhaps an environmental modification might be an easy solution. Some students struggle with core strength, and sitting on a carpet without back support can be very uncomfortable for them. This makes carpet time a challenge. Behaviors noted might, in fact, be the child's way of saying "I am not comfortable!"

Some possible environmental changes such as offering the student a chair with a back or an oversized cushion might bring about a change in behavior in that setting. Other possible environmental conditions such as classroom or outside noise, room lighting, room temperature, or even room smells (art room, classroom proximity to the lunchroom) might be environmental triggers for sensitive students.

As environmental conditions are identified, begin to make needed adjustments. Reaching out to related service providers in the building (occupational therapists, physical therapists, etc.) can provide guidance for planning modifications. These steps should be taken before any systems of behavioral reinforcement are put in place.

In addition to an analysis of environmental conditions on behavioral changes, it is critical to identify and address any instructional conditions that may be impacting classroom behavior. Collaboration with academic specialists (e.g., reading and math specialists, special education teachers) may provide some insight into possible academic triggers and some effective modifications for the classroom to reduce a student's anxiety during direct instruction.

Behavioral specialists may provide insight into social anxieties for students who struggle when working collaboratively with peers in classroom situations. Planful adjustments made to the immediate environment are the requisite first steps when developing a successful student-centered intervention plan.

Adjusting or changing environmental, academic, and/or social conditions can support student needs and impact behavior. These considerations should be addressed prior to any systems of reinforcement being put in place. Making changes to the classroom environment can increase student participation and successful access to education.

First, consider the students' needs. Using data collected, analyze some possible triggers and identify possible distractions. Manipulating the environment may take some trial and error. Give modifications some time before trying something else. If you notice any adverse effects, those should be changed immediately. Here are some suggestions for possible environmental modifications:

1. Seating:
   a. Preferential seating will depend on the needs of the student. The student may need to be closer to the area of instruction and/or far away from areas of distraction (i.e., windows, doors, computers, etc.).
   b. Modifications to seating can also include seating students near peer buddies or models, alternative seating options such as a standing desk, or the use of a buddy band.
   c. Adjust the actual seating to meet the needs of a particular student.

2. Classroom layout:
   a. Rearrange the classroom furniture so there is a quiet area for students to take breaks.
   b. Create an open space between desks/tables for students to move around and access materials easily.

3. Visual stimulation:
   a. Eliminate extraneous signs/posters on walls that could be distracting.
   b. Add signs/posters that can be used as visual reminders of appropriate behavior for students.

4. Sensory stimulation:
   a. Dim or brighten lights.
   b. Lower or increase the classroom noise level.

STEP 4: EXPLORE INTERVENTIONS BASED ON THE DATA ANALYZED
To generate behavior change, an understanding of "motivating operations" is necessary. Motivating operations are the reasons for or the causes of motivations for our behavior—specifically reasons/causes that encourage or discourage behavior to occur. There are two types of motivating operations: abolishing operations and establishing operations.

Abolishing Operations: Discourage or decrease the value of a reinforcer (satiation). Providing the student with open access to reinforcers will decrease the likelihood of trying to earn the reinforcer during specific tasks or time periods.

Example: A student gets to use the iPad to watch a movie in the morning. When asked to do math to earn the access to the iPad, the student might be less motivated because he or she already watched a show on the iPad before math.

Establishing Operations: Encourage or increase the value of a reinforcer (deprivation).

Not giving your student access to a reinforcer will increase motivation to earn the reinforcer during specific tasks or time periods.

Example: A student is not allowed to use the iPad to watch a movie in the morning. When asked to do math to earn the access to the iPad, the student will be more motivated to complete math to watch a movie.

Reinforcement. The definition of *reinforcement* is "a behavior that is followed closely in time by a stimulus and, as a result, the future frequency of that type of behavior increases in similar conditions" (Cooper et al., 2007, p. 36). A stimulus is any object or event that elicits a behavioral response in an organism. Reinforcement will increase the future frequency of behavior. Positive reinforcement is one type of reinforcement; positive reinforcement increases the frequency of the behavior.

Positive reinforcement. Positive reinforcement occurs "when a behavior is followed immediately by the presentation of a stimulus and, as a result, occurs more often in the future" (Cooper et al., 2007, p. 36). Some examples of positive reinforcement are displayed in table 3.6.

Table 3.6. Examples of Positive Reinforcement

Functions of the Behavior	Attention	Tangible	Sensory
Reinforcer	A teacher gives her student praise (reinforcing stimulus) for completing a task (behavior).	The class receives a marble in a jar (reinforcing stimulus) for every kind act that is observed (behavior). When the jar of marbles is full, the class earns a pizza party.	A student gives a friend a high five (reinforcing stimulus) for sharing his toy (behavior).

REINFORCEMENT VERSUS PUNISHMENT

Reinforcement occurs when you add or remove a stimulus to increase the future likelihood of behavior. Punishment occurs when you add or remove a stimulus to decrease the future likelihood of behavior (see table 3.7).

Table 3.7. Examples of Punishment and Reinforcement

	Reinforcement	Punishment
Add Stimulus (Positive)	Add a pleasant stimulus to increase behavior **Example:** Getting a hug/high five; receiving time on the iPad	Add an aversive stimulus to decrease behavior **Example:** Assigning extra homework
Remove Stimulus (Negative)	Remove an aversive stimulus to increase behavior **Example:** No homework	Remove pleasant stimulus to decrease behavior **Example:** Taking away recess time

When considering students' needs, it is crucial to move forward in a mindset of *least to most*. Often, when facing challenging student behaviors, we want immediate change, but the most effective methods of behavior change take place when we start slow.

ABA in the Classroom: Creating a Strategy Toolbox

There are many proactive strategies that classroom teachers can effectively use on a daily basis in their classrooms to create and maintain a supportive learning environment for all students. Oftentimes, these strategies—when implemented with consistency and fidelity—eliminate the need to conduct a full functional behavior assessment and create a behavior intervention plan for many students. The following pages detail eleven strategies to use in the classroom.

Toolbox Strategy #1: Prompting

A prompt is a stimulus that directly guides the performance of a specific behavior (Kazdin, 2013). A prompt provides a cue to a specific skill or behavior. When a student does not engage in a requested behavior, a prompt allows the teacher to show the student how, what, and when to engage in that behavior. Prompts are broken down into the following categories: verbal, visual, physical, gestural, and modeling (see table 3.8).

Table 3.8. Types of Prompts

Verbal Prompt: A verbal prompt occurs when a teacher provides a verbal direction or cue to a student. Verbal prompts take on the guise of a "direction," such as "Sit on the rug," "Take out your book," and "Raise your hand."

Visual Prompt: A visual prompt provides the learner with a tangible clue—whether a picture, a sign, or an object—that directly guides the student to engage in the targeted behavior. Examples of visual prompts include the following: to-do lists, visual schedules, written directions (including classroom signs), and Post-its. Examples of specific academic visuals include writing prompts.

Physical Prompt: A physical prompt occurs when the teacher physically guides the student to engage in the desired response or behavior. Partial prompts are one type of physical prompting and occur when a teacher provides some assistance to a student to encourage engagement in part of a requested activity or task. Full physical prompting—another type of physical prompting—occurs when assistance is provided to a student from initiation to completion of the activity or task. Examples of physical prompting include hand-over-hand prompting and physical guidance of a student's hand to point to the correct answer.

Gestural Prompt: A gestural prompt is a physical gesture provided without the use of any language to engage a student in the desired response or behavior. Examples of gestural prompting include pointing, nodding, or reaching to cue the student or learner to engage in the desired behavior.

Modeling: Modeling is also considered a prompt and occurs when a teacher performs the targeted response for the learner. By seeing the modeled target behavior, the student can then replicate it. Modeling can be done in person or through video. Video modeling demonstrates behavior that is not live but presented through a video platform. If the student is able to attend to the model and imitate skills, then modeling is beneficial. Reinforcement is important after the student demonstrates the desired behavior. Eventually, the reinforcement should be faded out.

Toolbox Strategy #2: Transition Preparation

Transitions represent the time between activities and are essential to the daily operation of every classroom. Transitions include movements between instructional activities within the classroom; moving from class to class; and going to and from the cafeteria, recess, special events, or even to lockers or cubbies. Transitions can account for a considerable proportion of the school day (Sainato, Strain, Lefebvre, & Rapp, 1987). In fact, transitions are a significant part of everyday life and a major facet of independent living. For some students, transitions can be anxiety provoking, eliciting inappropriate behaviors, and are therefore problematic for teachers when managing a classroom.

There are several strategies that classroom teachers can effectively use to support students who struggle with transitions throughout the academic day. Verbal preparation strategies such as a verbal cue that includes a specific end time are effective for some students. An example of a verbal cue might be, "In five minutes, at 10:40, we will be leaving for music. Please close your books and take out your music folder." Other students might require visual preparation strategies. A visual preparation strategy can include the use of a visual timer, a visual countdown, visual schedule, or visual transition cards.

Technology is helpful for classroom-wide visual timers and visual countdowns. A technology teacher or a district-wide technology consultant would be a valuable resource for a classroom teacher. In addition, teachers can create their own visuals for use by an individual student or for full-class use.

Figure 3.1 illustrates examples that are created with the intention of having each number be physically removed from the countdown. This tool should be used if the transition time needs to be flexible. When all sections are removed, it prompts the student that it is time to transition.

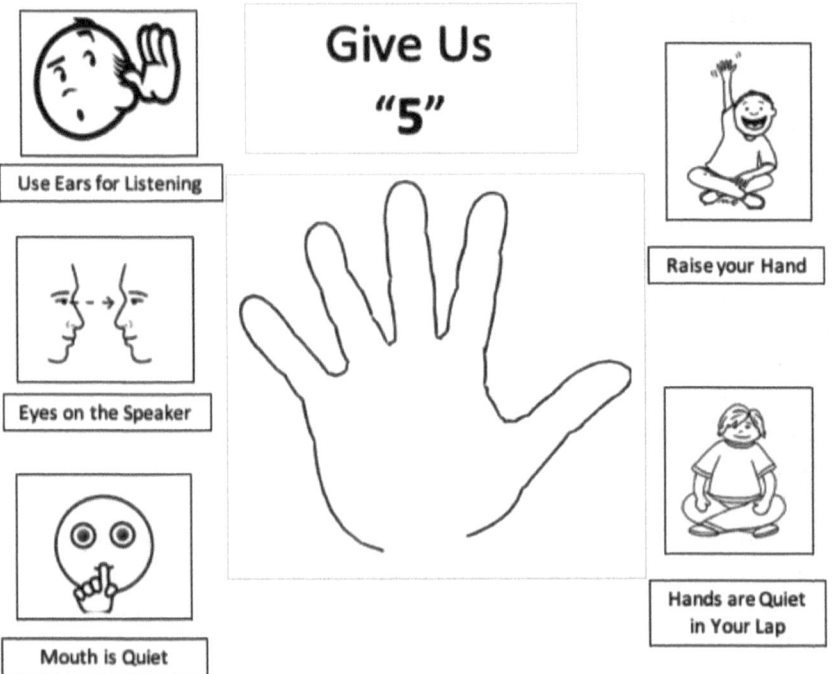

Figure 3.1. The Rug Rules

Toolbox Strategy #3: Behavior-Specific Praise

Behavior-specific praise is a powerful way to increase positive behavior in the classroom. Identified as an evidence-based classroom management strategy (Gable, Hester, Rock & Hughes, 2009), it has been shown to improve student behavior by telling students what they are doing correctly. When pairing praise specifically to the prosocial behavior, students make connections between reinforcement (praise) and the expected, appropriate behavior.

Before incorporating behavior-specific praise in the classroom, ask yourself this question: "What behaviors would I like to see more of in my classroom?" The following are possible teacher responses:

- I want to see more students participate in the classroom.
- It would be great to see fewer students calling out.
- It's important for my students to remember to take turns in class.
- I would love to see more students raise their hands when they are confused.

After making the list, pay attention in class for when these behaviors do occur and provide verbal, behavior-specific praise. This is a positive way to reinforce the behavior you'd like to see while sharing an example for other students to notice and follow. It is common for students to want their teacher to notice them. For many, the praise (reinforcement) is enough for them to repeat a positive behavior.

Here are additional examples of behavior-specific praise:

1. "I like the way you have been sharing your materials with your tablemate, Patrick."
2. "Peter, nice job taking turns!"
3. "Wow, Francesca! I love the way you have been participating in class."
4. "Ryan, I really admire the way you raised your hand when you did not understand the math problem!"

This is a strategy that should be a common classroom practice. As a reminder, adding visuals around the classroom for positive behavioral expectations is another way to display and manifest desired behaviors.

Toolbox Strategy #4: Replacement Behaviors

"Stop that!"
"If you do that one more time, you won't go out for recess!"
"That's enough!"
"Do I need to call your mom?"
"You need to stop calling out!"

Do these statements sound familiar? You've probably heard them when you were a student in school, and maybe you have even said them yourself. Let's consider a way to rephrase these statements while teaching students a replacement behavior. For example, instead of saying "Stop calling out," a replacement behavior might be "Raise your hand" (see table 3.9).

Table 3.9. Examples of Replacement Behavior Statements

Typical Response	Replacement Behavior
"Stop getting out of your seat!"	"Sit in your seat."
"You need to stop shouting!"	"Use a low voice."
"No hitting!"	"Hands are down."
"Don't stomp your feet!"	"Walk with quiet feet."

Here is an example: Tommy is a student who destroys personal property during challenging tasks. The teacher provides Tommy with an index card that reads, "I need help." Tommy is prompted to read the card, and when he does, he immediately receives help from the teacher. Tommy has been taught a replacement behavior that is more appropriate and will help him to communicate his needs. It is very important to redirect negative behaviors by providing the student with a more appropriate behavior that will benefit the student across multiple settings.

Toolbox Strategy # 5: Differential Reinforcement

Differential reinforcement is the process of reinforcing a specific response in a particular context and not reinforcing other responses. Below are two forms of differential reinforcement:

a. Differential reinforcement of alternative behavior: Determine a behavior that is not the target behavior and instead reinforce an alternative behavior. Example: A student is reinforced for raising a hand (alternative behavior), and reinforcement is withheld for calling out (target behavior).
b. Differential reinforcement of other behavior: When the target behavior does not occur for a predetermined amount of time, provide reinforcement. Example: A student is reinforced for not having occurrences of yelling for three minutes.

Toolbox Strategy #6: Consistency and Timing

Consistency and timing are crucial in behavior change. The student should obtain reinforcement immediately following the desired behavior. For example, a student raises a hand to speak. The teacher says, "Great job, Johnny. You earned a sticker on your chart." The teacher immediately places a sticker on Johnny's chart. Johnny sees the immediate consequence of his action, which will increase the probability that he will demonstrate that behavior again in the future.

In comparison, Bobby raises his hand to speak. The teacher says, "Great job, Bobby. I will put a sticker on your chart after this lesson." Bobby waits and waits while the lesson goes on. During this time, Bobby calls out to speak. Since the teacher did not provide Bobby with the sticker in an appropriate time frame, the appropriate behavior was not reinforced.

While a classroom teacher must be consistent and timely when delivering reinforcers each time an appropriate behavior is practiced, it is unrealistic for a teacher to be able to give such individualized reinforcement to each student. Therefore, it is very important for the teacher to consider which target behaviors are the most impactful behaviors to focus one's attention on, as well as to carefully consider the most realistic type of reinforcement plan to implement and the anticipated time frame for effective implementation.

If a teacher has one student who is working on raising his hand, providing a sticker each time he raises his hand might be considered "step 1" in targeting that behavior. This step would last for a predetermined period of time, perhaps two to three days. Then the teacher should move on to step 2 to reinforce hand-raising behavior every other time it is demonstrated. Again, this step might be implemented for a predetermined period of time, perhaps two to three days. Next, the teacher would move on to step 3 where stickers are awarded on an intermittent schedule when hand raising is demonstrated. Again, this step would be implemented for a predetermined amount of time.

The final step should involve fading stickers out completely and reinforcing hand-raising behavior with behavior-specific praise. Decisions regarding the implementation and fading of a positive reinforcement plan should be discussed with the school team.

Additional factors for teacher consideration when analyzing consistency and timing of individual reinforcers might include the size of the class; the number of students requiring reinforcement; and the availability of ancillary, support personnel in the classroom. Being consistent with the implementation of positive reinforcement and delivering reinforcement immediately are two essential pieces of behavior analysis that support the learning and maintenance of behavior change.

Toolbox Strategy #7: High-Probability Requests

A high probability ("high-p") request allows a teacher to prompt a student to engage in a behavior wherein there is a high probability that the student will engage in that behavior. A beneficial technique to use in the classroom is to present a high probability request followed by a low probability ("low-p") request. By presenting a high-p request first, you build the momentum of the learner to engage in a demand or task that has a history of low compliance, the low-p request.

Consider a student who has difficulty cleaning up after playtime. The teacher is aware of the tasks that the student has a high probability to engage in. These should be brief tasks; usually less than 5 seconds, such as, high fives, answering a question about a favorite sport, or giving the teacher an object. Sequentially presenting a high-p request (giving high fives) just prior to a low-p request (cleaning up toys) increases the likelihood that the student will complete the low-p task as requested.

Some commonly used high-p requests include, "Give me a high five," "Who won last night's game?," "Hand me the train!," and "Can you find the yellow truck?" It is important to reinforce for compliance on low-p requests.

Toolbox Strategy #8: Token Economies
Token economies have played an essential role in the advent of ABA, remaining one of the most successful, behaviorally based applications in the history of psychology (Ayllon & Azrin, 1968). Since the early 1800s, token economies have been implemented as behavior management and motivational tools in educational settings (Kazdin, 2013). Used to address a variety of behaviors, token reinforcers are used to increase the frequency of a desired behavior and reduce or eliminate inappropriate behaviors.

When a behavior is rewarded or reinforced, it is likely to be repeated. In the workplace, we are paid and our salary becomes our reinforcement. The money itself can be later exchanged for things we want and need. The things we choose to buy with our money—food, shelter, luxury items—are seen as the backup reinforcement. Token economies in classrooms work the same way. Students are awarded "tokens" for positive behaviors and are able to exchange their tokens for personally selected items or activities (backup reinforcers).

Example of a token economy:

1. Paul gets a token for every math problem he completes during class. After he earns five tokens, he gets access to a tangible item (iPad, class computer).
2. Jake gets a token for every one-minute interval where he exhibits "a quiet mouth" while doing classwork (intervals are subject

to change and should be increased). Once he has collected ten tokens, he can choose to exchange his tokens for an allotted time frame to play on the iPad.

Toolbox Strategy #9: Classwide Token Economy

Building a classroom-wide token economy has proven to be a successful practice to ensure effective classroom management practices. When implementing a classroom-wide token economy, the teacher must identify the behaviors that would be highly desirable in the classroom.

Backup reinforcers must be based on the student(s) and what they prefer collectively. These backup reinforcers can include tangibles such as iPads, toys, or games; edibles including food parties, snacks, or drinks (may need to be provided from home); sensory reinforcers such as music, pop tubes, or stuffed animals; and social reinforcers such as praise or attention, high fives, extra recess time, running errands, being a line leader, or even spending quality time with the teacher as part of a small lunch-bunch.

The teacher must then decide how many tokens students will collectively need to earn for a class reward (individual student backup reinforcers are determined separately) and what kind of token system will be used for the class.

Toolbox Strategy #10: Social Stories

Social Stories began in 1990 when Carol Gray, a consultant in a Michigan school district, decided to write a story to help her kindergarten student, Tim, understand the expectations and rules of a game played in gym class (Gray, 2000). Tim read over the Social Story every day and just before the next gym class. During his next gym class, Tim was able to play the game with competence and ease. After one story was effective, Gray began to address different topics using Social Stories (Gray, 2000).

Social Stories continue to be used today by teachers—typically in tandem with other strategies. They are used to describe social norms, manage expectations, enable smooth transitions, increase flexibility, and describe events. Usually short, Social Stories are meant to define criteria for a specific setting and provide students cues to adapt to new settings. Social Stories are created by anyone who knows a particular student well, and the stories are most often used to simplify social expectations. Social Stories are also used to address transitions (e.g., from one classroom to another), fire drills (e.g., loud noises), unexpected changes in daily schedules (e.g., schedule changes, substitute teacher), or even school events and class trips.

According to Carol Gray (2000), when writing a Social Story, we must "assume an invitation into the mind of a child." Social Stories are written in response to an individual student. You must use directive or descriptive sentences and sometimes a mixture of both. Descriptive sentences describe a social situation, while a directive sentence gives a step-by-step list of expected responses to a situation (Gray, 1992). The text is typically written in first person and should incorporate positive language while addressing the who, what, where, when, and why of the situation.

For younger students or nonreaders, it might be helpful to incorporate photos of the student within the story. Including visuals will also enhance the student's ability to understand and apply the text. Since the story is being used for the student, try to customize the story based on their abilities and include statements that will let readers know what will happen if or when they can accurately present the target behavior.

Toolbox Strategy #11: Functional Communication Training

Functional communication training is implemented by using a more appropriate replacement communication to achieve the same goal. Communication can be aided by the use of pictures, visuals, gestures, and signs. If a nonverbal child throws a tantrum to access a toy, the teacher might model the following actions: either pointing to the toy or prompting a verbal utterance of "toy." After the child engages in the modeled action, the teacher would then present the child with the desired toy.

The teacher might also choose to teach the child to complete a picture exchange communication. The child is taught that whenever he wants his favorite toy, he can select a card with the picture of the toy and give it to the teacher in exchange for the toy. In each situation, the child learns that he can get his favorite toy by communicating his request.

Functional communication can be used across grade levels. For example, an older student gets up and runs out of the classroom every time he needs to use the bathroom. Instead of blocking the student and engaging in a power struggle, the teacher may provide the student with a bathroom pass that he can simply hold up to leave the classroom to access the bathroom.

When a student is engaged in a crisis, the most important decision a teacher makes is how to react to the exhibited behavior. Table 3.10 proposes a checklist of things to do and not to do for effective classroom management.

Table 3.10. Classroom Management—Dos and Don'ts

What will de-escalate behavior?
DO

- Model behavioral regulation: remain calm and regulate breath
- Use body language and voice tone that reduces tension
- Provide communicative support to the student
- Support the student with calming redirection
- Offer choices
- Offer a short break
- Support the students with active listening
- Stop and wait

What will escalate behavior?
DON'T

- Use a loud voice
- Engage in power struggles
- Assume the students know why they are engaging in the behavior
- Use negative statements/threats (e.g., "You made your choice, now you need to go to the principal!")
- Humiliate the student in front of others
- Take away preferred or comforting materials or activities
- Physically redirect (If you are engaging in physical redirection of a student, this should be under the supervision of a clinician and written formally in a behavior intervention plan.)
- Bring up unrelated events or past behavior (e.g., "Remember last time when you acted like this?")
- Use an angry vocal tone or angry body language

If a student is still engaging in maladaptive behaviors after the teacher has exhausted all toolbox strategies, then an expert should conduct a functional behavioral assessment to determine if a behavior intervention plan is needed.

Conclusion

This chapter did an overview of the positive impact that ABA theory and practice can have on classroom management. It was written for both novice and experienced classroom teachers. Understanding behavior and the science behind behavioral change can empower classroom teachers to meet the needs of all students with insight and empathy.

If we begin to look at our students through a positive lens, we can easily acknowledge that students want to be members of their learning communities. We can also acknowledge each student's need to be recognized and validated in this setting. If we take the time to methodically analyze observed behaviors for their inherent functions, oftentimes we find that behaviors can be one way students communicate basic needs and wants.

This chapter provides teachers with the tools necessary to identify, analyze, plan, and monitor proactive interventions that have both immediate and long-term benefits for students. Focusing on the behavior itself—rather than the student—is essential when promoting an inclusive setting where all students are successful at accessing an education in the least restrictive environment.

Challenging behaviors in the classroom can be overwhelming. It is important to always consider the social significance of the behavior. The initial step of behavior modification should identify any potential environmental modifications and implement positive reinforcement systems. Data can guide making informed decisions on students' needs. A team approach can support decision making. Each student is unique and communicates wants and needs differently, so this toolbox of strategies can help with understanding that.

Making ethical decisions is an invaluable part of an educator's role. By using proactive strategies and reactive strategies, any behavior can be modified to foster a positive classroom environment and student success. ABA continues to be a growing field of evidence-based interventions, and updated research can allow the implementation of the most effective strategies in the classroom.

Additional Resources

Behavior Analyst Certification Board: https://www.bacb.com/about-behavior-analysis/.

Journal of Applied Behavior Analysis: https://onlinelibrary.wiley.com/journal/19383703.

Positive Behavioral Intervention Supports: https://www.pbis.org.

References

Alberto, P. C., & Troutman, A. C. (1999). *Applied behavior analysis for teachers* (5th ed.). Merrill.

Ayllon, T., & Azrin, N. H. (1968). Reinforcer sampling: A technique for increasing the behavior of mental patients. *Journal of Applied Behavior Analysis, 1*(1), 13–20.

Bijou, S., Peterson, R. F., & Ault, M. H. (1968). A method to integrate description and experimental field studies at the level of data and empirical concepts. *Journal of Applied Behavior Analysis, 1*, 175–91.

Bloh, C., & Axelrod, S. (2008). IDEIA and the means to change behavior should be enough: Growing support for using applied behavior analysis in the classroom. *Journal of Early and Intensive Behavior Intervention, 5*(2), 52–56. doi: 10.1037/h0100419.

Briesch, A. M., & Briesch, J. M. (2016). Meta-analysis of behavioral self-management interventions in single-case research. *School Psychology Review, 45*(1), 3–18. https://doi.org/10.17105/SPR45-1.3-18.

Cooper, J., Heron, T. E., & Heward, W. L. (2007). *Applied behavior analysis*. Merrill Publishing.

DuPaul, G. J., Stoner, G., & O'Reilly, M. J. (2002). Best practices in classroom interventions for attention problems. In A. Thomas & J. Grimes (Eds.), Best practices in school psychology IV (pp. 1115–27). National Association of School Psychologists.

Gable, R., Hester, P., Rock, M., & Hughes, K. (2009). Back to basics: Rules, praise, ignoring, and reprimands revisited. *Intervention in School and Clinic, 44*, 195–205.

Gray, C.A. (2000). *Writing social stories with Carol Gray*. Future Horizons.

Hanley, G. P., Iwata, B. A., & McCord, B. E. (2003). Functional analysis of problem behavior: A review. *Journal of Applied Behavior Analysis, 36*, 147–85. doi:10.1901/jaba.2003.36-147.

Kazdin, A.E. (2013). *Behavior modification in applied settings* (7th ed.). Waveland Press.

Pavlov, I. P. (1927). *Conditioned reflexes: An investigation of the physiological activity of the cerebral cortex*. Oxford University Press.

Sainato, D., Strain, P., Lefebvre, D., & Rapp, N. (1987). Facilitating transition times with handicapped preschool children: A comparison between peer mediated and antecedent prompt procedures. *Journal of Applied Behavior Analysis, 20*, 285–91.

Understanding the Role of Emotions in the Classroom   4

TYCE NADRICH, CANDICE R. CRAWFORD, DAVID JULIUS FORD, HEATHER C. ROBERTSON, AND AMY WEINSTOCK

EFFECTIVE TEACHING AND CLASSROOM MANAGEMENT require myriad intrapersonal and interpersonal skills. Even the most knowledgeable and experienced educators encounter pedagogical issues secondary to difficult classroom dynamics. Regardless of how classroom dynamics are impacted—whether by peer conflicts, school-related events, or broad community-based or societal trends—an underlying factor is often emotions. That is, the teacher's emotional reactions to their lived experiences can be highly influential to the individual student and the overall classroom.

As this chapter proposes, emotions are a normal and integral part of the human experience; consequently, emotions can (and often do) influence people to behave in specific ways, affecting interpersonal dynamics with conducive and detrimental effects on all parties involved. The classroom is no exception.

The role of emotions in the classroom can be significant. Educators are often expected to navigate students' emotions, in addition to their own, with limited formal training in interventions focused on emotional and mental health. It is not (and should not be) expected for teachers to serve as professionally trained emotional and behavioral interventionists; the task of teaching already requires vast physical, cognitive, emotional, and temporal resources. However, it is important to note the supports that are often available to teachers within and outside of the school system related to managing emotions.

This chapter provides a framework for understanding emotions and their effects on interpersonal and classroom dynamics. Of particular interest is the intersection of culture and emotions—the ways in which external variables and stimuli (e.g., substances, social media, etc.) affect our emotions, and the ways that emotions (e.g., sadness and anxiety) present and influence our social worlds. The chapter concludes with recommendations to foster best practices and overall wellness in the classroom.

The Helping Professionals

There are often multiple professionals within and outside of the school whose job is to support the success of the academic process. While these professionals' specific titles and duties sometimes vary by school and/or district, this section provides an overview of the professionals most commonly available to offer emotional and behavioral interventions. The aim is to increase educators' awareness of the resources available to them, their students, and the greater school system.

School counselors are highly involved with students and tend to be quite visible within the school system. Historically, the title of *guidance counselor* has been used for those we now prefer to call *school counselors*, as it is more inclusive of the vast duties and services provided by these professionals (Gysbers, 2010; see also Lambie & Williamson, 2004). According to the American School Counselor Association (n.d.a.), school counselors possess training in a variety of areas related to counseling as well as human and career development.

Although their specific duties vary by school, school counselors are trained and qualified to provide academic and career advisement, social and emotional support, and program assistance across many levels within the school system (American School Counselor Association, n.d.b.). School counselors can be a vital resource in supporting students academically and emotionally, and they can aid teachers in determining whether specialized interventions and/or supports are warranted for the student.

School social workers are also highly involved with students and educators within the school system; they have specialized training applicable to the school system. According to the School Social Work Association of America (n.d.), school social workers can provide a variety of direct and indirect support to students and personnel within the school system, and they often serve as the liaison for services between school, home, and the broader community.

School psychologists are specifically trained to provide in-depth support within the school system and work directly with school social workers, school counselors, students, teachers, parents/guardians, and other school personnel to support academic, emotional, and behavioral success (sometimes this collective group of people may be referred to as a school-based support team).

School psychologists are trained to provide a variety of services, including psychological assessment and intervention planning. In addition, they serve as an excellent resource for support regarding learning or behavioral issues and will likely work closely with the school counselor and social worker. School psychologists will likely be intimately involved with the creation and/or execution of a student's Individualized Education Plan.

Other mental health professionals include professional counselors (e.g., licensed professional counselor, licensed mental health counselor), clinical social workers, and licensed clinical psychologists. These professionals sometimes work within the school system itself but more often operate within the community and collaborate and consult with school personnel (e.g., school psychologist, school social worker, or school counselor).

As such, the primary support persons for teachers within the school are school counselors, social workers, and psychologists, as well as their well-informed colleagues. When engaging with these trained mental health professionals, teachers should remember that their specific duties and responsibilities will likely vary by district, so some duties in a school district that are performed by a school counselor may have been performed by a school social worker in another district. Despite the benefits and limitations of school bureaucracy, these professionals are all trained in providing mental health services, and their duty is to help foster the success of all students.

Understanding Emotions

Emotions, also known as feelings, are known to everyone and yet are difficult to define. Our bodies react to emotions at three basic levels: physiological, psychological, and behavioral. It is important to note that although these are discussed separately, they are all inextricably connected and should be viewed as co-occurring.

Emotions affect our physiology in numerous ways. When we experience emotions, neurological responses are triggered and are visible via neuroimaging technology (e.g., brain scan, MRI). We can detect how certain emotions activate specific parts of the brain (Celeghin, Diano, Bagnis, Viola, & Tamietto, 2017). These neurological reactions evoke physiological responses such as facial expressions (e.g., smiling, frowning, grimacing), physical reactions (e.g., crying, nausea, rapid heart rate), and may contribute to disease states over prolonged time (e.g., stress contributes to heart disease; trauma contributes to mental health disorders).

These physiological reactions are a combination of overt and covert responses; it is not possible to readily see a student's neurological response, although some physical reactions might be visible. While facial expressions are informative, the emotional reactions that are typically noticed within the classroom are psychological and behavioral.

Psychological responses to emotion are categorized by the feeling words used to describe emotions. There are a wide range of feeling and emotion words with varying levels of intensity. It is proposed that there are "basic" or "primary" emotions—namely, fear, anger, joy, sadness, surprise, and disgust. The theory of basic emotions emphasizes that these pure emotions do not contain any other emotion combinations (Celeghin et al., 2017).

Emotions beyond these basic emotions, such as guilt or worry, may be a combination of emotions such as fear, sadness, anger, or others. Thus, emotions are complex and may consist of combinations or layers of various emotions. Understanding the complexity of emotions is critical to working with children and adolescents, especially since they often struggle to describe their emotions and may lack both the vocabulary and awareness to share what they are feeling. In the absence of words, students may exhibit behavioral responses to emotion.

Behavioral responses are the ways in which we express our emotions through our actions and are as varied and diverse as our students. Behavioral responses to emotions are impacted by the cognitive and developmental age of the student, as well as the student's cultural norms. Children experiencing difficulties recognizing or communicating their emotions may exhibit behaviors such as stomping their feet, screaming, throwing things, hitting peers, ignoring others, and many others.

The behavioral response is often the final result of emotional processing and is a representation of how a student is feeling. Just because the connection between the behavior and the emotion may not be understood does not make the emotion any less valid or important. Emotion processing and expression is complex, and not all emotions are the same.

State Emotions versus Trait Emotions

Emotions may be triggered by a temporary event or may be a longer-standing condition of character. As discussed, emotions may have physiological, psychological, or behavioral manifestations. *Manifestation* describes the embodiment of the emotion, whereas *onset* helps illuminate the origin of the emotion. The onset of emotion is often described as either state or trait emotion. State emotions describe a temporary state or mood, sometimes in reaction to environmental stimuli (Chaplin, John, & Goldberg, 1988).

For example, elementary school-age students excluded from a peer group may feel sad or angry until they are invited to another activity. Middle school students who gossiped about a friend may feel guilt or shame until confessing their behavior to the friend and seeking forgiveness. High school students may feel joy or excitement over outstanding performance during an athletic season, only to sustain an injury later in the season that removes them from play.

These examples represent emotional states that were triggered by external stimuli. The duration of these emotions is typically temporary. When the triggering event is more significant—such as the death of a loved one—the emotional state may last longer or be more intense and yet is still viewed as a temporal reaction to an event. Notably, state emotions may lack a clearly identifiable stimulus or trigger, such as simply "being in a good/bad mood." Regardless of the duration, intensity, or trigger, the person is experiencing an emotional state that is temporary.

Trait emotions, on the other hand, are considered stable, long-standing, and are viewed as a condition of an individual's personality (Chaplin et al., 1988). A person's character, personality, and temperament are often defined using emotional terms. For example, the parent of an elementary student describes the student as "timid" and "nervous" who often appears uncomfortable with others.

A school social worker describes a middle school student as "hostile" or "aggressive" who regularly engages in physical altercations with other children. A high school student describes their friend as often being "always kind of down and gloomy" who prefers to be alone. Are these emotional terms being used to describe the students' temporary state of mind, or are they describing personality traits of the individual that are long-standing and consistent? Trait emotions cannot be tested for stability or longevity over time (Chaplin et al., 1988) but represent a consistent pattern of emotional characteristics within an individual.

There is controversy as to whether emotions are innate in an individual or are conditioned by one's environment (Celeghin et al., 2017). It should be noted that environmental stimuli—such as parenting styles, adverse childhood experiences, and traumatic events in childhood—may contribute to long-standing emotional traits. Educators are not expected to know specifically if a student is experiencing a state or trait emotion, but they can help students learn to manage their emotional responses productively.

Furthermore, teachers' emotional expectations and goals for students should be congruent with their developmental status.

Emotional Development through Early Childhood

There are key characteristics of children aged between approximately three and six years old. During this period, children's social and emotional development is in the beginning stages. Early school-age children are beginning to develop their skills for self-control. Children during this age are starting to develop language skills to express their emotions. However, their emotions can change rapidly and are generally situation specific. If children are unable to regulate their emotions, they may be more notably expressive while lacking the skills to articulate their feelings, resulting in outbursts or tantrums.

Emotional Development through Middle Childhood

Middle childhood can be classified as children between the ages of six and twelve years old. During this period, emotional development progresses significantly compared to early childhood. The emotional development changes of middle-aged children include the ability to suppress negative emotional reactions, an improved emotional understanding, and the ability to understand that more than one emotion can exist for one particular situation. It is not uncommon for students to recognize and reconcile that they can have one particular feeling or emotion and their peers might have a different emotion in response to the same situation.

Emotional Development through Adolescence

As emotional development continues to progress through adolescence, students become more emotionally competent (Wong, Hall, Justice, & Wong Hernandez, 2015). During adolescence, students are able to assess and understand their emotions more effectively than they were able to during early and middle childhood. However, this increased emotional understanding should not imply the absence of strong or intense emotions. In fact, adolescents often experience heightened, complex (e.g., mixed) emotional states, as well as strong emotional reactions to stress (McLaughlin, Garrad, & Somerville, 2015).

In addition, adolescents tend to experience increased social sensitivity and self-consciousness compared to younger children. Understanding the emotional development of school-aged children and adolescents will better serve teachers, staff, and administrators to more accurately assess students' emotional state and provide an appropriate plan of intervention for students.

Emotional Reactions and the Classroom

Despite the ubiquity of references to feelings and emotions, truly understanding emotions is complex and difficult. Consider the classic example of a two-year-old child's "temper tantrum." Children at that age have not developed the cognitive or linguistic abilities to problem solve beyond simple tasks. When they encounter a situation that they cannot resolve, they may experience frustration, anger, sadness, or other distressing emotions (i.e., psychological reactions), but lack the linguistic, cognitive, and social development to express their emotional needs.

Their response to these emotions may be physiological (e.g., crying, grimacing, body tension) and/or behavioral (e.g., throwing themselves on the ground, throwing items, yelling, screaming). As children grow, their cognitive, linguistic, social, and emotional development increases, and they learn a wider array of tools to use in response to their emotion. In the classroom, however, the behavioral response to emotions may be less obvious than a temper tantrum.

Behavioral responses to emotion are often mislabeled as "acting out" behavior by educators and met with disciplinary responses. Disciplinary responses do not promote increased understanding of emotions and fail to provide students with an alternative mechanism to manage their emotions. It helps for educators to look beyond the observed behavior and begin to explore the emotional context of the behavior.

For example, sadness or fear may manifest as withdrawing from class activities, not interacting with peers or teachers, isolating, lacking focus, or refusing to do work. Anger or disgust may manifest as yelling, shouting, shoving, inability to sit still, or any of the behaviors described for sadness and fear. Joy and surprise may be manifested by shrieking, laughing, talking out of turn, inability to sit still, and lacking focus.

Complex emotions such as grief, worry, anticipation, helplessness, loneliness, guilt, shame, and others have different and varied behavioral manifestations. Examples of more dangerous behavioral responses to emotions include violence, self-harm, suicide attempts, and risky behavior (e.g., substance abuse, unsafe sex practices).

While the educator cannot be expected to perfectly read the emotion behind a student's behavior, every educator can take time view the student's behavior as a response to their emotion, as opposed to their character. It is strongly recommended to lead with a critical examination of the intersection of emotions and behaviors and consider collaborative interventions (e.g., consulting with school counselors, social workers, and/or psychologists), as opposed to immediate disciplinary actions.

Managing Emotions

Managing emotions is a critical component of human functioning. Emotional functioning allows us to interact with one another, communicate effectively, and sustain meaningful relationships. It also impacts our ability to maintain healthy interactions within our homes, schools, workplaces, and communities. There are multiple factors that contribute to our ability to manage our emotions, including emotional intelligence, emotional regulation, and distress tolerance.

- *Emotional intelligence* is defined as "the ability to identify, assess, and control the emotions of one's self, of others, and of groups" (Wong et al., 2015, p. 324).
- *Emotional regulation* is described as the ability to control one's emotions (American Psychological Association, 2020) and "involves teaching children to identify emotions, helping them identify what triggers those emotions, and teaching them to manage those emotions by themselves" (Pelini, 2020, para. 19).
- *Distress tolerance* describes the ability of an individual to tolerate and endure various levels of physical and psychological distress (Leyro, Zvolensky, & Bernstein, 2010).

People often mistake "healthy" emotional functioning as portraying only positive emotions such as strength, joy, love, and confidence. However, being able to share difficult emotions with others—and having others receive those emotions nonjudgmentally—helps individuals feel validated, heard, and respected. These concepts of emotional intelligence, emotional regulation, and distress tolerance demonstrate the importance of managing emotions in relation to overall well-being.

The inability to manage emotions, however, can be damaging to one's well-being. Many students struggle to manage their emotions for a variety of reasons. One of these reasons may be modeling. We know that children learn from what they observe and experience (Pelini, 2020). Children who witness an adult's inability to manage emotions may model the adult's behavior, such as a parent who gives the silent treatment or a teacher who yells when frustrated.

Similarly, students can learn from observing peers. A sibling who uses an illegal substance due to sadness over the parents' fighting might be modeling that coping strategy for the younger sibling. Peers who respond with violence when they are angry or embarrassed model that behavioral response for nonviolent peers. These negative responses to emotion may result in damaged relationships, physical harm, and criminal consequences.

Negative responses to emotions can also be fatal. Adolescent substance use and abuse can have long-term health, financial, and criminal consequences, as well as death. Nonsuicidal self-injury (NSSI) is the act of self-inflicted bodily injury that is intended to be nonfatal, including carving, cutting, scratching, burning, and other activities. According to the Cornell Research Program on Self-Injury and Recovery (n.d.), the average age of NSSI onset is fifteen, and those who engage in NSSI report doing so to deal with anxiety, relieve stress, and cope with trauma, among other reasons.

While NSSI is not intended to be fatal, those who engage in NSSI often do not seek medical attention when needed. Suicide is now the second leading cause of death in the United States among fifteen- to twenty-four-year-olds, and suicide rates have increased 30 percent among that age group between the years 2000 and 2016 (Miron, Yu, Wilf-Miron, & Kohane, 2019). There is a prevalence of mental illness among those who engage in NSSI (Cornell Research Program on Self-Injury and Recovery, n.d.) and those who attempt suicide (American Foundation for Suicide Prevention, n.d.).

Finally, children, adolescents, and adults may struggle to manage their emotions due to mental illness, also known as mental health disorders. While educators are not expected to recognize or diagnose mental health disorders, a broad understanding of mental health disorders—specifically pertaining to children and adolescents—is beneficial. The *Diagnostic and Statistical Manual*, 5th edition (*DSM-5*) is used by mental health professionals to diagnose mental health disorders in children, adolescents, and adults.

The neurodevelopmental disorders section of the *DSM-5* describes disorders often diagnosed in childhood while the brain is developing. Some of these disorders include intellectual disabilities, language disorders, autism spectrum disorders, and attention deficit/hyperactivity disorders (American Psychiatric Association [APA], 2013). Children and adolescents may also be diagnosed with other mental health disorders, including depressive disorders, anxiety disorders, trauma-related disorders, obsessive-compulsive disorders, feeding and eating disorders, and elimination disorders, among others.

Students may or may not have a formally diagnosed mental health disorder. A student with a diagnosis who receives academic accommodations may have an Individualized Education Plan, a 504 Plan, or none. Students with a diagnosed mental health disorder may or may not be receiving counseling or taking psychotropic medications. In fact, a student may meet all the criteria to be diagnosed with a mental health disorder, but financial, cultural, or familial factors prevent the student and their family from seeking and receiving mental health support.

Similarly, students may have many symptoms (but not enough to be formally diagnosed) and still experience emotional distress (Auger, 2011). Regardless of whether a student has a diagnosis, mental health symptoms can impact a student's emotional functioning and academic performance. However, the teacher–student relationship can be a powerful tool in supporting students and reducing stigma.

Student–Teacher Communication

Students bring emotions to the classroom. Whether state or trait emotions, diagnosed or undiagnosed mental health conditions, student emotions will present with psychological, physiological, and/or behavioral symptoms. Students form trusting relationships with teachers based on regular contact, class schedules, supportive feedback, and ongoing discussions. As a result of these relationships, students often feel comfortable disclosing their emotions to a trusted teacher. Conversely, teachers may be the first to notice changes in student behavior or academic performance that is rooted in emotional distress. Even in the absence of these disclosures and observations, educators can positively impact their students by using trauma-informed and empathetic responses.

Trauma-informed teaching recognizes that students may come to the classroom having experienced a variety of traumatic events, including poverty, abuse, neglect, violence, substance abuse, incarceration, illness, and death (Crosby, Howell, & Thomas, 2018). These events may also include systemic and historical trauma in relation to race, gender, religion, socioeconomic status, and other factors (Kendi, 2017).

Trauma-informed approaches require educators and administrators to recognize the impact of these events on academic learning and performance. Trauma-informed educators engage in professional development and commit to developing school policies and educational curricula that address student needs in response to trauma (Crosby et al., 2018). When a student struggles academically or behaviorally, a trauma-responsive educator examines the student's personal, historical, societal, and emotional factors contributing to that struggle and considers those factors when supporting and responding to the student.

An educator's response to a student's emotion can enhance or erode the student–teacher relationship. As stated, younger children often do not have the language or awareness of their emotions to describe what they are experiencing. Students need help identifying emotion, learning the triggers for their emotion, and learning to respond to emotion (Pelini, 2020). Young children can use feeling charts with words and pictures to help identify emotions, while adolescents and adults may prefer a feeling chart or feeling wheel with a wider variety of emotion words.

To help students learn emotional triggers, teachers can introduce the ABC model developed by Albert Ellis in 1957 (see The Albert Ellis Institute, n.d.). In this model, A is the antecedent, or the activating event that may include being excluded by peers, seeing parents fighting, or performing poorly in academics or athletics. The B is the belief, or thought, that follows the antecedent.

Using the examples above, a student being excluded may think that they have no friends, or a student who does poorly on an assignment may think that they will fail the class. This belief triggers an emotional response such as sadness, worry, or anger. The C is the consequences of that belief, which may include behaviors such as pouting, fighting, or yelling.

The ABC model teaches that although we cannot change the antecedent, we can change the belief. Students understand how their negative thoughts lead to negative feelings and behaviors. Once they have this awareness, educators can help them explore alternative thoughts, which could lead to alternative feelings and more productive behaviors. These skills can be further enhanced through work with other helping professionals within and outside of the school, too.

Some families and cultures discourage discussing emotions outside of the family or church community. In addition, society often minimizes emotion—specifically, negative emotions. This is evident in the minimizing responses people receive when displaying negative emotions (e.g., sadness = "cheer up," anxious = "relax," angry = "calm down"). As opposed to minimizing emotions, educators can build relationships by validating emotions. Simple statements such as "I can see that you are sad," "I understand that you are angry," "I hear that you are scared," or "It is clear you are feeling hurt" allow students to feel heard, validated, and to know that their emotion has worth.

Students also learn that it is appropriate to feel and experience negative emotions. Students learn that they do not need to "stuff" or cover up their negative emotions, and they can share how they feel without judgment. Being nonjudgmental is critically important to students feeling heard and respected. It is best to avoid statements such as "Don't be sad" or "There's no reason to be scared" because these statements not only minimize emotion but also judge the student for displaying the emotion.

To assist students in developing emotional distress tolerance, it is helpful to acknowledge the difficult emotion and express support (e.g., "I know you are really angry right now, and I'm proud of you for coming to talk to me" or "I sense that you are really sad, and I'm just going to sit with you and let you know that I'm here to listen"). These strategies can aid educators in mitigating complex emotional encounters while establishing trust with students to facilitate appropriate referrals and connections with helping professionals.

At the foundation of all educator communication is empathy for their students and positive regard for their well-being. Communicating empathy requires the educator to attempt to understand their students' perspective and connect to their emotion. Brené Brown describes empathy as "feeling with someone," as opposed to sympathy in which we feel for someone (RSA, 2013). Brown also discusses the importance of avoiding judgment, seeking to understand what someone is feeling, and communicating that understanding to the person.

Educators display positive regard when they believe that all students can learn and change. Positive regard supports the belief that all students deserve respect, caring, and acceptance, despite the struggles or obstacles that present in the classroom. Empathy and positive regard allow students to trust and build relationships with educators. Finally, educators should not act beyond their professional role and competence because mental health professionals—such as school counselors, social workers, and psychologists—are available in schools if a referral or consultation is needed. Furthermore, these professionals can connect students with community resources such as professional counselors or psychologists if needed.

Student Identity, Emotions, and the Classroom

Emotional expression is contingent on a variety of factors unique to the student, including the student's personal identities. There are a multitude of identities that contribute to who we are: race, ethnicity, gender, sexuality, socioeconomic status, age, disability status, and spirituality, among others. Furthermore, these identities are intersecting both within the individual and throughout society. The combination and expression of these identities contributes to everything that we are (e.g., our worldview, sense of self). For the purposes of this chapter, all these identities are referred to as *culture*. This is an oversimplification of the human experience; in reality, the role of each identity likely warrants its own chapter, if not its own book!

Culture is omnipresent, highly influential, and at the core of the human experience. Culture is also infused in the myriad ways we understand ourselves and our emotions. As such, culture can (and does) influence the classroom experience and pedagogy. The job of an educator is not to know about the nuances of every aspect of human culture. In fact, that borders on an impossibility. However, the job of an effective educator is twofold: (1) foster an environment where differing cultures do not impede on learning, and (2) teach content that includes various cultural worldviews to a multicultural audience.

Understanding Culture

Culture is defined as the norms, practices, and values of a group of people (Hays & Erford, 2017). Culture also comprises the many cultural groups a student belongs to. For example, a student's racial group may be Black or African-American, the sexual identity group may be female, the religious/spiritual identity group may be Christian, and the socioeconomic identity group may be middle class. Each cultural group has its own norms, practices, and values, contributing to a student's unique identity and worldview.

Culture is taught both explicitly and implicitly throughout our lives. An excellent resource to help understand the levels in which culture exists is through Bronfenbrenner's Ecological Systems Model (Bronfenbrenner, 1979; see also Guy-Evans, 2020). The model depicts the various levels in which influential factors exist. For example,

- the *microsystem* includes the environments occupied by students most frequently (such as home, day care, and school);
- the *mesosystem* represents the interactions between multiple microsystems, such as the interaction between students' home and school (i.e., communication and involvement between parents/guardians and teachers/school administrators); and

- the *exosystem* is expressed as students' indirect environment and includes settings that affect students without their directly interfacing with the environment. This can include the broader neighborhood in which students reside, where there are many aspects that are not experienced directly (e.g., neighborhood policies, social services within the community).

The largest level within the model is the *macrosystem*, which refers to overarching, wide-reaching ideas and belief structures that impact students and all of society. Examples of the macrosystem include political ideologies and the climate of an entire city, state, and/or nation. Finally, the chronosystem highlights temporal factors and changes. For example, identifying how students express emotions across time (e.g., grade and school levels) is valuable toward understanding their experience.

We recognize the depth of this model and how it can seem unwieldy for educators to use regularly. However, we share this model to serve as a framework for understanding the role of culture and emotions within the classroom. That is, if we begin to recognize the different influences and demands of the various cultures we exist in across location and time, we can begin to interpret emotions within the context in which they exist and occur, as opposed to through only our frame of reference.

As educators, we do not want to perceive students through an ethnocentric perspective, or the perspective that one's own worldview is the correct one and the comparison point for all other perspectives and behaviors (Hays & Erford, 2017). For example, if an educator holds the belief that "boys don't cry," the educator may not react with empathy if a male student begins to cry in the class but respond more empathically to female students expressing the same emotions.

The Role of Power, Privilege, and Oppression within Culture

Earlier in this chapter, we discussed what emotions are and why they exist. However, despite the commonalities of various emotions (i.e., we all have a general understanding of what sadness and happiness look and feel like), we experience and understand emotions differently. This differentiation is interconnected to culture; our culture and the cultures we exist in have taught us how we experience emotions.

In addition, certain cultures place value on the expression and inhibition of certain types of emotions. Again, it is not the job of the teacher to know every culture and common emotional belief system. However, recognizing that culture and emotion vary and can influence school dynamics is important for classroom management.

Implicit within culture is the role of power, privilege, and oppression. Power and privilege refer to the "unearned . . . access to resources, advantage, and social position based on cultural group memberships" (Hays & Erford, 2017, p. 5). Likewise, those lacking power and privilege are oppressed. The effects of power, privilege, and oppression are informed by both historical and ongoing issues within society (Kendi, 2017; see also Tatum, 2017).

We encourage all teachers to engage in both structured/formal education (e.g., diversity, equity, and inclusion training programs) and unstructured/informal education (e.g., readings) regarding these topics. We also encourage educators to recognize what they may represent to a specific student and how that can contribute to their emotions within the classroom.

The role of teacher comes with inherent authority and power over students (this can also intersect with one's other privileged identities), which can contribute to a student's distrust, unease, or even fear. For example, a female student may present as avoidant or withdrawn around a male educator if the student has experienced abuse by a male.

This example illustrates the intersectional consequences of both societal issues (e.g., males hold power and privilege over females [Hays & Erford, 2017]) and situational issues (e.g., the student is experiencing issues of transference with the male teacher due to her traumatic experiences). The identities we hold have meaning on how our students engage within the classroom, and not acknowledging the effects of power and privilege is a disservice to students.

Our relationship with emotions (both our own and the emotions of others) will inform how we navigate emotion-laden situations. Furthermore, our relationship with emotions may change across settings. What may be viewed as acceptable in some situations may be unacceptable in others. For example, some may view it as appropriate for a child to cry in the privacy of the home but not in public and around strangers. The notion of appropriateness may directly connect with the classroom experience, especially because some emotions can be disruptive or distracting within a school environment.

The School-to-Prison Pipeline

The school-to-prison pipeline describes how students are pushed out of schools and into prisons (Cole, 2020). This process might be the worst-case scenario of cultural incongruence between the school (e.g., teachers, administration, policies) and the student. Students are criminalized by disciplinary policies and practices in schools that place them in contact with law enforcement.

Once students have contact with law enforcement secondary to school disciplinary actions and policies, they are pushed out of educational settings and into the juvenile and criminal justice systems. Some policies and practices that created and maintain the school-to-prison pipeline include zero-tolerance policies that mandate harsh punishments for minor and major offenses, excluding students from educational settings through punitive suspensions and expulsions, and the presence of school resource officers (Cole, 2020).

This fact highlights the potentially significant consequences of ethnocentrism, racial biases, prejudices, and stereotypes. The school-to-prison pipeline primarily affects Black students, and students receiving harsh punishments within school are less likely to graduate high school and more than twice as likely to be arrested while being away from school. Consequently, these students are more likely to experience significant depression, anger, and stigma—secondary to suspension or expulsion.

In-school disciplinary action may lead to additional disciplinary responses within the community, further exacerbating their emotions. As such, we strongly urge teachers (and all those within the school system) to address issues related to culture (e.g., race, socioeconomic status, sex/gender), power, privilege, and oppression within the school. Furthermore, these actions should occur across all levels within the school system, from the individual interactions between teachers/school staff and students to the policies governing the entire school district. Again, not acknowledging and addressing the effects of power and privilege within the school system is a disservice to our students.

Sadness, Depression, and the Classroom

Sadness is an emotion that all people experience at multiple points in their lives. Although sadness is an emotion that most do not want to experience, it is a part of the emotional spectrum and should not inherently indicate a significant problem. In fact, a significant percentage of the population reported experiencing sadness throughout their lives (Tebeka, Geoffroy,

Dubertret, & Le Strat, 2021). However, the normalcy of experiencing sadness does not mean that sadness is without consequences or the need for intervention.

Colloquially, sadness is often described as someone feeling "sad, blue, depressed, or down" (Tebeka et al., 2021, p. 51). However, sadness can also be described through specific actions, observations, and behaviors. Sadness often presents as a combination of presentations, including feelings of sadness or depression; decreased concentration, energy, and interest in activities; and disruptions in sleep and appetite (APA, 2013; see also Leventhal, 2008).

As with all emotions, sadness is theorized to serve an evolutionary purpose. For example, sadness may serve as a signal for dissatisfaction with events or not accomplishing goals (Leventhal, 2008). However, despite the theoretical utility of sadness, there can be undesired consequences to experiencing sadness while in the classroom.

Depression, also referred to as clinical depression, major depressive disorder, or unipolar depression, is a mental health disorder that resembles sadness in many ways. In fact, essentially all the salient aspects of sadness are present within depression as well. Differentiating between sadness and depression should be done by a trained mental health professional, but aspects such as intensity and duration are notable factors.

Educators may be some of the first to notice depressive symptoms in their students. Students presenting with notable declines in performance, concentration, mood, and activity may be showing signs of depression. Educators should also be aware that depression in children and adolescents can present as irritability, as opposed to sadness. Also, in some cases of depression, individuals may exhibit NSSI or express suicidal ideations (e.g., thoughts, plans, or intent to kill themselves). These are clear signs to seek additional support from mental health professionals within the school system.

There are a myriad of ways a student experiencing sadness or depression can affect a classroom. In more traditional cases, a student might be significantly more withdrawn and disengaged from the class. This will certainly impact the student's own academic performance, but it may also pull the attention and energy of peers away from class lessons and toward interpersonal dynamics (e.g., checking in with the student experiencing sadness or depression, feeling concerned or sad due to their peers shifting in mood).

This shift away from the class agenda may be exacerbated by the student's status within the class (e.g., popularity or typical visibility/presence within the classroom). Also, if the student is experiencing irritability instead of sadness or depression, the emotions may manifest more overtly. Irritability can present as conflict with peers, classroom disruption, and other forms of "acting out."

As an educator, it can be easy to lose sight of the underlying cause for these shifts in the classroom and become overwhelmed. We recognize the difficult task of being an educator (especially since we are mostly educators as well). Foremost, we encourage teachers to do their best to manage their classes and lessons as effectively as possible. We also encourage educators to engage with students, offering whatever degree of support they deem appropriate, considering their individual resources and professional rules and ethics.

We strongly encourage educators to utilize the resources they have available to them when noticing a shift in a student's behavior that may resemble sadness or depression. This is especially important because sadness and depression may sometimes present with harmful ideations (e.g., thoughts about death, thoughts or plans to commit suicide).

If harmful ideations are present, safety protocols will likely need to be administered by a trained mental health professional. As such, educators should consider consulting with and/or referring to their school counselor, social worker, or psychologist—depending on the specific institution. While we assume most educators reading this text would not engage in this manner, we discourage challenging the validity of a student's emotional state. For example, statements such as "What do you have to be sad about?" or "You have no reason to act this way" can be minimizing and exacerbate a student's mood and well-being.

Loss, Grief, Bereavement, and the Classroom

The grief and bereavement process is one that many, if not all, will encounter throughout their lives. As such, students are no exception to this rule, and they may be processing grief while attending school. Despite the ubiquity of loss, grief, and bereavement, the meaning and nature of the terms are sometimes not fully understood.

Loss is central to the grief and bereavement process and is quite self-explanatory: an individual has experienced a loss of some kind. It is important to note that while we often think of grief and bereavement in response to the loss of an individual (i.e., death), people may experience grief and become bereaved for myriad types of losses: loss of relationship status, social status, home, identity, and so on. Loss should not be exclusively conceptualized as death.

Following a notable loss, a person is bereaved; that is, the literal experiencing of a loss is the process of bereavement (Howarth, 2011). However, all people experience loss differently with varying degrees of intensity. Grief is the "individual's personal response to loss and has emotional, physical, [behavioral], cognitive, social, and spiritual dimensions" (Buglass, 2010, p. 44). Furthermore, there are many ways someone may grieve, and grief is often informed by the individual's unique identities and culture (Cicchetti, McArthur, Szirony, & Blum, 2016; see also Howarth, 2011).

Sadness and depression commonly accompany grief, loss, and bereavement. While there is this distinct overlap, grief and bereavement are presumed to subside over time (e.g., state emotions). However, as the individual is actively experiencing the grief and bereavement, there may be notable presentations and effects that are different from sadness or depression. Grief and bereavement are likely to present with varying intensity throughout the process.

As individuals reencounter the loss, their emotional state will likely change in response. This is sometimes referred to as "grief pangs" and is considered typical throughout the grieving process. In addition, grief and bereavement may present with more prominent feelings of loss or emptiness, as opposed to overt sadness or depression (APA, 2013). Lastly, educators may notice emotional or behavioral shifts within a grieving and bereaved student, such as an increased involvement or engagement with things that are morbid or macabre (e.g., sense of humor [APA, 2013]).

Many descriptions of how sadness and depression may affect the classroom hold true for grief and bereavement, as do the recommendations: do your best to manage the class, provide appropriate support, and utilize available resources. We also discourage educators from providing narrow (or ethnocentric) advice to students about processing grief. There are numerous theories for grief and bereavement, with many emphasizing a staged process (e.g., Kübler-Ross five stages of grief [Buglass, 2010]).

However, helping professionals have adopted many different ways to approach and find resolution for the bereaved and grieving that require specific mental health training. Mental health referrals may be especially important because sometimes individuals do not effectively process their grief and experience a prolonged, distressing bereavement period. This is sometimes referred to as complicated bereavement and may require more significant mental health interventions.

Anxiety and the Classroom

The word *anxiety* has increasingly become reflective of someone's poor emotional regulation in our current society. Despite the colloquial co-opting of anxiety, there is significance behind the term and notable potential effects on the classroom. Anxiety can be defined as excessive worry or apprehension (APA, 2013).

It is important to distinguish between anxiety and fear. Fear is a response to a known and unambiguous stimulus, whereas anxiety is a response to an ambiguous stimulus. For example, a student may exhibit fear if a larger peer says, "I'm going to beat you up after class." The student is responding to a clear situation with real consequences. A student may exhibit anxiety about a potential confrontation due to concern about having talked over a larger peer during class. The student may note having potentially offended the larger student and becomes worried about consequences, even in the absence of a clear and defined rationale.

Experiencing anxiety is nearly universal. Common anxieties in response to a situation may include nervousness related to taking a test or social interactions. This emotion can manifest as restlessness, irritability, sleep disturbance, fatigue, and/or muscle tension, among other symptoms. Anxiety is often a state emotion; an individual feels anxious in response to a specific situation.

Anxiety can manifest both visibly and invisibly. For example, visible anxiety may present as jitteriness or difficulty speaking or breathing. However, some are able to effectively hide their anxiety from others and will experience difficulties with concentration and sleep—in private. In more severe instances of anxiety, students may present in a panicked state. This may be an isolated incident or it may be evidence of an anxiety disorder, which tends to be more intense, long lasting, and have more notable impacts on an individual's lived experience.

For school-aged children, anxiety may present itself as failure to complete assignments, overcompensating on assignments, and tardiness. Recognizing that these presentations or behaviors may be manifestations of anxiety is critical to note for teachers and other educators. Failure to complete assignments may not be indicative of a student's intellectual ability but instead a product of worries about how their performance may be judged, also known as performance anxiety.

Furthermore, students may develop certain study habits that could be a result of their anxiety. Some students might utilize their anxiety to exhibit better study habits, while others may find themselves debilitated by anxiety and not studying sufficiently. Lastly, peer pressure can also lead to student anxiety. That is, a student may feel pressured to live up to the expectations or standards of their peers, possibly resulting in anxiety about underperforming.

Educators encountering students with anxiety should aim to validate their emotions. Educators should avoid statements such as "What are you so worried about?" or "You have nothing to worry about," as they may be minimizing the student's emotions. Instead, educators should inquire about the student's emotions and offer space and time to speak about feelings. However, if teachers notice symptoms of panic or symptoms of anxiety across multiple areas of the student's life (e.g., anxiety among peers, academics, and performance), there should be a consultation with the mental health professionals in the school system.

Social Media and the Classroom

Technology is constantly evolving and new social media platforms are rapidly developing. Students of all ages are exposed to and engage with various social networking sites. It is important to acknowledge and address how social media impacts a student's mental and emotional health, and subsequently, what implications these have in the classroom.

Students turn to social media for a variety of reasons. Some children utilize social media platforms as a form of self-expression and creativity. In addition, through these networking sites, students can share their personal stories and stay up-to-date with popular cultural trends, peers, and family. Students of all ages can find a sense of connectedness and belongingness through the unique communication offered via social networking sites.

As educators, there is an opportunity to utilize social media to help students foster a sense of self and identity, and to include social networking sites as a tool in the classroom. For example, when working with high school students who are exploring their career and education opportunities after graduation, educators can highlight the utility of creating and maintaining professional social media accounts (e.g., LinkedIn).

Despite the myriad of benefits available to students and educators, it is imperative to be aware of the potential drawbacks of social networking. In fact, some researchers indicate that students who engage in high social media usage can have lower levels of connectedness to school and academic performance (Sampasa-Kanyinga, Chaput, & Hamilton, 2019).

One major concern to educators and students is cyberbullying and harassment. Cyberbullying is defined as bullying that occurs via digital devices, including through social media (US Department of Health and

Human Services, n.d.). Negative experiences on social media platforms, including cyberbullying, can affect a student's self-esteem and can consequently impact their performance in the classroom.

Another issue related to social media and the classroom is that of privacy and security. Students might want to share academic successes or extracurricular achievements on social media platforms, exposing their personal information to the public. However, sometimes this information can be used against students, such as sharing their location and interests with unintended parties. It may be useful for educators to explain the importance of privacy settings and information sharing to their students. We recommend that educators recognize the consequences of extended time spent on social media and take preventative measures to avoid excessive time on social networking sites (Sampasa-Kanyinga et al., 2019).

Body Image and the Classroom

Body image can be defined as the perception of one's own body. From birth until late adolescence, students are rapidly developing socially, emotionally, and, just as importantly, physically. It is also during late childhood and early adolescence that students are more aware of their own bodies, particularly during puberty (approximately ages ten to fourteen for females and ages eleven to sixteen for males). This heightened sense of awareness sometimes co-occurs with judgment of self and others.

The judgment of one's own body and the bodies of others has become more commonplace and culturally acceptable due to the way in which body image is presented in our society. The concept of body image is essentially in everything that we see, do, and encounter. One area in which body image is presented is in the media. In music, artists describe the bodies of their perfect partner or critique the bodies of individuals.

Likewise, movies also evoke particular reactions from viewers when actors of different shapes and sizes are shown on the screen. Across many areas of popular culture, the bodies of people (particularly famous people) are presented without the context of how these individuals attained and maintain their physique, implying their physique to be near commonplace.

Social media also contributes to how body image is perceived. Due to the accessibility of social media, students can compare themselves to what they view on different social media sites. Often what is highlighted on social media is generally idealized or only the best version of an individual, but individuals will compare their current self to another's best self on social media. For example, Instagram influencers who professionally curate their photos and spend multiple hours per day attending to their physical appearance may present themselves as having done no preparation at all and never share themselves as sad, upset, or stressed.

In addition to the role of body image within media, the perception and judgment of body image can occur in everyday interactions. For example, school dress codes may be better suited for certain body types and shapes, resulting in ridicule for those not suited to the mandated attire. Even in the home, a student's body may be scrutinized by loved ones commenting on their eating habits or their way of dress.

Included in the perception of body image are other physical presentations, such as hair types and hair styles. There are numerous reports of discrimination against women—particularly Black women—and how they decide to wear their hair. Society often discriminates against women who choose to wear their hair in their natural state versus their hair being straightened. These judgments and discriminations about body, hair, and dress can all lead to issues related to body image.

When individuals are faced with a negative self-concept or a negative sense of self due to how they feel about their bodies, there are a variety of issues that may arise. Some manifestations can include depression or anxiety, as discussed earlier in this chapter. However, in some situations, eating disorders or disordered eating can result from a negative body image.

It is significant to differentiate between eating disorders and disordered eating. Disordered eating is an unhealthy relationship an individual has with food. This is common and can be seen in behaviors such as fad diets, fasting, or other signs of not maintaining a healthy relationship with food. Disordered eating can present with varying emotional and physical symptoms.

If students are not partaking in a healthy diet, they may experience symptoms of fatigue and difficulty concentrating. They may also experience increased stress or peer pressure over food choices. In more severe instances, students may be suffering from an eating disorder. Signs of an eating disorder include extreme food avoidance (insofar as students are significantly below expected weight for their age and height), binge eating (eating in extreme excess), or purging behaviors (e.g., intentionally vomiting or ingesting laxatives after eating).

Eating disorders are mental health disorders, classified within the *DSM-5* (APA, 2013), and will warrant support from trained mental health professionals. Another important consideration related to body image includes the role of sociocultural factors such as athletics. Students may feel pressured to attain and maintain a certain physique based on their athletic community (e.g., a bigger body size is likely to be rewarded in football, whereas a smaller body size may be rewarded in ballet and gymnastics).

When a student is experiencing notable body image issues, this might have effects on the classroom. In addition to feelings of depression or anxiety connected to low self-esteem, eating disorders may result in a student feeling powerless to certain behaviors, such as food restriction, binging, or purging. For example, a student may miss class time due to the need to engage in purging, and this absence can negatively impact a student's overall performance in that class. Also, a student's absence or insistence on leaving the classroom could potentially be disruptive for other students. There are also notable health effects due to eating disorders and disordered eating, including a decrease in blood pressure, dental problems, intolerance to cold, dry skin, and anemia, among others. A student suffering from these health effects may have difficulty focusing and being alert in class, which would ultimately impede the student's ability to perform well in class.

Even if teachers are unaware that a student is experiencing disordered eating or has an eating disorder, they can implement certain strategies to encourage healthy habits. Some schools may not encourage eating in classrooms due to health factors and other reasons, but if a school does allow students to eat in classrooms, educators should encourage and model healthy snacking.

Educators can also find ways to have conversations with students about healthy relationships with food. There can be a collaborative effort with mental health professionals within the school to effectively engage students with accurate information about healthy eating habits. Lastly, if educators notice overt signs of eating disorders (i.e., binge eating or purging), they are strongly encouraged to consult with school-based mental health professionals.

Emotions, Substance Use, and the Classroom

Substances—also known as drugs—include a wide variety of products such as prescription medication, over-the-counter medication, illegal drugs, marijuana, alcohol, tobacco, synthetics, inhalants, and other items. Substances are used to treat diagnosed medical conditions and may also be used for feelings of euphoria or "highs."

Prior versions of the *DSM* utilized the terms *substance use, substance abuse,* and *substance dependence.* In the current version of the *DSM*, all substance use disorders are classified as either mild, moderate, or severe (APA, 2013). This language indicates that substance use may or may not be problematic based on how the substance is used. Substances are often referred to as *alcohol, tobacco, and other drugs* (ATOD). The *DSM-5* classifies substance use disorders into ten substance categories: alcohol, caffeine, cannabis, hallucinogens, inhalants, opioids, sedatives, stimulants, tobacco, and other substances (APA, 2013).

Substance Misuse and Illicit Substance Use

Substance misuse is a growing problem among children and adolescents. Many substances impact the dopamine receptors in the brain, which regulate feelings of pleasure to create a high (Fisher & Harrison, 2018). Adolescents and children may use ATOD to get high for a variety of reasons, including socialization, peer relationships, or emotion management.

Although alcohol, tobacco, vapes, and marijuana are legal for adults to purchase, they are illegal for individuals under age eighteen or twenty-one and would be classified as substance misuse. Even substances that are obtained legally, such as prescription medication, over-the-counter medications, and household products used as inhalants, can be used to get high and constitute substance misuse.

Other categories of substances may include synthetic cannabinoids (e.g., K2, spice), synthetic cathinones (e.g., bath salts), and designer drugs or club drugs (e.g., MDMA, ecstasy, molly). The challenge with all drugs, but specifically synthetics and designer drugs, is the changing nature of the chemical compound. Drug makers regularly change the contents of the drug, which impact how the drug affects the brain, the body, and the individual.

Adolescent rates of substance misuse vary. According to the Substance Abuse and Mental Health Services Administration (2019), while tobacco and alcohol use has declined among twelve- to seventeen-year-olds, binge drinking has remained steady. Illicit drug use has also remained constant, and prescription medications have been the second most widely used substance following marijuana (excluding alcohol and tobacco).

Adolescent substance use contributes to significant issues in later adulthood, including increased likelihood for substance abuse (Merline, O'Malley, Schulenberg, Bachman, & Johnston, 2004), higher levels of unemployment (Hyggen, 2012), lower levels of education attainment, and higher welfare dependence (Fergusson & Boden, 2008).

Adolescents are most likely to abuse prescription opioids received from a friend or family member or prescribed by a doctor (Hudgins, Porter, Monuteaux, & Bourgeois, 2019). Most significantly, substance use can lead to overdose and death. In fact, adolescent deaths due to drug overdose more than doubled between 1999 and 2015 (Curtin, Tejada-Vera, & Warner, 2017).

Educators are not expected to be substance abuse counselors; however, they may be the first to recognize some of the early warning signs of substance use and misuse. Some of these early warning signs include changes in academic performance; attitudes toward school, mood, peer groups, hygiene, and eating and sleeping habits; as well as breaking rules, engaging in risky behavior, and low self-esteem (Sikes, Cole, McBride, Fusco, & Lauka, 2009).

In response to these warning signs, educators can talk with students and express concern about these changes. It is important to remember that adolescent substance use may be a coping strategy for managing difficult emotions such as fear, depression, or anxiety, or may be a response to a specific trigger such as trauma, relationships, or peers. Educators can use the communication skills discussed earlier, including listening empathically, responding without judgment, validating the student's emotions, using trauma-informed approaches, and referring the student to specialized school personnel when needed.

Psychotropic Medications

Children and adolescents with mental health disorders, such as attention deficit/hyperactivity disorders (ADHD), depression, anxiety, and other disorders, may be prescribed psychotropic medication to manage their symptoms. The use of medication in children and adolescents is an important decision that students and families make with their medical providers. Yet, because educators may have students in class who are using psychotropic medication, a brief understanding of these medications is appropriate.

Psychotropic medications—like other drugs—regulate brain chemistry yet target brain functions that address mental health disorder symptoms. The most common medication classifications prescribed to children and adolescents include ADHD medication, antidepressants, antipsychotics, mood stabilizers, antianxiety medications, and sleep medications (American Academy of Child and Adolescent Psychiatry, 2017). Children and adolescents may be prescribed one or more of these medications, specifically if they have more than one mental health diagnosis (Olfson, He, & Merikangas, 2013).

Medication is usually prescribed by a medical doctor, psychiatrist, or psychiatric nurse practitioner after appropriate evaluation. The medical professional, the student, and the family must consider both the benefits and risks of the medication. Students endure a trial period during which they see how they respond to the medication. Dosages may need to be increased or decreased.

Most medications take time before symptoms start to improve, and not every medication works for every student. While medications are designed to assist students with their mental health symptoms, side effects may be unpleasant or undesirable. Depending on the medication, side effects may include headaches, decreased appetite, or obesity. Other side effects among youth may include restlessness and irritability, depending on the medication (American Academy of Child and Adolescent Psychiatry, 2012).

Newer, long-lasting medications allow students to take only one dose per day, which avoids students needing medication in the middle of the school day and the fatigue that may follow (American Academy of Child and Adolescent Psychiatry, 2017). Different side effects can emerge when a student is stopping or changing medication.

Educators can be supportive and flexible as students adjust to their medication. Using both trauma-responsive and empathic communication, educators can help students feel supported about the decision to improve their mental health symptoms. Ideally, psychotropic medication can improve students' ability to manage their emotions, which will likely improve their academic outcomes.

Medication, when properly prescribed, can assist students to improve their mood, focus, attention, and functioning. Some medications, such as stimulants for ADHD, have the propensity for abuse either by the students or their family and friends. As with substance misuse, educators can discuss their concerns with students, demonstrate positive regard, and refer them to school mental health professionals.

Resources and the Classroom

Students need their basic needs met to be successful academically (Kline, n.d.). Maslow's hierarchy of needs (Maslow, 1943) provides the framework for educators that depicts students' (and people's) basic needs. A person's basic needs include physiological needs (e.g., food, water, warmth, air, clothing, and rest) and safety needs (personal security, health, and safety [Kurt, 2020; see also McLeod, 2020]). Physiological needs are prioritized and must be satisfied for students to engage effectively within the classroom (Kurt, 2020).

A student will likely be significantly distracted when immediate needs are not met and will prioritize them over their education. Students' immediate needs determine their immediate action. If they are hungry, they may seem distracted and/or exhibit rule-breaking behavior because hunger is their priority, not school. If they are sleep deprived, they may fall asleep during class instead of doing their work (Kurt, 2020). Students from families with low socioeconomic status may experience not having their basic needs met.

Teachers cannot possibly meet the physiological needs of their students (nor should they be expected to), but they can impact macrosystemic changes such as advocating for programs that provide food and clothing for students to help meet these needs. They can also be more sensitive to students and not be as punitive when these students exhibit distracting behavior. Teachers should also partner with mental health professionals within the school, such as school counselors and school social workers, to advocate for these students and connect them with services.

Safety needs are the next level in Maslow's model. Rules and discipline should be consistent and culturally sensitive, especially for students who experience discrimination and oppression. We recommend that teachers advocate for and with students, even if doing so puts them at odds with the administration.

For students who return to school from suspension and/or expulsion, teachers must create an environment that is welcoming and help reduce the stigma and bullying these students experience upon returning. Teachers must also check their own biases. If a student's safety needs are not being met at home, teachers should partner with school counselors, school social workers, and parents to address these needs so the student's academics will not be negatively affected.

Psychological needs include belongingness and love needs (e.g., intimate relationships, friends, and a sense of connection) and esteem needs (e.g., prestige, a feeling of accomplishment, self-esteem, status, recognition, strength, and freedom [Kurt, 2020; see also McLeod, 2020]). Students can feel disconnected from their school and academic community for a variety of reasons (e.g., peer conflicts, social anxiety, disability status, discrimination, oppression).

However, educators can make efforts to ensure that they are competently trained to recognize exclusionary practices within the school systems (both official and unofficial), as well as identifying their own biases. Unfair policies and procedures can rapidly disconnect the victimized from the school system.

In addition, bias and discrimination of any kind (e.g., racism, sexism, ableism) will target those without privilege, and push them out of the classroom and away from a sense of community and belongingness (Bryan, 2017). We strongly encourage educators and school systems to engage in trainings focused on equitable practices. Teachers should also seek out and implement anti-deficit frameworks that assist them in challenging stereotypes and biases.

Emotional Catharsis

In a classroom setting, teachers will undoubtably experience a multitude of emotional expressions from their students, particularly during developmental stages where emotional regulation is not fully developed. The teacher has a significant role in helping students express themselves emotionally. Have you ever heard students call their teacher Mom or Dad?

Teachers are often the authoritative figure that students spend the most of their time with and are often looked to for emotional and moral support, similar to their parents. Students also look to teachers for validation. Because of this, educators tend to be confidants for students. The role of being a confidant for a student can be simultaneously honoring and humbling; however, it can also be taxing.

It is expected that navigating different roles and encountering students' different emotional states can be exhausting and overwhelming at times. In some cases, feelings of overwhelm can result in burnout or a loss of interest in an activity due to physical and/or emotional exhaustion and stress (Mayo Clinic, n.d.). Burnout can result in the loss of excellent educators, many that the profession cannot afford to lose. As such, if symptoms of burnout are beginning to emerge, we recommend engaging in self-care practices that will allow for rest and rejuvenation.

Self-Care

The concept of *self-care* is commonly discussed and has a multitude of meanings, expectations, and sometimes misconceptions. Self-care is engagement in behaviors of taking care of oneself in a mental, physical, emotional, or spiritual way. Generally, self-care is likened to vacations or trips to the beach. While those are specific examples of self-care, it is not limited to that particular vision. Self-care should be feasible and accessible to all. Below are some tips on how to engage in self-care in various ways:

- Mental: Talking to a therapist, reading, journaling, being more organized
- Physical: Engaging in regular exercise; improving sleep hygiene; including more fruits, vegetables, and vitamins in diet
- Emotional: Spending time with a supportive friend, stating positive affirmations
- Spiritual: Meditating, praying, connecting with nature

Educators are often asked to "do it all," which is both unreasonable and impossible. Educators should re-evaluate their boundaries within their work because as much as serving students can be taxing, it can be equally rewarding. It is especially important to reexamine the situation if the boundaries are fluid (e.g., staying exceptionally late after classes end, missing appointments or tasks within and outside of school) because the consequences connected to fluid boundaries can also lead to stress, exhaustion, and burnout.

Summary of Strategies for Navigating Student Emotions in the Classroom

Recognizing the depth and breadth of content in this chapter, below are three other suggestions for navigating emotions in the classroom.

ASK STUDENTS WHAT THEY KNOW ABOUT THEIR EMOTIONS

Having honest conversations with students about their emotions can allow open dialogue to discuss what emotions might look like for them. Even if students are not able to identify their emotions specifically, they can have healthier emotional development and improved self-regulation by recognizing what various emotions look like. Also, emotion-focused dialogue may serve as effective modeling for students to engage in emotional conversations with other important persons.

IDENTIFY AND UNDERSTAND TRIGGERS

Emotions can be exhibited by students in a variety of ways. As you learn to identify the visible and nonvisible emotional reactions, it is equally important to identify the triggers or the catalyst to students' emotional reactions. Identifying triggers can help prepare teachers to provide supportive intervention with students. In addition, sharing triggers with students can aid in their emotional development, fostering their emotion regulation.

NORMALIZE EMOTIONS

Normalization is key in navigating students' emotions. For teachers, administrators, and other school staff, it is of the utmost importance to recognize that emotional expression is critical in childhood development. Therefore, normalizing emotions and offering support for students who are emotionally expressive can improve overall development.

Conclusion

This chapter discussed the multiple helping professionals available to teachers within schools and provided a foundation for understanding emotions. We overviewed how students experience and understand emotions differently as they develop and the relationship between culture, power, privilege, oppression, and emotions. We shared how internal factors (e.g., mental health, self-perception) and external factors (e.g., society, substances) influence emotional expression and how emotions can affect classroom dynamics. Lastly, we shared the importance of teacher self-care and summarized our overall recommendations.

We believe it is necessary to share one final factor related to emotions and the classroom: global health crises. This chapter was written during the COVID-19 pandemic, during which many classrooms have moved out of physical spaces and into virtual ones. The management of virtual classrooms is starkly different compared to physical classes and brings about many new challenges for teachers.

Due to the shift in teaching formats, students are now forced to balance school life with home life. They no longer have the benefits afforded by physical school, including friends, peers, resources (academic or otherwise), and direction (e.g., students can avoid home and community distractions while in school). Instead, they must now navigate school simultaneously with their home and community distractions, which likely adds stressors.

COVID-19 has also directly affected the emotional and mental health of all people. People have reported increases in multiple mental health concerns, including symptoms of anxiety, depression, trauma responses, substance use, and thoughts of self-harm or suicide (Czeisler et al., 2020). In addition, there has been a notable rise in mental health emergencies (i.e., emergency room visits) since the onset of the pandemic (Leeb et al., 2020). The COVID-19 pandemic is undoubtedly taxing students and teachers in unprecedented ways.

While we encourage educators to use our recommendations throughout this chapter, we believe our section on teacher self-care is likely of the utmost importance. We (the authors of this chapter) are also mental health professionals, and in mental health, we often give the analogy of the oxygen mask on an airplane (an oldie but a goodie).

When the safety procedures are overviewed on an airplane, passengers are told to put their own oxygen mask on before helping others. The rationale here is that if one is unable to breathe, he or she cannot assist anyone else. As such, if a teacher is experiencing burnout, he or she will be less effective (if not ineffective) in working with and supporting the students. Thus, we urge all teachers to take care of themselves the best they can by finding time for self-care so that they can take care of those that they love and that need them—their students included.

References

The Albert Ellis Institute. (n.d.). *REBT in the context of modern psychological research.* Retrieved from https://albertellis.org/rebt-in-the-context-of-modern-psychological-research/.

American Academy of Child and Adolescent Psychiatry. (2012). *A guide for community servicing agencies on psychotropic medications for children and adolescents.* Retrieved from https://www.aacap.org/App_Themes/AACAP/docs/press/guide_for_community_child_serving_agencies_on_psychotropic_medications_for_children_and_adolescents_2012.pdf.

American Academy of Child and Adolescent Psychiatry. (2017). *Psychiatric medications for children and adolescents: Part II–types of medications.* https://www.aacap.org/AACAP/Families_and_Youth/Facts_for_Families/FFF-Guide/Psychiatric-Medication-For-Children-And-Adolescents-Part-II-Types-Of-Medications-029.aspx.

American Foundation for Suicide Prevention. (n.d.). *Top ten things we've learned from research.* Retrieved from https://afsp.org/what-we-ve-learned-through-research.

American School Counselor Association. (n.d.a). *State certification requirements.* Retrieved from https://www.schoolcounselor.org/About-School-Counseling/State-Requirements-Programs/State-Licensure-Requirements.

American School Counselor Association. (n.d.b). *The role of the school counselor.* Retrieved from https://www.schoolcounselor.org/getmedia/ee8b2e1b-d021-4575-982c-c84402cb2cd2/Role-Statement.pdf.

American Psychiatric Association. (2013). *Diagnostic and statistical manual of mental disorders* (5th ed.). https://doi.org/10.1176/appi.books.9780890425596.

American Psychological Association. (2020). *APA dictionary of psychology: Emotion regulation.* Retrieved from https://dictionary.apa.org/emotion-regulation.

Auger, R. (2011). *The school counselor's mental health sourcebook: Strategies to help students succeed.* Corwin.

Bronfenbrenner, U. (1979). *The ecology of human development: Experiments by nature and design*. Harvard University Press.

Bryan, N. (2017). White teachers' role in sustaining the school-to-prison pipeline: Recommendations for teacher education. *The Urban Review, 49*(2), 326–45. https://doi.org/10.1007/s11256-017-0403-3.

Buglass, E. (2010). Grief and bereavement theories. *Nursing Standard (Royal College of Nursing (Great Britain), 24*(41), 44–47. https://doi.org/10.7748/ns 2010.06.24.41.44.c7834.

Celeghin, A., Diano, M., Bagnis, A., Viola, M., & Tamietto, M. (2017). Basic emotions in human neuroscience. *Frontiers in Psychology, 24*, 1432. https://doi.org/10.3389/fpsyg.2017.01432.

Chaplin, W. F., John, O. P., & Goldberg, L. R. (1988). Conceptions of states and traits: Dimensional attributes with ideals as prototypes. *Journal of Personality and Social Psychology, 54*, 541–57.

Cicchetti, R. J., McArthur, L., Szirony, G. M., & Blum, C. R. (2016). Perceived competency in grief counseling: Implications for counselor education. *Journal of Social, Behavioral, and Health Sciences, 10*(1), 3–17. https://doi.org/10.5590/JSBHS.2016.10.1.02.

Cole, N. L. (2020, October 21). *Understanding the school-to-prison pipeline*. Retrieved from https://www.thoughtco.com/school-to-prison-pipeline-4136170.

Cornell Research Program on Self-Injury and Recovery. (n.d.). *Self-injury basics*. http://www.selfinjury.bctr.cornell.edu/perch/resources/self-injury-basics.pdf.

Crosby, S. D., Howell, P., & Thomas, S. (2018). Social justice education through trauma-informed teaching. *Middle School Journal, 4*, 15–23. https://doi.org/10.1080/00940771.2018.1488470.

Curtin, S. C., Tejada-Vera, B., & Warner, M. (2017). *Drug overdose deaths among adolescents aged 15–19 in the United States: 1999–2015* (NCHS Data Brief No. 282). Retrieved from https://www.cdc.gov/nchs/products/databriefs/db282.htm.

Czeisler, M. É., Lane, R. I., Petrosky, E., Wiley, J. F., Christensen, A., Njai, R., et al. (2020). Mental health, substance use, and suicidal ideation during the COVID-19 pandemic–United States, June 24–30, 2020. *Morbidity and Mortality Weekly Report, 69*(32), 1049–57. http://dx.doi.org/10.15585/mmwr.mm6932a1.

Fergusson, D. M., & Boden J. M. (2008). Cannabis use and later life outcomes. *Addiction, 103*. 969–76. doi:10.1111/j.1360-0443.2008.02221.x.

Fisher, G. L., & Harrison, T. C. (2018). *Substance abuse information for school counselors, social workers, therapists, and counselors*. Pearson.

Guy-Evans, O. (2020). *Bronfenbrenner's Ecological Systems Theory*. Retrieved from https://www.simplypsychology.org/Bronfenbrenner.html.

Gysbers, N. (2010). *Remembering the past, shaping the future: A history of school counseling*. American School Counselor Association.

Hays, D. G., & Erford, B. T. (2017). *Developing multicultural counseling competence: A systems approach* (3rd ed.). Pearson.

Howarth, R. (2011). Concepts and controversies in grief and loss. *Journal of Mental Health Counseling, 33*(1), 4–10. https://doi.org/10.17744/mehc.33.1.900m56162888u737.

Hudgins, J. D., Porter, J. J., Monuteaux, M. C., & Bourgeois, F. T. (2019). Prescription opioid use and misuse among adolescents and young adults in the United States: A national survey study. *PLoS Med, 16*(11): e1002922. https://doi.org/10.1371/journal.pmed.1002922.

Hyggen, C. (2012). Does smoking cannabis affect work commitment? *Addiction, 107.* 1309–15. doi: 10.1111/j.1360-0443.2012.03796.x.

Kendi, I. X. (2017). *Stamped from the beginning: The definitive history of racist ideas in America.* Bold Type Books.

Kline, T. (n.d.). *Applying Maslow's hierarchy of needs in our classrooms.* Retrieved from http://www.changekidslives.org/actions-4.

Kurt, S. (2020). *Maslow's hierarchy of needs in education: Applying Maslow's hierarchy of needs.* Retrieved from https://educationlibrary.org/maslows-hierarchy-of-needs-in-education/.

Lambie, G. W., & Williamson, L. L. (2004). The challenge to change from guidance counseling to professional school counseling: A historical proposition. *Professional School Counseling, 8*(2), 124–31.

Leeb, R. T., Bitsko, R. H., Radhakrishnan, L., Martinez, P., Njai, R., & Holland, K. M. (2020). Mental health–related emergency department visits among children aged <18 years during the COVID-19 pandemic–United States, January 1–October 17, 2020. *Morbidity and Mortality Weekly Report, 69*(45), 1675–80. http://dx.doi.org/10.15585/mmwr.mm6945a3.

Leventhal, A. M. (2008). Sadness, depression, and avoidance behavior. *Behavior Modification, 32*(6), 759–79. https://doi.org/10.1177/0145445508317167.

Leyro, T. M., Zvolensky, M. J., & Bernstein, A. (2010). Distress tolerance and psychopathological symptoms and disorders: A review of the empirical literature among adults. *Psychological Bulletin, 136*(4), 576–600. https://doi.org/10.1037/a0019712.

Maslow, A. H. (1943). A theory of human motivation. *Psychological Review, 50*(4), 370–96. https://doi.org/10.1037/h0054346.

Mayo Clinic. (n.d.). *Job burnout: How to spot it and take action.* Retrieved from https://www.mayoclinic.org/healthy-lifestyle/adult-health/in-depth/burnout/art-20046642.

McLaughlin, K. A., Garrad, M. C., & Somerville, L. H. (2015). What develops during emotional development? A component process approach to identifying sources of psychopathology risk in adolescence. *Dialogues in Clinical Neuroscience, 17*(4), 403–10. https://doi.org/10.31887/DCNS.2015.17.4/kmclaughlin.

McLeod, S. (2020). *Maslow's hierarch of needs.* Retrieved from https://www.simplypsychology.org/maslow.html.

Merline, A. C., O'Malley, P. M., Schulenberg, J. E., Bachman, J. G., & Johnston, L. D. (2004). Substance use among adults 35 years of age: Prevalence, adulthood predictors, and impact of adolescent substance use. *American Journal of Public Health, 94*, 96–102.

Miron, O., Yu, K., Wilf-Miron, R., & Kohane, I. S. (2019). Suicide rates among adolescents and young adults in the United States, 2000–2017. *JAMA, 32*, 2362–64. doi:10.1001/jama.2019.5054.

Olfson, M., He, J., & Merikangas, K. (2013). Psychotropic medication treatment of adolescents: Results from the National Comorbidity Survey–Adolescent. *Journal of the American Academy of Child and Adolescent Psychiatry, 52*, 378–88. https://doi.org/10.1016/j.jaac.2012.12.006.

Pelini, S. (2020). *An age-by-age-guide to helping children manage emotions.* Retrieved from https://www.gottman.com/blog/age-age-guide-helping-kids-manage-emotions/.

RSA. (2013, December 10). *Brené Brown on empathy.* Retrieved from https://www.thersa.org/discover/videos/rsa-shorts/2013/12/Brene-Brown-on-Empathy.

Sampasa-Kanyinga, H., Chaput, J., & Hamilton, H. A. (2019). Social media use, school connectedness, and academic performance among adolescents. *The Journal of Primary Prevention, 40*(2), 189–211. https://doi.org/10.1007/s10935-019-00543-6.

School Social Work Association of America. (n.d.). *Role of school social worker.* Retrieved from https://www.sswaa.org/school-social-work.

Sikes, A., Cole, R. F., McBride, R., Fusco, A., & Lauka, J. (2009). Addressing the needs of substance abusing adolescents: A guide for professional school counselors. *Journal of School Counseling, 7.* Retrieved from https://files.eric.ed.gov/fulltext/EJ886163.pdf.

Substance Abuse and Mental Health Services Administration. (2019). *Key substance use and mental health indicators in the United States: Results from the 2018 National Survey on Drug Use and Health* (HHS Publication No. PEP19-5068, NSDUH Series H-54). Rockville, MD: Center for Behavioral Health Statistics and Quality, Substance Abuse and Mental Health Services Administration.

Tatum, B. D. (2017). *Why are the Black kids sitting together in the cafeteria? And other conversations about race (revised and updated).* Basic Books.

Tebeka, S., Geoffroy, P. A., Dubertret, C., & Le Strat, Y. (2021). Sadness and the continuum from well-being to depressive disorder: Findings from a representative US population sample. *Journal of Psychiatric Research, 132*, 50–54. https://doi.org/10.1016/j.jpsychires.2020.10.004.

US Department of Health and Human Services. (n.d.). *What is cyberbullying?* Retrieved from https://www.stopbullying.gov/cyberbullying/what-is-it.

Wong, D. W., Hall, K. R., Justice, C. A., & Wong Hernandez, L. (2015). *Counseling individuals through the lifespan.* Sage.

Integrating Gender Equity into Positive Classroom Culture

5

DONNA CEMPA-DANZIGER, TRICIA KRESS, AND MAUREEN T. WALSH

Schools play crucial roles in the nurturing and promotion of both academic and socio-emotional learning. As society evolves and changes, the support of gender diversity and inclusivity in the classroom has become an essential part of the learning process. This support includes the need for educators to present material that acknowledges the intersections of gender with race and class, as well as ability.

Despite many advances toward gender equity, gender bias and stereotyping still exist, leading to altered student participation, decreased academic outcomes, lower self-esteem, and decreased retention (Nduagbo, 2020). A foundation for positive classroom environments can be set by attending to gender and diversity within the school curriculum, beginning in early education.

Conversations about gender diversity, as well as race and class, may be uncomfortable, but avoidance can have detrimental outcomes for learners. It is not uncommon to avoid addressing issues of gender or race as an indicator of diversity support, but this position can be more harmful than good. This lack of acknowledgment and discussion may lead students to feel rejected and invisible, and it can perpetuate stereotyping.

Educators must closely examine their own classroom practices to ensure they are providing equitable support to all students. It is also crucial for educators to be self-reflective of their own biases throughout their career. This is an ongoing process and may not be easy, but it is necessary to promote a positive learning environment for all students.

Lack of instructor support can be founded on subconscious bias. It is well documented that the female presence in science, technology, engineering, and mathematics (STEM) courses of study is lower than that of males (Botella, Rueda, López-Iñesta, & Marzal, 2019; see also Kinskey, 2020). This marginalization of females begins around middle school due to beliefs that male students are better in math and science than females.

Other research has shown that teachers call on male students more often than female students and will interact with the sexes differently. This form of sexism may be unconscious or due to the belief that boys need more attention than girls. In either case, the foundation for oppression of females may be established.

Students of color are at an even greater disadvantage in that they may be discriminated against because of their race as well as gender. For example, the representation of Black males as criminals in movies and television shows positions them for a lifetime of disadvantage. Black female students face the dual discrimination of sex and race, which is also promoted by negative representation in entertainment media. They are less likely to be placed in honors classes, more likely to be suspended, and cite choosing to be "invisible" as a coping mechanism (Pietri, Johnson, & Ozgumus, 2018).

Sexual diversity in the classroom must also be examined as students are becoming more vocal about their sense of identity. Lesbian, gay, bisexual, transgender, questioning, queer, intersex, asexual, pansexual, and allies (LGBTQIA+; see table 5.1 for an explanation of terms) students are at a higher risk for discrimination by other students within binary-gendered learning environments (Mangin, 2018). Risk factors associated with gender-diverse students include higher drop-out rates, poor self-esteem, low achievement, and suicide. Higher rates of bullying and physical abuse are also reported by LGBTQIA+ students (Brody, 2020).

The provided examples establish the urgency of the need for change. As young children become aware of gender differences, they are more attuned to societal expectations. For educators, teacher–student interactions will impact student participation, ultimately affecting workplace behaviors. The foundation for gender stereotyping begins in school and is perpetuated throughout life. The goal of this chapter is to provide an awareness of gender differences in the classroom and suggestions to create a positive and inclusive learning environment for all by celebrating student diversity.

Table 5.1. Summary of Terminology Related to Gender and Sexual Orientation

Term	Definition
Ally	People who support the LGBTQIA+ community but may not identify with it
Bisexual	Individuals attracted to both men and women
Cisgender	Individuals whose gender identity matches their biological sex
Cisnormative	The belief that gender is binary and that almost all individuals are cisgender
Gay	Individuals attracted to the same sex
Gender	A cultural and social construct that includes social expectations of how people should behave based on their biological sex
Gender expression	An individual's outward presentation of his or her gender
Gender fluid, nonbinary, nonconforming	Individuals whose behavior and gender identity are viewed as nonstereotypical
Gender identity	The way which individuals view and feel about themselves
Gender typing	When a child learns awareness of his or her gender
Heteronormativity	The belief that heterosexuality is the acceptable or normal sexual orientation
Lesbian	Women who are sexually and emotionally attracted to other women or who have an attraction toward womanhood
Queer	Individuals with gender and sexual identities that do not conform with cisgender
Sexual orientation	Who you are physically and emotionally attracted to
Transgender	Individuals whose sense of gender identity differs from their biological sex

Gender: A Social Construct

Sex and *gender* are vastly different terms and yet are typically used interchangeably. One's sex is biologically determined by the presence of specific chromosomes: XX for female and XY for male. A person's biological sex includes the physical characteristics that differentiate males from females. When looking at gender, descriptions may include the terms "male and female" and the presupposed behaviors associated with the biological identity of being male or female. When identifying another person's gender, people may state factors such as genitalia at birth, how a person dresses, how people look, or ways that people act with others (Berkowitz, Manohar, & Tinkler, 2010).

Gender is not to be confused with one's biological sex. Expectations of how people dress or behave based on their biological structures is a social construct, meaning society, or a culture, has collectively decided what behaviors and traits should be exhibited by males or females (Ellemers, 2018). Gender is therefore defined as a socially constructed set of expected behaviors that characterize being male or masculine and female or feminine (Heller, 2019). Deviations from assumed gendered behaviors may be viewed negatively and reinforce societal expectations of boys and girls or men and women.

The American Psychological Association attributes gender typing, where children learn awareness of their gender, to social and cultural expectations of people's behaviors based on their biology, sex, or the process through which individuals impute such assumptions (VandenBos, 2007). Gender is learned through interactions with other people. People's first experiences of gender occur as a toddler and are based on how their parents dressed them, what toys they were given to play with, or what behavioral cues they received such as "girls don't play rough" or "boys don't wear pink."

As one attends preschool or nursery school, these behavioral cues are reinforced through interactions with teachers as well as with the friends they play with and in relationships they form. People do not "have" a gender. They are not born with a gender. People "do gender" (West & Zimmerman, 1987). As time passes, people's interactions with one another change, leading to changes in societal expectations of one another. This means the definition and role expectations of gender can change and evolve as a society changes.

Over the past several decades in the US context, an evolution of gendered expectations has occurred, with students being more aware and vocal about their sense of identity as well as their positioning in gendered roles. Those who have gender identities that do not match their birth/biological sex may identify as "gender fluid, nonbinary, nonconforming" or "transgender." People who are gender fluid do not perceive their gender as fixed or static, feeling that their perceptions of self can change over time.

Gender-fluid people identify with both masculine and feminine characteristics, depending on how they are feeling. While this may align with the term *nonbinary*, it is more specific. Nonbinary is a blanket term in the gender spectrum. A prime difference between the terms is that nonbinary individuals do not see their gender as changing or fluid.

People who do not adhere to societal expectations of gender may identify as gender nonconforming. This means that while they may identify with a specific gender, their gender expression—or how they present themselves or act—does not align with their gender identity. The term *transgender* describes individuals whose personal identity differs from their biological sex assigned at birth. For example, a transgender man who was assigned the biological sex of female at birth due to anatomy now lives as a male.

A person's sense of gender identity may align with or differ from their sexual orientation. US society's general viewpoint is that of *heteronormativity*, the belief that heterosexuality is the "normal" or "preferred" sexual orientation (Page & Peacock, 2013). Individuals whose gender identity aligns with their biological sex are referred to as *cisgender*. Heteronormativity is reinforced through actions such as media representations of heterosexual couples and forced pronoun designations of individuals based solely on anatomy.

Terms associated with sexual orientation include *heterosexual, bisexual, homosexual,* and *asexual*. People who are heterosexual are attracted to individuals of the opposite biological sex. Homosexual individuals are attracted to those of the same sex. Asexual individuals have a lack of or low interest in sexual activity with others.

Labeling individuals as a specific gender categorizes them according to difference—specifically, that men and women are different from one another. However, people are not organized solely by gender; they are also identified by race, class, ethnicity, religion, and sexual orientation. These categories are intertwined and intersect with gender. Discussing gender without taking into account the intersection of the aforementioned social layers would be an incomplete discussion.

Tying different identifiers together enables people to group various intersections with gender and examine how inequality, oppression, and dominance are perpetuated in a culture. For example, Collins (1998) points out the plight of Black women who experience double layers of social oppression. The use of an intersectional approach examines gender not as an individual category but rather as a social position whose meaning deepens through the interrelations with other social categories (Crenshaw, 1989).

Teachers may look at their students in a gender-binary fashion and are cognizant of ensuring gender equality, but are they considering other social factors intersecting with their students' genders? Students arrive at school bringing differing experiences of these intersections and influencing how teachers interact with and engage in the classroom with them. For educators, it is not only important to promote equity and inclusion in the classroom environment but also to avoid unconscious bias and stereotyping.

Gendered Stereotyping

Stereotyping refers to a set of fixed, overly simplified beliefs about individuals or groups of people that may not be fully accurate. Stereotypes alter not just how people think about other people but also how they act toward them. Some classifications of stereotyping include gender, race, culture, sexuality, and class. It may lead to self-doubt, fear of poor performance or of physical attack, and the oppression of groups of people. Many perceptions people harbor are due to implicit bias, meaning they are subconscious attitudes that people hold without thinking about them. Through biased thinking, a social hierarchy is maintained, positioning people who do not conform to an accepted set of beliefs into an oppressed role.

Gendered stereotyping begins at birth. Infants are positioned into specific gender roles through the mode of dress, room decorations, hair styles, and ear piercing (for girls.) Parents may dress children in a gendered way to avoid being asked what the child's sex is. Furthermore, genderism and stereotyping are promoted through television shows and advertisements. Trucks are geared toward men, while women are shown driving children in minivans. Men are shown doing construction, while women are teachers. In schools, teachers and administrators separate students into the boys' and girls' lines and the boys' and girls' gym classes.

Consumerism promotes gender stereotypes in store displays and imagery. The boy and girl toy aisles are separate and push the idea of boys being athletic or tough and playing with trucks, footballs, and other similar items. Girl toy aisles are filled with dolls, kitchen sets, and crafts—thus preparing girls for a role of domestic care. Separate gym classes (where sports differ based on a child's sex) and toy display aisles imply a preparation of boys for competitive activities and assertive or leadership roles, perpetuating the hierarchy of male dominance.

Gender typing includes the expectations of males and females to have traits attributed to their biological sex. As children grow, their sense of identity can change. Having the physical construction of a female does not mean that one has to feel conformed to society's view of being female, nor does having male body parts mean that a person has to feel "manly."

People's perceptions of their gender can be categorized under *gender identity*, or the way individuals view and feel about themselves. Broken down into male, female, and gender queer, people's gender identity does not have to align with their biological sex. Gender typing may negatively alter individuals' behaviors by suppressing their true identities. While gender identity describes how people feel in their mind, *gender expression* is how people present their gender by the way they dress, act, and engage with other people. Categories of gender expression include feminine, masculine, and androgynous (neither masculine nor feminine).

Cisnormative societies and cultures view cisgender individuals, whose personal perceptions of self and gender correspond with their birth sex, as the majority or norm. Reading materials, sex typing, television shows, and media reinforce this heteronormative standpoint. An additional assumption is that individuals who are heterosexual are automatically cisgender. This is not always the case as there is a gender spectrum, with individuals identifying between categories.

Heterosexual females do not have to identify with hyperfemininity, nor do heterosexual males need to identify with hypermasculinity. Familiarity with and acceptance of the gender spectrum means not limiting individuals to expected binary behaviors. Expected behaviors also include an alignment of gender and sexual preference. Sexual orientation stereotyping refers to opinions and perceptions about the sexual preference of LGBTQIA+ individuals.

When gender is positioned as binary, the opposing sexual orientations complement each other in heterosexuality (Klysing, Lindqvist, & Björklund, 2021). An intersectional approach allows one to examine how sexual minorities relate to gender normative groups. According to the Stereotype Content Model (Fiske, Cuddy, Glick, & Xu, 2002), socially constructed binary gender stereotypes position men as possessing agency or leadership and women as being communal or warm and empathetic.

Sexual orientation stereotyping also differs based on race (Klysing et al., 2021). Sexual minority males (as a social subgroup) are viewed more as possessing inverted stereotypes, meaning homosexual males are viewed as more communal. Sexual minority women are not as likely to be viewed as having gender inversion traits (Mize & Manago, 2018). Discrimination against gender nonconforming and transgender individuals occurs due to a societal view that heterosexuality is "normal" and "good" (Mize & Manago, 2018).

Another type of stereotyping people may be guilty of relates to student race and ethnicity. Racial stereotyping leads to inaccurate perceptions of people based on their race. Media plays a role in creating some racial stereotypes, with TV crime shows portraying criminals more often as Black men or Black women, who are portrayed as single mothers or in illegal job roles. Individuals of Middle Eastern descent may be portrayed as terrorists.

Children are prey for racial stereotyping in television shows as well. Black male teenagers may be depicted as violent, while Black females may be shown talking back to their teachers. Hispanic teenagers might be depicted as gang members, while Asian children are presented as the model minority by being good in STEM courses.

People may subconsciously absorb these biased portrayals, leading to the continuation of a cycle of oppression and discrimination. The examples presented also exemplify the intersection of race and gender. Studies suggest that in the United States, teachers have higher expectations of White students than minority students—especially Black students—altering their academic outcomes (Holder & Kessels, 2017; Papageorge, Gershenshon, & Kang, 2020). Students of color are less likely to be placed in honors or other higher-level courses. Children of color are more likely to be harshly disciplined with detention or suspension.

According to the National Center for Education Statistics (2019), a greater percentage of the students suspended from school are Black as opposed to White, although they make up about 17 percent of the student population. Girls of color may be punished because of their demeanor in an attempt to "teach" them the acceptable behaviors of White, middle-class norms (Skelton, Francis, & Smulyan, 2006).

Differences in gender, race, and class are interconnected (Eaton, 2017, p. 9), establishing the need to look at gender-based racial bias in an attempt to eliminate its pervasiveness and open up critical discourse. Bias and stereotyping can carry across one's lifetime, leading to gender gaps and continued discrimination. Early education, resources, and support services can set the foundation for breaking discriminatory biases and promoting inclusivity.

Appearance and Impact of Gender Bias and Stereotyping in Schools and Classrooms

The education system in the United States is one of hegemonic, heterosexual, and White dominance. Textbooks, curriculum, pedagogy, and learning resources promote the dominant social order. There are few resources that present diversity, be it gender, race, or culture. Most science books still favor contributions by male researchers. Math books present problems that children from other cultures may not find relevant or tangible. Family dynamics in stories position heterosexual couples as the norm.

Gendered stereotyping may appear through teacher practices with instructor bias directed at gender-based student personalities and behaviors. Teachers expect boys to be louder, more aggressive, less emotional, and more physically assertive than girls. Girls are expected to be kinder, more empathetic, quieter, and more likely to answer questions than boys.

For example, a teacher may reflect on these questions at the beginning of a new school year: What are your thoughts about classroom dynamics if there are more boys than girls? (Some teachers might think it will be a tough year because of potential discipline issues.) What if there are more girls than boys in the classroom? (Some teachers might think it's going to be a drama-filled year, especially if it is middle school or high school.)

The example above presented a stereotype of gendered behaviors. The assumption is that boys will act in an agentic way and girls will act in a more communal way due to their gender, but we know this is not the case. Students are very aware of their sense of self-identity, which may not conform to binary stereotyping. Stereotyping may also affect academic outcomes of girls and boys in the classroom. Implicit or explicit bias and stereotyping on the part of teachers may have perpetuated this mindset and contributed to students experiencing stereotype threat.

A definition of *stereotype threat* is a "socially premised psychological threat that arises when one is in a situation or doing something for which a negative stereotype about one's group applies" (Steele & Aronson, 1995, p. 614). Furthermore, this stereotype threat can confirm negative stereotypes as related to students' gender, race, cultural background, and is often due to situational factors that can strengthen or weaken the effect of a threat.

Teachers, thinking they are being supportive, may say to girls, "It's okay if you don't do well; girls aren't very good at math" or to boys, "Boys don't write very well." Stereotype threat was first explored in Black male students as a theoretical mechanism to explain achievement gaps. It is encompassing, affecting any marginalized group regardless of culture or gender. Anxiety brought on by fear of validating stereotypes may lead to their confirmation. Examples of behaviors brought on due to negative stereotyping include low achievement in math scores by girls based on the belief that they are less capable at math or the belief that males should act with assertion and should not act with sensitivity (Zawisza, 2018).

Whether negative stereotypes are related to race or gender, these can have adverse effects on students as well as on the classroom environment. Individuals may internalize anxiety brought on by feelings of inferiority, leading to discomfort in the classroom. Gender stereotypes may further perpetuate gender inequity issues in the classroom as students often follow the societal or culturally prescribed expectations for their behavior and choices.

For example, negative stereotypes may limit students' inclinations to pursue or explore subjects usually viewed as typical for a specific gender. This is seen in research where there are fewer females in STEM-based majors and careers (Botella et al., 2019). Males may choose not to value literature or writing courses due to the perceptions that these are "girl" courses or that males lack the same competence in verbal and writing courses as females (Voyer & Voyer, 2014).

Students may not take full advantage of learning opportunities or educational assistance programs for fear of fulfilling a certain stereotype. A final effect of stereotype threat may be students taking on a role of "victim identity" (Steele & Aronson, 1995, p. 798). Students may use stereotype threat to create this position as an external locus of control, resulting in lowered motivation. While negativity associated with stereotype threat within academia may lead to fewer job options due to limitations in courses of study (Stroessner & Good, 2011), it also significantly impacts classrooms on a daily basis.

Marginalized students face a dual bias based on gender as well as race. Stereotyping and bias against Black males position them to be more likely placed in remedial or lower-level classes; miss more school than White males due to suspensions; be reprimanded more in lower grade levels than White males; be more likely punished for loudness and disrespect than White students; and suffer greater academic losses when moving from middle school to high school and therefore remain in a lower-class rank, ultimately affecting college acceptance (McGrady & Reynolds, 2013; see also Perszyk, Bodenhausen, Richeson, & Waxman, 2019; Sutton, Langenkamp, Muller, & Schiller, 2018).

Although there are many studies on continued discrimination and marginalization of Black boys, there are far fewer studies on the discrimination against Black girls (Pietri et al., 2018). Black girls and women are faced with a dual discrimination brought on through their race as well as gender, leading them to be positioned in needing to work twice as hard to earn half the recognition. In school, teachers may unconsciously view Black female students based on perceived abilities rather than actual abilities.

Teachers may not recognize maladaptive behaviors exhibited by their Black female students as actually being coping mechanisms. Black females have very unique needs brought on by socioeconomic and gender oppression, as well as cultural expectations and stereotype threat. As students, they are less likely to be placed in gifted classes despite ability, due to potential teacher bias.

Black female students are also more likely to be victims of school-related violence. This combination of factors with a lack of culturally relevant curriculum, fear of not achieving, and drive for perfectionism leads Black female students to take on a role of "invisibility" in order to cope (Anderson, 2020). In choosing silence over the risk of not achieving academic success, teachers may view Black female students as "lazy" or not putting in the effort. In addition, cultural upbringing within the family and Black community teaches Black girls to be strong and resilient (Leath, 2019). This combination of pressures can be especially hard and ultimately dampen academic success.

Gender nonconforming, transgender, or LGBTQIA+ students may face bias from students as well as faculty. Many marginalized students may choose not to express who they truly are for fear of not conforming, being ostracized, or of being bullied. Marginalized students who are surrounded by the pressure to conform to binary/heterosexual ideals can feel isolated and confused.

Some students may act out due to resentment to conform to expected behaviors they do not identify with. Other students may take on personas and hyper-express expected gender roles to prevent being "outed." Fears and concerns lead to a higher likelihood of LGBTQIA+ students facing student aggression, depression, failing, dropping out, and/or suicide (Gnan et al., 2019). Student acceptance and retention begins with establishing a welcoming classroom environment that facilitates and promotes equity and inclusion through conversations, education, and support of all students.

Promoting Positivity in a Gender-Diverse Classroom

Teachers' bias, subconscious or not, often presents itself in everyday teaching. Considering the fact that students spend most of their day in the classroom being influenced by their teachers as well as other students, it is important to promote a positive learning environment inclusive of all students.

Reflexivity

To be agents of change, educators need to be reflective and mindful of the classroom environment, since the way they teach students affects how the students perceive the world. Teachers need to reflect heavily on their own biases and stereotypes. While harboring biases may be subconscious and not meant to be harmful, the effects may still be detrimental and long lasting.

Self-reflection and honesty with oneself about subconscious biases are the first steps in diminishing teachers' own stereotyping. Since students look to teachers as role models, having open conversations with students and colleagues to discuss bias and stereotyping is always a good proactive step. Having dialogue about bias and admitting when you have acted in a biased way sets a positive example for students to follow.

To create a positive classroom environment, teachers need to begin with themselves, starting with being brutally reflective of their own beliefs and potential biases. The reality is that many teachers are not prepared to teach in a culturally responsive manner. Increasing one's own awareness through professional development programs or diversity trainings can be beneficial here. Learning what other teachers or districts are doing to promote inclusivity can assist in eliminating stereotypes and bias, as well as incorporating learned techniques into the classroom.

Getting to Know the Students

Another way to promote awareness and reflection is creating safe spaces in the classroom to have "courageous conversations." Using students' diversity and the intersectionality of their life experiences as a lens to eliminate biases can help them gain a greater understanding of who they are and how they learn. Nowadays, students are more comfortable in expressing their own preferences for gender and sexual identity. Being open and suspending potential assumptions about student gender identity or sexual orientation can help teachers break the initial barriers in getting to know them.

Inclusive Classroom Environment

There are steps that can facilitate creating an open, inclusive classroom environment. Starting on day one, teachers can establish their classes as safe, judgement-free zones. Within those zones, students can be assured of welcoming and bullying-free spaces, where they can express themselves freely without the fear of being judged or criticized.

In elementary classrooms, clarifying definitions and openly answering questions about various terms and issues can further promote trust and open communication with students. Many children use words they have heard at home, on the school bus, or in the media without fully understanding what they mean.

In middle school or high school, the first day of classes can be an opportunity to ask students about preferred pronoun use. Students who are gender fluid may prefer "they/them." Those who are gender neutral may use "ze" or "zir." Acknowledging and respecting the identities of all students and exploring teaching materials for diversity is the first step for teachers in creating an inclusive environment.

Exposure to Diverse Authors and Ideas

To promote various points and perspectives, teachers should review teaching materials and go beyond promoting a heteronormative mindset by including gender and sexual diversity. It is important for educators to ask these questions: Do the textbooks currently used in the classroom focus on writings, accomplishments, or stories of White males, or are they diverse in their content? How do you interact with diverse students?

Teacher Expectations

Diverse students may have difficulty establishing a positive relationship with their teachers, especially those of a different race. This impedes their connection in the classroom and may lower academic outcomes. In cases where teacher achievement expectations are not equally distributed, teacher expectations can undermine students' view of themselves.

Deficit mindsets, based on ability stereotyping, position students for lower academic outcomes through decreased teacher expectations, thus supporting the maintenance of high academic standards. Even if achievement bias is unconscious, there are "more errors when you expect to see more errors" (Staats, 2016). The tone and body language when speaking to students are also to be considered, especially in cases where teachers may subconsciously alter them when working with students of color.

Teachers can ensure that students, regardless of sex, are supported in all subject matters. Instilling a growth mindset viewpoint that encourages students to take on challenges and learn from the process leads to the development of skills and knowledge (Dweck, 2008). Teachers can help students overcome the false beliefs such as "girls can't do math" or "boys aren't good at English—it's a girl's subject" and shift to a "can do" attitude for all students.

Communication and Feedback to Students

Instances like students using inappropriate language or name calling can be turned into great opportunities to prevent future verbally hurtful interactions between students. Thus, allowing students to explore conversations on how gender and culture intersect in their lives can help everyone to capitalize on the richness of experience they bring into the classroom.

Negative interactions among students can be a function of not understanding and appreciating people other than those of their own gender, race, and culture. Students emulate what they see, so it is crucial for a teacher to be a model to the students. Role-playing as a strategy can allow

Table 5.2. Teacher Suggestions for Promoting Classroom Positivity

Students	• Avoid grouping students by gender such as "boys' line" or "girls' line." • Gendered language should be altered. Avoid gender-specific terms when speaking to children (e.g., "guys"), and instead use expressions such as "scholars," "students," or "class." • Ask students for their preferred pronoun to be used. • Role-play to promote student understanding. • Acknowledge appropriate behaviors.
Classroom	• Act as a role model. • Have "courageous conversations" about gender diversity. This resource explains what can be difficult terms to understand: https://www.genderbread.org/. • Create the class as a "safe space" to have open dialogue. • Provide literature, lessons, and assignments that present males and females outside of the expected gendered roles and domains. • Limit the focus on gender. Have activities and curriculum be as gender-neutral as possible. This can diminish the notion of certain interests and courses of study as being for "girls" or for "boys." Students should be encouraged to explore any endeavors they find of interest, such as poetry or domestic activities for boys and science or contact sports for girls. • Teachers should provide students with examples of role models (Steele & Aronson, 2015; see also Stroessner & Good, 2011). Gender stereotypes are formed based on role models seen by children. The use of counter-stereotype role models can break the ideas of gender-specific domains (Olsson & Martiny, 2018). • Discourage demeaning comments from other students, and be sure to use any disparaging words as a learning opportunity.
Institution/ Policy	• Establish gender-neutral bathrooms. • Eliminate dress codes. • Advocate for students both inside and outside of the classroom. • Attend workshops and professional development opportunities to learn how to assist students who may be transitioning their gender. Organizations such as Gender Spectrum or the Gay, Lesbian & Straight Education Network (GLSEN, 2015) provide professional development seminars to instructors in supporting LGBTQ students, including how to intervene when a student is being bullied: https://www.glsen.org/. • Complete diversity trainings offered within the district and offsite. • Research what other districts are doing to create positive classroom environments. • Help establish gender-supportive policies.

students to embrace diverse people through the understanding and appreciation of their identities. Table 5.2 provides some additional suggestions on how to promote classroom positivity at the student, classroom, and institution levels.

Schools and educational settings should be places of inclusivity. It is crucial to the learning process that students feel a sense of belonging, welcome, and safety. A positive classroom environment begins with instructors through their self-reflection of personal biases, stereotyping, and noninclusive classroom practices. Eliciting change is not a speedy process; it takes work, perseverance, and dedication, but it is necessary for promoting positive student outcomes. The combined efforts of educators and administrators can establish educational institutions as positive learning environments.

References

Anderson, B. N. (2020). "See me, see us": Understanding the intersections and continued marginalization of adolescent gifted Black girls in US classrooms. *Gifted Child Today, 43*(2), 86–100. https://doi.org/10.1177%2F1076217519898216.

Berkowitz, D., Manohar, N. N., & Tinkler, J. E. (2010). Walk like a man, talk like a woman: Teaching the social construction of gender. *Teaching Sociology, 38*(2), 132–43. https://doi.org/10.1177/0092055X10364015.

Botella, C., Rueda, S., López-Iñesta, E., & Marzal, P. (2019). Gender diversity in STEM disciplines: A multiple factor problem. *Entropy, 21*(1), 30. http://dx.doi.org/10.3390/e21010030.

Brody, S. (2020). Gender-inclusive children's literature as a preventative measure: Moving beyond a reactive approach to LGBTQ+ topics in the classroom. *Bank Street Occasional Paper Series, 44*. Retrieved from https://educate.bankstreet.edu/occasional-paper-series/vol2020/iss44/7?utm_source=educate.bankstreet.edu%2Foccasional-paper-series%2Fvol2020%2Fiss44%2F7&utm_medium=PDF&utm_campaign=PDFCoverPage.

Collins, P. H. (1998). *Fighting words: Black women and the search for justice* (Vol. 7). University of Minnesota Press.

Crenshaw, K. (1989). Demarginalizing the intersection of race and sex: A black feminist critique of antidiscrimination doctrine, feminist theory and antiracist politics. *University of Chicago Legal Forum, 1.* Retrieved from https://chicagounbound.uchicago.edu/cgi/viewcontent.cgi?article=1052&context=uclf.

Dweck, C. S. (2008). *Mindset: The new psychology of success*. Random House Digital.

Eaton, O. (2017). *It's just good teaching: Creating inclusive elementary classrooms through feminist pedagogy*. Unpublished master's thesis, University of Toronto. Retrieved from https://tspace.library.utoronto.ca/bitstream/1807/76994/1/Eaton_Olivia_201706_MT_MTRP.pdf.

Ellemers, N. (2018). Gender stereotypes. *Annual Review of Psychology, 69,* 275–98.

Fiske S. T., Cuddy A. J. C., Glick P., & Xu J. (2002). A model of (often mixed) stereotype content: Competence and warmth respectively follow from perceived status and competition. *Journal of Personality and Social Psychology, 82*(6), 878–902. http://dx.doi.org/10.1037/0022-3514.82.6.878.

GLSEN. (2015). *The 2015 national school climate survey.* Retrieved from https://www.glsen.org/sites/default/files/2019-10/GLSEN%202015%20National%20School%20Climate%20Survey%20%28NSCS%29%20-%20Executive%20Summary.pdf.

Gnan, G. H., Rahman, Q., Ussher, G., Baker, D., West, E., & Rimes, K. A. (2019). General and LGBTQ-specific factors associated with mental health and suicide risk among LGBTQ students. *Journal of Youth Studies, 22*(10), 1393–408.

Heller, J. (2019). Constructed gender but unconstructed sex? Historical roots of sociological practice. *The American Sociologist, 50*(1), 38–62.

Holder, K., & Kessels, U. (2017). Gender and ethnic stereotypes in student teachers' judgments: A new look from a shifting standards perspective. *Social Psychology of Education, 20*(3), 471–90. http://dx.doi.org/10.1007/s11218-017-9384-z.

Kinskey, M. (2020). Girls in STEM. *Science and Children, 57*(7), 56–59.

Klysing, A., Lindqvist, A., & Björklund, F. (2021). Stereotype content at the intersection of gender and sexual orientation. *Frontiers in Psychology, 12.* https://dx.doi.org/10.3389%2Ffpsyg.2021.713839.

Leath, S. (2019, August 15). How the expectation of strength harms Black girls and women. *Scholars Strategy Network.* Retrieved from https://scholars.org/contribution/how-expectation-strength-harms-black-girls-and.

Mangin, M. (2018). Supporting transgender and gender expansive children in school. *Phi Delta Kappan, 100*(2), 16–21.

McGrady, P. B., & Reynolds, J. R. (2013). Racial mismatch in the classroom: Beyond black-white differences. *Sociology of Education, 86*(1), 3–17. https://doi.org/10.1177/0038040712444857.

Mize, T. D., & Manago, B. (2018). The stereotype content of sexual orientation. *Social Currents, 5*(5), 458–78. https://doi.org/10.1177/2329496518761999.

National Center for Education Statistics. (2019). *Status and trends in the education of racial and ethnic groups.* Retrieved from https://nces.ed.gov/programs/raceindicators/indicator_rda.asp.

Nduagbo, K. C. (2020, July). *How gender disparities affect classroom learning.* Retrieved from https://www.ascd.org/el/articles/how-gender-disparities-affect-classroom-learning.

Olsson, M., & Martiny, S. E. (2018). Does exposure to counterstereotypical role models influence girls' and women's gender stereotypes and career choices? A review of social psychological research. *Frontiers in Psychology, 9,* 2264.

Page, A. D., & Peacock, J. R. (2013). Negotiating identities in a heteronormative context. *Journal of Homosexuality, 60*(4), 639–54.

Papageorge, N. W., Gershenson, S., & Kang, K. M. (2020). Teacher expectations matter. *Review of Economics and Statistics, 102*(2), 234–51. http://www.nber.org/data-appendix/w25255.

Perszyk, D. R., Lei, R. F., Bodenhausen, G. V., Richeson, J. A., & Waxman, S. R. (2019). Bias at the intersection of race and gender: Evidence from preschool-aged children. *Developmental Science, 22*(3), e12788. DOI: 10.1111/desc.12788.

Pietri, E. S., Johnson, I. R., & Ozgumus, E. (2018). One size may not fit all: Exploring how the intersection of race and gender and stigma consciousness predict effective identity-safe cues for Black women. *Journal of Experimental Social Psychology, 74*, 291–306. https://doi.org/10.1016/j.jesp.2017.06.021.

Skelton, C., Francis, B., & Smulyan, L. (Eds.). (2006). *The SAGE handbook of gender and education.* Sage.

Staats, C. (2016). Understanding implicit bias: What educators should know. *American Educator, 39*(4), 29.

Steele, C. M., & Aronson, J. (1995). Stereotype threat and the intellectual test performance of African Americans. *Journal of Personality and Social Psychology, 69*(5), 797.

Stroessner, S., & Good, C. (2011). *Stereotype threat: An overview.* Retrieved from http://www.teachercollaborate.org/uploads/2/1/8/1/21813164/stereotype_threat_overview.pdf.

Sutton, A., Langenkamp, A. G., Muller, C., & Schiller, K. S. (2018). Who gets ahead and who falls behind during the transition to high school? Academic performance at the intersection of race/ethnicity and gender. *Social Problems, 65*(2), 154–73. https://doi.org/10.1093/socpro/spx044Washington, DC: American Psychological Association.

Voyer, D., & Voyer, S. D. (2014). Gender differences in scholastic achievement: A meta-analysis. *Psychological Bulletin, 140*(4), 1174.

West, C., & Zimmerman, D. H. (1987). Doing gender. *Gender & Society, 1*(2), 125–51. http://links.jstor.org/sici?sici=0891-2432%28198706%291%3A2%3C125%3ADG%3E2.0.CO%3B2-W.

Zawisza, M. (2018). *The terrifying power of stereotypes—and how to deal with them.* https://theconversation.com/the-terrifying-power-of-stereotypes-and-how-to-deal-with-them-101904.

Technology as a Classroom Management Asset 6

MADELINE CRAIG AND LINDA KRAEMER

Since 2010, there has been an enormous increase in the use of technology in classrooms. Generally, most schools offer some type of technology instruction and/or classroom technology access. The changes to education due to the COVID-19 pandemic have demanded the use of instructional technology. The requirements and use of technology have varied widely across the United States during this health crisis, but all teachers have had to rise to this challenge in one way or another.

In many cases, school districts dictate technology use in classrooms, but often teachers must decide for themselves which technology is likely to improve student learning and their classroom environment. Since classroom management tends to be a challenging aspect of teaching, various types of educational technologies may provide teachers with additional support and serve as an asset in their classrooms.

When considering which technologies to integrate into a classroom, a teacher may consider a standards-based approach or one of a few theoretical frameworks. If using a standards-based approach, the International Society for Technology in Education (ISTE) is a well-known resource; it provides detailed standards for educators and students to use as a common set of expectations across states to clarify how educators can support student learning with technology.

ISTE (2017) states that teachers need to be both "empowered professionals" and "learning catalysts" in the classroom. For the empowered professional category, ISTE provides standards that categorize the educator as a learner, leader, and citizen. For the learning catalyst category, ISTE includes standards for the educator as a collaborator, designer, facilitator, and analyst. The ISTE Standards for Students "provide a support framework across the grades and for all subject areas that serve as a groundwork for what's possible in learning using technology" (ISTE, 2016). Furthermore, the ISTE Standards for Educators and for Students maintain that they are about learning and not about devices or tools.

There are several theoretical models to help educators think about technology integration in meaningful ways, in addition to the ISTE standards. These models vary in their approach, but all supply a systematic method to help educators make decisions about technology integration. The most well-known and often utilized in schools are the TPACK model, the SAMR model, and the Triple E framework (Kolb, 2017; see also Mishra & Koehler, 2006; Puentedura, 2006).

The TPACK model seeks to provide educators with a framework for understanding technology's role in education. This framework shows how three types of knowledge (technological knowledge, pedagogical knowledge, and content knowledge) combine and interact in important ways (Mishra & Koehler, 2006).

The SAMR model, which stands for substitution, augmentation, modification, and redefinition, is designed to help educators create digital lessons to improve student learning (Puentedura, 2006). Last, the Triple E framework helps educators measure how well technology tools are integrated into lessons to engage, enhance, and extend learning goals (Kolb, 2017).

Technology for Classroom Management

The number of cloud-based technologies available for classroom management continues to grow. Many educational technology companies develop their products based on teacher needs. Without a doubt, teachers at both the elementary and secondary levels tend to need help in the realm of managing their classrooms. Technology can assist teachers to better manage their classrooms to a degree.

Of course, technology cannot solve every classroom management need, but it can provide support for both new and experienced teachers looking for assistance. Using technology in a classroom should be a conscious choice that educators make intentionally to improve student learning. There are several approaches to technology integration, including a standards-based approach as well as research-tested models.

There are important differences in classroom management for elementary and secondary students due to many factors, including students' developmental levels, class logistics, school environment, and students' ages. Although both elementary and secondary teachers struggle with managing their classrooms, the needs are different. Secondary teachers usually have more students and more classrooms to manage than elementary teachers. On the other hand, elementary teachers work with their students for longer periods of time, which comes with its own classroom management challenges.

This chapter outlines technology that can be used to manage both elementary and secondary classrooms. Although some educational technology tools are designed specifically for the elementary or for the secondary level, the majority of the tools can be used for any grade level. The tools reviewed are organized into categories based on their use for managing classrooms. Categories include classroom environment, home–school connection, student-centered instructional tools, and learning management systems.

Classroom Environment

Creating and sustaining a positive classroom environment is key to effectively managing a group of students. A positive environment relies on structure and includes an agreed-upon set of rules, productive communication, and a clearly articulated daily structure. There is clear evidence that "classrooms with more structure have been shown to promote appropriate academic and social behaviors such as greater task involvement, proper peer interaction, helpful behaviors, and less aggression" (Riden, 2019, p. 134). There are apps and other technologies that can assist teachers in achieving these goals (see table 6.1).

Table 6.1. Classroom Environment Technology Tools

Tool Name	Brief Description	Website
Noise Monitoring		
Too Noisy	App using a visual stimulus to monitor classroom noise.	https://toonoisyapp.com/
Too Loud	Noise meter and timer to graphically display the noise level.	https://apps.apple.com/us/app/too-loud-kids-noise-meter/id1073746536
Bouncy Balls	Noise meter that responds to a microphone and displays noise levels using fun themes.	https://bouncyballs.org/
Volume Lights	Different colored lights offer a visual and audio option for monitoring sound either automatically or manually.	https://www.acousticalsurfaces.com/talklight/quiet_light.html

(continued)

Table 6.1. *(Continued)*

Tool Name	Brief Description	Website
Transitioning		
Wireless Doorbell	Remote-controlled wireless doorbell uses various chimes to signal instructions to the class.	https://www.sadotech.com/pages/classroom
Traffic Light App	Simple app uses different colored lights to indicate the transition to a new activity.	https://edshelf.com/tool/traffic-light/
Timing		
Best Sand Timer	App offering a visual indicator of time remaining to complete a task.	https://apps.apple.com/us/app/best-sand-timer/id501940934
Timer for YouTube	Timer limits access to YouTube.	https://support.google.com/youtubekids/answer/6130558?hl=en
Happy Kids Timer	Visual timer app that helps to establish routines by turning chores into a game.	https://happykidstimer.com/
Name Selection		
Popsicle Sticks App	App randomly selects and groups students as well as scoring discussions and creating classroom tournaments.	https://apps.apple.com/us/app/popsicle-sticks-teacher-picks/id1139826444
Team Maker	Simple app that allows quick and random sorting of the class into groups or teams.	https://apps.apple.com/us/app/team-maker-lite/id1435742770
Team Shake	Choose random or balanced teams based on predetermined criteria using either conventional buttons or a shake of a device.	https://www.amazon.com/Team-Shake-Pick-Random-Groups/dp/B01M4KKK18
Seating		
Smart Seat	Helps in creating digital seating charts and tracking attendance.	http://www.cornsoftapps.com/smartseat/
Teacher Kit	Feature-rich app that supports a seating chart as well as a grade and attendance log.	https://www.teacherkit.net/
Mega Seating Plan	Generates a seating plan based on teacher-supplied data.	https://www.megaseatingplan.com/

Tool Name	Brief Description	Website
Rewards		
HeroK12	Collaborative tools to set up desired behaviors and merit-based rewards while students are provided clear expectations regarding attendance, tardiness, on-task behavior, and other classroom rules.	https://www.herok12.com/
Live School	App to track behavior allowing for schoolwide setup.	https://www.whyliveschool.com/
ClassDojo	Website sharing feedback among teachers, students, and parents.	https://www.classdojo.com/
Classcraft	Website offering a personalized, cooperative game that tracks students' behavior by allowing students to play the role of a character.	https://www.classcraft.com/

Noise Monitoring

Too Noisy, an app that monitors classroom noise, can assist teachers in managing the noise level in their classrooms (Walsall Academy, n.d.). By having the teacher use this technology on the projector in the front of the room or on individual students' devices, the noise level of the class can be kept to an acceptable (customizable) level so that the teacher can work individually with some students while others work in groups. Too Loud is a comparable app that also has a built-in timer (Idea4e, n.d.).

Bouncy Balls browser app works similarly, but instead of a noise meter, this app has the students keeping the balls in balance to maintain the noise level in the classroom (Naeve Interactive, 2019). When the noise level gets too loud in the classroom, the balls are too high on the screen and an alert sounds to tell students to lower their volume.

For a "lower tech" option, as opposed to the "high tech" options already offered above, teachers might choose to use small lights to indicate to students the expected volume level in the classroom. Sticking these small lights to the classroom wall can help students physically see the specific classroom management technique. Teachers might use three lights—red, yellow, and green—to indicate the appropriate levels of noise for each activity. Red would indicate that silence is required, such as during an exam. Yellow might indicate that students are permitted to whisper with a neighbor, while green encourages conversation.

Transitioning

Efficient transitions in a classroom have been shown to increase students' time on-task and thereby improve achievement (Ardoin, 1999). Simpler technologies could be used to support transitioning from one activity to the next. A wireless doorbell placed in the classroom with a handheld remote for the teacher can more easily help students make the move from one subject or activity to another. Students are trained to stop what they are doing when they hear the doorbell and return to their desks or some variation of that process.

Many wireless doorbells come with multiple bell options (dogs barking, music playing, chiming bells, etc.) so teachers might use the different bell options for different needs. For example, dog barks might indicate that students should return to their seats, whereas a certain song might let students know it is time to pack up for the day. The volume lights discussed above might signal the time to transition to a new activity.

Similarly, teachers might choose to use lights in an app format instead, such as the Classroom Traffic Light app, to indicate specific desired actions (Easdown, n.d.). The Classroom Traffic Light application has three color options: red, amber, and green. For example, a teacher might use red to indicate to be quiet while the teaching is talking, amber for quietly working alone, and green as talking time while working with others.

Timing

Using apps for timing students offers similar support for easing transitions. Setting timers for class activities sets expectations, builds classroom routines, and keeps students on-task. Timer applications include Best Sand Timer, Happy Kids Timer, and a variety of other options for both Android and iOS devices. Best Sand Timer is one of many hourglass sand timers available that depicts sand to show the passage of time (Simkovskyi, n.d.). Happy Kids Timer helps to time activities to create a routine (Evoprox, 2019). Timers can be used on a projector displayed in the front of the classroom or eventually on students' own devices as they transition to managing their own time.

Name and Team Selection

Various tools are available to randomize name selection. These tools, such as the Popsicle Sticks app, can allow the teacher to choose students to share or respond to a prompt (Daly, 2016). Similarly, there are apps available that can support fair and random team selection. Team Maker or Team Shake allow for the quick and simple selection of teams (Kikowi Solutions, 2018; see also Rhine-o-Enterprises, 2016).

Team Shake helps choose random or balanced teams based on predetermined criteria (such as skill level or gender) using either conventional buttons or a shake of a device (Rhine-o-Enterprises, 2016). Team Maker is an app that has the user enter names and form teams by shaking the phone (Kikowi Solutions, 2018). These technologies limit bias and assure that no students are being neglected or ignored.

Seating Arrangements

Teachers can use seating arrangements to manage their classrooms by separating chatty students from one another or putting together students to help support their learning. There are a number of apps available to help teachers carefully arrange the seating chart for their classroom, such as Teacher Kit, Smart Seat, and Mega Seating Plan. Teacher Kit helps teachers manage their classes through the app by taking attendance, adding behavior notes, tracking grades, and creating a seating chart (ITWorx Egypt SAE, 2010).

Smart Seat is similar and helps in creating seating charts and tracking attendance (Quinn, 2011). Mega Seating Plan is a website that helps teachers create seating charts based on room layout (Cowen, 2015). It also allows the teacher to upload student photos and has a built-in random-student-selector tool.

Reward Systems

Reward systems can stimulate learning and motivate positive behavior. Incentives can instill a feeling of personal pride, thereby enhancing self-esteem. All of this leads to improved outcomes for students. Technology tools can support this by keeping track of behaviors and privileges over time. Some examples of this type of tool include Hero K12 (Schoolmint, 2019), Live School (Liveschool, 2016), ClassDojo (Don & Chaudhary, 2012), and Classcraft (Classcraft Studios, 2019).

Tools like HeroK12 allow the setting up of desired behaviors and merit-based rewards to provide equitable, nondiscriminatory discipline (Schoolmint, 2019). Students are provided clear expectations regarding attendance, tardiness, on-task behavior, and other classroom rules. Teachers can quickly track behaviors and further analyze progress and issues with a review of behavior analytics data.

Classcraft is a cooperative game that tracks students' behavior and motivates students to achieve more in the classroom (Classcraft, 2019). This tool offers a gamified storyline that lets students engage in teams, with each student playing a character in the story. Students earn points to level up for real-life privileges customized by the teacher. Teachers determine the rewards and consequences based on the needs of their classroom to encourage or discourage certain behaviors.

A study involving forty-four elementary students and fifteen teachers finds an increase in student engagement from the use of Classcraft (Mustafa, 2018). Another study conducted in Poland in a high school history class finds that Classcraft "improve[s] pupils' social skills and their involvement in a lesson" (Janiec, 2015). These types of technology tools can help teachers reward students for positive behavior in a fun and engaging way.

Home–School Connection

Involving students' home lives into their school lives is a key factor for student success in the classroom. Keeping parents or guardians informed regularly and connected to their child's school helps students succeed academically (Dodd & Konzal, 2003). The more support the guardian gives to a child at home, the better the student will perform in school.

Making these important connections between school and home can aid in classroom management. Common Sense Education (2019) suggests tips for more proactive parent communication, including consistently sending out general classroom updates, using a technology that meets parents' needs, and empowering students to lead the connection between teachers and parents.

As indicated in Table 6.2, there are numerous tools for helping to make the connection between home and school, such as messaging and announcement apps, portfolio tools, and websites and class blogs.

Table 6.2. Home–School Connection Technology Tools

Tool Name	Brief Description	Website
Messaging and Announcement Tools		
Remind	An easy-to-use communication app where information can be shared without disclosing anyone's personal information.	https://www.remind.com
Bloomz	Full featured communication app to easily connect home and school, including scheduling conferences and reviewing student achievement.	https://www.bloomz.net

Tool Name	Brief Description	Website
ClassDojo	Communication app through which reports can be shared between parents and teachers. The app allows teachers to share information regarding the student's conduct and performance as well as a feed for photos and videos during the school day. Students can take part in the communication by adding artifacts themselves.	https://www.classdojo.com
ClassTag	Messaging tool that allows teachers to create announcements and activities or schedule events and conferences.	https://home.classtag.com

Portfolios		
Seesaw	Student-driven portfolio and communication tool to unlock student creative thinking, differentiate student learning, and engage families.	https://web.seesaw.me
Sesame	A portfolio, assessment, and parent communication tool on an app and the web.	https://sesamehq.com
Fresh grade	A flexible tool with portfolios, lesson planning, communication, and gradebook capabilities.	https://freshgrade.com
Bulb	A simple yet powerful digital portfolio to organize and showcase learning.	https://www.bulbapp.com

Websites and Blogs		
Weebly	Powerful free website with customizable website designs.	https://www.weebly.com
Google Sites	Simple-to-use website creation that integrates with the Google suite of tools.	http://bit.ly/googlesiteslearningcenter
Strikingly	A tool to make a creative website with a wide array of free templates and blogging capabilities.	https://www.strikingly.com
Blogger	A blog-publishing website owned by Google.	https://www.blogger.com
EduBlogs	A robust blog creation tool that allows the teacher to create and link each student's individual blog to create a community.	https://edublogs.org

(continued)

Table 6.2. *(Continued)*

Tool Name	Brief Description	Website
Social Media		
Twitter	A social networking site in which users interact with "tweets" in which they can post, like, and retweet.	https://twitter.com
Instagram	A social networking site in which users can share photos and videos.	https://www.instagram.com
Facebook	A social networking site to connect friends, family, and others one knows through photos, videos, messages, and updates.	https://www.facebook.com

Messaging

Messaging and announcement tools allow schools to share alerts, important dates, upcoming events, and even photos or handouts. Some of the existing messaging and announcement tools include Remind (Kopf & Kopf, 2013), Bloomz (Appalabattula, 2016), ClassDojo (Don & Chaudhary, 2012), and ClassTag (Lotkina, n.d.). All students can use some reminding when it comes to their schoolwork, especially middle schoolers as they transition out of their elementary school routines.

Teachers can use technology to inform parents or guardians or older-aged students of upcoming assignments and changes to the schedule. By using technology to send out these updates, teachers can better manage the valuable limited time they have in class with their students. In addition, many middle and high schoolers use their cell phones on a regular basis, so it is best to reach out to students on an existing platform.

There are several tools that teachers can use to reach their students or their guardians through an app or text messaging. The Remind app can reach out to students and parents through their mobile devices (Kopf & Kopf, 2013). It is efficient because students and parents receive the message simultaneously and teachers can choose to accept replies to their messages or not. On Remind's website (www.remind.com/resources), there are numerous case studies and testimonials on the successful use of Remind in school districts.

Some of the touted benefits include schoolwide communication, community engagement for safety and support, streamlined communication to improve oversight, increased attendance among chronically absent students, and a bridging of existing gaps in diverse communities. Nisbet and Opp (2017) find that the usage of Remind leads to higher response rates from parents and guardians in a mixed-income middle school. Success is attributed to the ease and the convenience of the tool.

Bloomz is a similar type of tool but has more functionality and interactivity than Remind (Appalabattula, 2016). It can connect guardians and teachers through a shared calendar, a student rewards system, and photos from the classroom or home. In a recent dissertation study, Castaneda (2019) finds that "Bloomz may help increase parent–teacher communication as a whole, but Bloomz was not effective for two-way communication at this time in the rural Idaho setting within the short implementation time frame of one quarter" (p. ix). Although this study does not find a significant increase in students' academic grades, the researcher acknowledges that if implemented correctly, Bloomz may help increase parent–teacher communication.

Portfolios

Similarly, portfolio tools offer another way to share information with parents. Digital portfolios house a collection of student work at different stages. These tools can store a variety of work samples, including writing drafts, creative projects, exams, and reflections. The content should demonstrate a wide range of skills and abilities. These portfolios can be shared with families so they can monitor progress and celebrate successes. Portfolios can offer parents a glimpse into their child's school experiences while giving the students and teachers the opportunity to engage in constructive reflection on their work (McLeod, 2009).

Technologies that are designed to be used as e-portfolios include Seesaw (Graham, Lin, & Sjogreen, 2012), FreshGrade (Merrifield, 2011), and Bulb (Petrick, 2011). Seesaw, for example, supports a student-driven portfolio that allows parents to stay in the loop by using an app or checking into the website. While teachers evaluate student work, parents gain insight and find ways to support their young learners. Similarly, FreshGrade is an integrated toolset that enhances learning, empowers students, and keeps families informed (Merrifield, 2011).

Websites and Blogs

Websites and blog tools can be used by teachers to support collaboration and communication and serve as an authentic audience for students' work (Hong, 2008; see also McGrail & Davis, 2011; McGurk, 2014). A class website is similar to a learning-management system that can serve as a repository for class assignments; a communication vehicle for guardians, teachers, and students; and a site for teacher and student blog posts. Teachers can easily create their own class website using Google Sites, Weebly, WordPress, or Strikingly, 2012; see also Google, 2008; Little & Mullenweg, 2003; Weebly, 2007).

These sites can be used to a limited degree to make basic class announcements and homework assignments, or these sites can be used to a more robust degree to build a class community and share student work with parents and students. Google Sites is easy to use for the creation of a simple website that supports multiple collaborators, and it allows for an easy integration of other Google tools such as Google Docs, Slides, Forms, and Drawings (Google, 2008). Many students, through their schools, have a Google account for easy login.

Blogs have been found to be effective for reflection, classroom dialogue, and social networking (McGrail & Davis, 2011). Examples of blog tools include EduBlogs (Farmer, 2005), Blogger (McIntosh, 2003), and KidBlog (Hardy, 2008). Teachers can host a blog that they write themselves to communicate with guardians, or they can have students create and maintain their own ongoing blogs. These tools give students and teachers an audience for their writing endeavors and a unique way to practice writing skills.

EduBlogs is a blog-creation tool that allows the teacher to create and link each student's individual blog. It is powered by WordPress, which is a full-featured website creation tool and thus is highly customizable. Blogs can be a valuable addition to a teacher's classroom management toolkit to increase home–school communication and to provide a public space for student writing.

Social Media

Social media use in education is varied and beneficial. The benefits include improved communication among students as well as between students and teachers, the promotion of students' engagement, and the fostering of collaboration as students work to achieve a common goal (Faizi, Afia, & Chiheb, 2013). In many cases, social media is viewed as a negative distraction, but it can also serve as a positive part of teaching and learning. Niehoff (2019) discusses ways that students are using social media for good: to make important connections with external agencies; gather survey data; collaborate with peers; research careers; and communicate with teachers, mentors, and experts.

Using a social media account that students and guardians are already using such as Twitter (Dorsey, Glass, Stone, & Williams, 2006), Instagram

(Systrom & Krieger, 2012), and Facebook, (Facebook 2004) can be an effective way to communicate using technology instead of time in class. Once teachers create a classroom account or use a class hashtag on social media, they can communicate expectations, show student work, and make class announcements easily. Teachers should always check with their administrators to make sure they are abiding by the technology and social media regulations set up by their districts.

Facebook can be used for communication among students, teachers, and families through the creation of a private group (Facebook, 2004). Guardians may be more likely to check Facebook than their emails or the website to follow their students' progress in the class and to communicate with the teacher. Building community inside and outside the classroom allows the teachers to maintain a more effective classroom. Through a literature review, Shaw (2017) finds Facebook to be an effective educational resource for creating community, promoting collaboration, enhancing communication, developing skills, and incorporating culture.

Student-Centered Instructional Tools

Student-centered learning, or active learning, keeps students actively engaged in their own learning, which can result in more effective classroom management. Educators can have students use technology to show their learning through creation while providing both differentiation of learning; this also gives the teacher an opportunity to work with students individually. Keeping students engaged by showing what they have learned in unique and interesting ways can lead to better learning outcomes.

Gardner's (2011) work on multiple intelligences demonstrates the importance of acknowledging students' assorted abilities such as musical-rhythmic, bodily-kinesthetic, and naturalistic among others. Assessing students on their "other" intelligences aside from the purely academic/intellectual can open up student possibilities in their learning and an opportunity for them to demonstrate their particular talents or strengths.

In addition, active learning has been shown to have a significant impact on student achievement. Freeman et al. (2014) found through a meta-analysis of 225 studies that active learning increases student performance across the STEM disciplines. Interactive presentations are a combination of the typical static presentations with built-in questions and activities: "Active learning engages students in the process of learning through activities and/or discussion in class, as opposed to passively listening to an expert. It emphasizes higher-order thinking and often involves group work"

(Freeman et al., 2014). This study examined a range of active-learning strategies, including student response systems, which is another term for interactive presentations.

Student-centered instructional technology tools include interactive presentations, discussions, and review games. These tools can be used to assess student learning, increase student motivation and engagement, and improve students' learning outcomes. Many of the technologies in this category can serve multiple purposes (see table 6.3 for details).

Table 6.3. Student-Centered Instructional Technology Tools

Tool Name	Brief Description	Website
Interactive Presentations		
Pear Deck	Integrates with Google Slides and Microsoft PowerPoint to easily create interaction for student engagement.	https://www.peardeck.com
Nearpod	Allows for interactive and assessment slides to be added to existing presentations, and has a library of ready-to-run lessons, including multimodal learning and virtual reality options.	https://nearpod.com
Buncee	A tool for student creation and communication for all ages.	https://app.edu.buncee.com
Socrative	A classroom app for student engagement and on-the-fly assessments.	https://socrative.com
Mentimeter	Interactive presentation software to engage learners through polling and questions.	https://www.mentimeter.com
Poll Everywhere	Live interactive audience participation tool that engages the audience and allows for instant results.	https://www.pollevery where.com
EdPuzzle	A tool that turns videos into a lesson to engage students, reinforce accountability, and track student comprehension.	https://edpuzzle.com
Discussions		
Parlay	Online and face-to-face discussion tool with visual analytics.	https://parlayideas.com
Flipgrid	Flipgrid is a video discussion tool that advocates for student voice. This free Microsoft product can be used for discussions, allowing for video contributions in response to the instructor's prompt and replies among students' video posts.	https://info.flipgrid.com

Tool Name	Brief Description	Website
Backchannel Chat	Backchannel Chat allows for real-time discussion, similar to group texting.	http://backchannelchat.com
Equity Maps	Equity Maps chart dialogue in an iPad app that allows the teacher to track group conversations by recording the discussion and giving the teacher the tool to tap on student symbols as each student speaks.	https://equitymaps.com
Classroom Q	Classroom Q is a virtual hand-raising tool that lets students join a session on their device and then tap a button to request assistance when they need it.	https://classroomq.com

Review Games		
Kahoot!	Kahoot! is a lively quizzing game to be used for testing students' knowledge or for in-class discussions.	https://kahoot.com/schools
Gimkit	Gimkit is a live quizzing game to test students' knowledge by involving strategy with in-game money students earn for correct answers and lose for incorrect answers.	https://www.gimkit.com
Quizlet	Quizlet's study sets allow students to study using digital flashcards or play a variety of games with the content, and it can be used in self-study or live in-class sessions.	https://quizlet.com
Quizizz	Quizizz has free, self-paced quizzes to do in class or at home to review, assess, or engage students.	https://quizizz.com

Interactive Presentations

Keeping students active and engaged in their own learning can be done by using interactive presentations or what is sometimes referred to as student response systems. Static presentations are typical presentations that consist of a series of slides that feature text and perhaps images. They are usually created on PowerPoint (Encyclopaedia Britannica, n.d.), Keynote (Apple, 2003), or Google Slides (Google, 2006), which provide needed content for students. The more popular interactive presentations available for use are Pear Deck (Showalter, Sweeney, Eynon-Lynch, & Eynon-Lynch, 2014) and Nearpod (Kovalskys, Abramzon, & Sommers, 2010).

Interactive presentations include built-in questions and activities that require students to pause, reflect, answer questions, or complete activities individually or with others. This switch from lecture-style presentation to interactive presentations demands student participation, which forces the student to stay alert and focused on the content. Freeman et al. (2014) found that 34 percent of students failed their course using traditional lecturing compared to 22 percent of students when using active learning.

There are also tools that have polls, multiple-choice and short-answer questions, word clouds, and other assessment options that can be added to any presentation. These tools include Socrative (Socrative, 2010), Mentimeter (Warstrom, 2014), and Poll Everywhere (Vydunda & Gessler, 2010). There are even technologies to make video watching engaging so that students must pause during the video to answer questions related to the video, such as EdPuzzle and YouTube Studio.

Pear Deck can serve as a good example of this type of interactive presentation technology, as it allows teachers to add interactivity to a typical content-rich presentation (Showalter et al., 2014). The interactivity could include a draggable drawing, text, number, multiple-choice question, or website. When a teacher presents with Pear Deck, students log in on their devices using a code and then their screens are taken over by the Pear Deck presentation. Teachers present as usual, but throughout the presentation, students will encounter interactive slides to which they must respond. The teacher can see the student responses in real time and get feedback on each student's understanding of the content. Pear Deck attempts to keep all students engaged in the content as they know they are being held accountable through their responses (Pear Deck, 2020). In this way, teachers are managing their classrooms using student engagement and the tracking of student responses.

Discussions

Discussion is a teaching method used in most classrooms to empower and transform learners (Ostroff, 2020). Using educational technologies for discussions can ensure that every student's voice is heard. The technology tools for discussion can be placed in two categories: technology to host discussions both in class and online, and applications to monitor discussions in class.

Technology to host discussions for use in class and online include Parlay (McDonald, 2016), Flipgrid (Flipgrid, 2012), and Backchannel Chat (Learnweaver Pty Ltd, 2014). Apps such as Equity Maps chart dialogue

(Nelson, 2019) and Classroom Q (virtual hand raising [ClassroomQ, 2019]) can assist teachers in managing their classroom discussions in a more effective and efficient manner.

Parlay is a fairly new technology designed to improve both online and in-class discussions by making the discussions more inclusive of all students (McDonald, 2016). In class, students participate in a roundtable live discussion but use the tool to tap in for their turn to participate. Teachers get reports in a variety of forms to track and improve future discussions. The online discussion tool is different from other online discussion forums because it focuses on peer feedback. Parlay's own research shows an increase in student participation; students are more comfortable participating in discussions, are more satisfied with their own communication, and are better respected by classmates (Parlay, 2018).

Games

Games can serve as a method of classroom management because they supply a competitive, engaging, hands-on strategy to learning content. Using games in the classroom can minimize distractions and increase engagement and motivation, thereby improving the quality of teaching and learning (Licorish, Owen, Daniel, & George, 2018). Studies show, on average, academic games result in a 20-percentile point gain in student achievement (Marzano, 2010). Some popular games include Kahoot! (Versvik, Brand, & Brooker, 2012), Gimkit (Feinsilber, 2017), Quizziz (Quizizz, n.d.), Quizlet (Sutherland, 2005), and ClassCraft (Young, Young, & Young, 2013).

Kahoot! is one of the more popular technology games used in both elementary and secondary classrooms (Versvik et al., 2012). The upbeat music, colorful squares for question responses, and the interactive nature in which students must use their devices to answer questions adds to the full engagement in this game. Ares et al. (2018) finds that using Kahoot! in a college-level chemistry course of eighty-seven students in Spain has led to an increase in students' grades and overall higher course passing rates.

Plump and LaRosa (2017) find an 88.7 percent positive response rate to 139 students' use of Kahoot! in college business law courses: "Overall, utilizing Kahoot! was a positive experience that imbued our classes with activity and focus and provided a way for all students, not just the extroverted students, to participate and contribute to the learning environment" (Plump & LaRosa, 2017, p. 156).

Quizizz, another popular gaming technology, tests students' knowledge at home or in class (Quizizz, n.d.). The benefit of this tool is that students can pick a ready-made quiz or make their own. They can complete the quiz on their own time and at their own pace. For teachers, there are many existing assessments on Quizizz to save creation time. This tool reduces grading time and integrates smoothly with Google Classroom.

In a study conducted with three sections of an accounting course including over 100 students, Zhao (2019) finds that when evaluating the tool's use, students' perceptions indicate that using Quizizz enhances their learning. In addition, this study finds that the class section in which Quizizz is used more frequently has higher scores on the satisfaction of using this app and higher scores on the students' evaluation of the instructor's teaching.

Learning Management Systems

Learning management systems (LMS) are designed to efficiently manage course content and communicate with students (Ackerman, Chung, & Sun, 2014; see also Lonn & Teasley, 2008). LMS track and store course content, including assessments, presentations, and activities. In fully online courses, LMS are essential as the means by which students navigate the course content. In traditional classes, LMS serve as a repository for the content so students can find whatever they need whenever they need it to succeed in the class.

Some LMS have logins for parent access and can thereby also serve as a communication vehicle from not only teacher to student but also teacher to parent. Some of the learning management systems used in K–12 include Google Classroom (Rochelle & Yeskel, as cited in Singer, 2017), Seesaw (Graham et al., 2012), Schoology/PowerSchool (Friedman, Hwang, & Trinidad, 2009), Canvas (Whitmer & Daley, 2008), and Edmodo (Borg & O'Hara, 2008). See table 7.4 for details.

One of the most popular LMS in K–12 is Google Classroom (Rochelle & Yeskel, as cited in Singer, 2017). It seems to be the most popular because it is free and integrates smoothly with the other Google suite of tools, such as Google Docs, Slides, Forms, and Drawings. Using Google Classroom helps educators better manage their classrooms by providing an online space for students to read or listen to instructions for upcoming assignments.

Students can see their assignment feedback and grades, locate their reading assignments and links to their readings differentiated by student, and store any other class materials in the form of documents, videos, links, or images. In addition, the Google suite of tools allows for not only

Table 6.4. Learning Management System (LMS) Tools

Tool Name	Brief Description	Website
Google Classroom	Full-featured learning management platform that integrates the Google Suite for Educators.	https://classroom.google.com
Seesaw	Manages student work, with an emphasis on feedback and sharing.	https://web.seesaw.me
Schoology/PowerSchool	Designed for K–12 to personalize learning and improve student outcomes (PowerSchool acquired Schoology).	https://www.powerschool.com/schoology-faq
Edmodo	Brings classroom tools together to communicate, share, and make learning accessible.	https://new.edmodo.com
Canvas	A virtual classroom that focuses on student development, scaled instruction, formative assessment, and learning paths.	https://www.instructure.com/canvas/k-12

collaboration among students both in and out of class but also between student and teacher for better feedback, as well as the revision of drafts.

Heggert and Yoo (2018) find that using Google Classroom improves classroom dynamics by increasing student participation and learning. These researchers acknowledge a lack of clarity for the definition of a learning platform and encourage educators to examine the potential of LMS by considering the following four concepts: ease of access, collaboration, student voice/agency, and pace.

Conclusion

Technology can be a distractor and an obstacle to effective classroom management, but it can also offer many learning benefits. Therefore, it is essential to build technology plans into class rules and guidelines at the start of the school year. Technology cannot be an afterthought for teachers.

Some tips from Common Sense Education (2019) for setting up a digital classroom include having a dedicated, secure, and organized area in the classroom for the technology that allows for the easy charging of devices. Another tip is to communicate clearly when and why students will be using in-class technology. Last, teachers should establish a digital workflow with clearly defined and understood procedures for managing students' digital work (Common Sense Education, 2018).

Teaching digital citizenship skills to students is an essential part of any curriculum. This digital curriculum may be the main responsibility of the technology teacher if the school has a dedicated technology bloc, but every teacher should be aware of and mandate the use of effective digital citizenship skills when using all types of technology, especially collaborative technology tools and social media (James, Weinstein, & Mendoza, 2019).

Many districts dictate the use of technology in their schools by providing their students and teachers access to devices, curriculum-related programs, and paid accounts to educational technology tools. Some teachers seek out their own technology options to meet their particular needs in the classroom. The number of educational technology tools available for free or paid subscriptions is overwhelming, and new tools are released often. Finding the "right" tool to solve a problem in the classroom or to enhance the learning of a particular content area is not an easy task.

There are many resources that teachers can use to learn more about new and existing educational technologies. The first very accessible option is Common Sense Education, an independent, national, nonprofit organization focused on helping making sense of the world of media and technology for educators, as well as for children and their families. The website has a comprehensive, well-organized database of EdTech, with reviews by teachers and the Common Sense staff along with details of the tool, images, and ratings based on engagement, pedagogy, support, and privacy.

Another good tool comes from a well-known blogger, podcaster, and educator, Jennifer Gonzalez. Every year, Gonzalez (2022) updates *The Teacher's Guide to Tech*, which is a user-friendly encyclopedia of educational technology. The guide is available for a cost through Gonzalez's website. This guide comes as a PDF with clickable links to videos and details about each educational technology available to educators free or at a cost.

Ultimately, educators looking to integrate technology should do so for sound pedagogical reasons. Whether the technology has the ability to solve an educator's problem, creatively meet a standard, engage students in an enlightening manner, or help with managing a classroom, technology should be just one of many assets in the educator's toolkit.

References

Ackerman, D., Chung, C., & Sun, J. C.-Y. (2014). Transitions in classroom technology: Instructor implementation of classroom management software. *Journal of Education for Business, 89*(6). 317–23. https://doi.org/10.1080/08832323.2014.903889.

Appalabattula, C. (2016). About Bloomz. *Bloomz*. Retrieved from https://www.bloomz.net/about/.
Apple. (2003). *Keynote*. Retrieved from https://www.apple.com/keynote/.
Ardoin, S. P. (1999). Using high-probability instruction sequences with fading to increase student compliance during transitions. *Journal of Applied Behavior Analysis, 32*(3), 339–51. doi:10.1901/jaba.1999.32-339.
Ares, A., Bernal, J., Nozal, M., Sanchez, F., Javier, F., & Bernal, J. (2018). *Results of the use of Kahoot! Gamification tool in a course of chemistry*. Paper presented at the 4th International conference on Higher Education Advances (HEAd'18) Universitat Politecnica de Valencia. Doi: http://dx.doi.org/10/4995/HEAd 18.2018.8179.
Borg, N., & O'Hara, J. (2008). *Edmodo*. Retrieved from https://go.edmodo.com/about/.
Castaneda, F. J. (2019). *The impact of Bloomz app on parent-teacher interaction in middle schools serving low-socioeconomic rural communities* (Unpublished doctoral dissertation). Northwest Nazarene University, Nampa, ID.
Classcraft (2022). About. *Classcraft*. https://www.classcraft.com/.
ClassroomQ (2019). About classroomQ. *ClassroomQ*. https://classroomq.com/about-us/.
Common Sense Education. (2018). *Set up your digital classroom*. Retrieved from https://www.commonsense.org/education/teaching-strategies/digital-classroom-management-set-up.
Common Sense Education. (2019). *Power up your parent communication*. Retrieved from https://www.commonsense.org/education/teaching-strategies/power-up-your-parent-teacher-communication.
Cowen, R. (2015). About Mega Seating Plan. *Mega Seating Plan*. Retrieved from https://www.megaseatingplan.com/.
Daly, N. (2016). *Popsicle Sticks: Teacher picks* [Mobile app]. Retrieved from https://apps.apple.com/us/app/popsicle-sticks-teacher-picks/id1139826444.
Dodd, A., & Konzal, J. (2003). *How communities build stronger schools: Stories, strategies, and promising practice for educating every child*. Palgrave Macmillan.
Don, L., & Chaudhary, S. (2012). About. *ClassDojo*. Retrieved from https://www.classdojo.com/.
Dorsey, J. (2006). About. *Twitter*. https://about.twitter.com/en/who-we-are/our-company.
Easdown, P. (n.d.). *Classroom traffic lights* [Mobile app]. Retrieved from https://apps.apple.com/us/app/classroom-traffic-lights/id1080976061.
Encyclopaedia Britannica. (n.d.). *Microsoft PowerPoint*. Retrieved from https://www.britannica.com/technology/Microsoft-PowerPoint.
Evoprox. (2019). *Happy Kids Timer* [Mobile app]. Retrieved from https://apps.apple.com/us/app/happy-kids-timer-chores/id978996118.
Facebook (2004). About. *Facebook*. https://about.facebook.com/technologies/facebook-app/.

Faizi, R., Afia, A. E., & Chiheb, R. (2013). Exploring the potential benefits of using social media in education. *International Journal of Engineering Pedagogy, 3*(4). 50–53.

Farmer, J. (2005). Edublogs. *CampusPress*. https://campuspress.com/about/.

Feinsilber, J. (2017). Work at Gimkit. *Gimkit*. Retrieved from https://www.notion.so/Work-At-Gimkit-b16813d67dc44d1ab8ddce08e6e034d9.

Flipgrid (2012). *Flipgrid*. https://info.flipgrid.com/.

Freeman, S., Eddy, S. L., McDonough, M., Smith, M. K., Okoroafor, N., Jordt, H., & Wenderoth, M. P. (2014). Active learning increases student performance in science, engineering, and mathematics. *Proceedings of the National Academy of Sciences of the United States of America, 111*(23), 8410–15. https://doi.org/10.1073/pnas.1319030111.

Friedman, J., Hwang, R., & Trinidad, T. (2009). *Schoology, now Power School*. Retrieved from https://www.powerschool.com/company/about-us/.

Gardner, H. (2011). *Frames of mind*. Basic Books.

Gonzalez, J. (2022). The teacher's guide to tech. *Cult of Pedagogy*. https://www.cultofpedagogy.com/store/books/.

Google (2006). Slides. *Google Workspace*. https://workspace.google.com/products/slides/.

Google (2008). Sites. *Google Workspace*. https://workspace.google.com/products/sites/.

Graham, A., Lin, C., & Sjogreen, C. (2012). Seesaw founders. *Seesaw*. Retrieved from https://web.seesaw.me/about.

Gray, C. (1992). *How to write social stories*. Jenison, MI: Jenison Public Schools.

Heggert, K., & Yoo, J. (2018). Getting the most from Google Classroom: Pedagogical framework for tertiary educators. *Australian Journal of Teacher Education, 43*(3). Retrieved from http://ro.ecu.edu.au/ajte/vol43/iss3/9.

Hong, W. (2008). Exploring educational use of blogs in U.S. education. *US-China Education Review, 5*(10), 34–37.

Idea4e. (n.d.). *Too Loud noise meter & timer* [Mobile app]. Retrieved from https://apps.apple.com/us/app/too-loud-noise-meter-timer/id1101856655.

ISTE. (2016). *Refining learning in a technology-driven world: A report to support adoption of the ISTE standards for students*. Retrieved from https://id.iste.org/docs/Standards-Resources/iste-standards_students-2016_research-validity-report_final.pdf.

ISTE. (2017). *ISTE standards*. Retrieved from https://www.iste.org/standards.

ITWorx Egypt SAE. (2010). *Teacher Kit*. Retrieved from https://www.teacherkit.net/.

James, C., Weinstein, E., & Mendoza, K. (2019). *Teaching digital citizens in today's world: Research and insights behind the Common Sense K–12 Digital Citizenship Curriculum*. Common Sense Media.

Janiec, J. (2015). *Use of gamification in the IB history class and as a tool for form teacher: New empirical research and solutions.* Retrieved from https://files.classcraft.com/classcraft-assets/research/Janiec.pdf.

Kikowi Solutions. (2018). *Team Maker app* [Mobile app]. Retrieved from https://play.google.com/store/apps/details?id=com.teammaker&hl=en_US.

Kolb, L. (2017). *Learning first, technology second: The educator's guide to designing authentic lessons.* International Society for Technology in Education.

Kopf, B., & Kopf, D. (2013). Strong relationships are at the heart of student success. *Remind.* Retrieved from https://www.remind.com/about.

Kovalskys, G., Abramzon, E., & Sommers, F. (2010). *Nearpod.* Retrieved from https://nearpod.com/about.

Learnweaver Pty Ltd. (2014). Backchannel chat. *LearnWeaver.* http://learnweaver.com/BackChannel-Chat.

Licorish, S., Owen, H., Daniel, B., & George, J. L. (2018). Students' perception of Kahoot!'s influence on teaching and learning. *Research and Practice in Technology Enhanced Learning, 13*(9). https://doi.org/10.1186/s41039-018-0078-8.

Little, M., & Mullenweg, M. (2003). The history of WordPress from 2003-2022 (with Screenshots). WordPress wpbeginner. https://www.wpbeginner.com/news/the-history-of-wordpress/.

LiveSchool. (2016). *LiveSchool app* [Mobile app]. Retrieved from https://www.whyliveschool.com/.

Lonn, S., & Teasley, S. D. (2008). Saving time or innovating practice: Investigating perceptions and uses of learning management systems. *Computers & Education, 53*(3), 686–94. https://doi.org/10.1016/j.compedu.2009.04.008.

Lotkina, V. (n.d.). We're on a mission to help teachers and parents make it happen. *ClassTag.* Retrieved from https://home.classtag.com/.

Marzano, R. J. (2010). The art and science of teaching/using fames to enhance student achievement. *Educational Leadership, 67*(5), 71–72.

McDonald, B. (2016). Why did we create Parlay? The reason=more meaningful discussions. *Parlay.* https://parlayideas.com/why-did-we-create-parlay/.

McGrail, E., & Davis, A. (2011). The influence of classroom blogging on elementary writing. *Journal of Research in Childhood Education, 25*(4), 415–37. http://dx.doi.org/10.1080/02568543.2011.605205.

McGurk, B. (2014). *The impact of blogging on K–12 student learning: Engagement, self-expression, and higher-order thinking.* Graduate Research Paper submitted to University of Northern Iowa 203. https://scholarworks.uni.edu/grp/203.

McIntosh, N. (2003). Google buys Blogger web service. *The Guardian.* Retrieved from https://www.theguardian.com/business/2003/feb/18/digitalmedia.city news.

McLeod, J. K. (2009). Electronic portfolios: Perspectives of students, teachers and parents. *Education and Information Technologies, 14*(1), 29–38. doi:10.1007/s10639-008-9077-5.

Merrifield, L. (2011). Leadership team. *FreshGrade.* Retrieved from https://freshgrade.com/company/leadership/.

Mishra, P., & Koehler, M. (2006). Technological pedagogical content knowledge: A framework for teacher knowledge. *Teachers College Record, 108*(6), 1017–54.

Mustafa, H (2018). *Can gamification or game based learning via BYOD increase active engagement in learning activities for student's age 8–11 years?* A research project submitted for the Master of Arts in Learning and Teaching Programme, Department of Education University of Roehampton London.

Naeve Interactive Ltd. (2019). *Bouncy Balls.* Retrieved from https://bouncyballs.org/privacy/.

Nelson, D. (2019). *Equity Maps* [Mobile app]. Retrieved from https://equitymaps.com/equity-maps-home/about/.

Niehoff, M. (2019, October). *9 ways real students use social media for good.* Retrieved from https://www.iste.org/explore/Digital-citizenship/9-ways-real-students-use-social-media-for-good.

Nisbet, K., & Opp, A. (2017). *Effects of the Remind app on parent-teacher communication at a mixed-income middle school.* Retrieved from https://sophia.stkate.edu/maed/227.

Ostroff, W. (2020). Empowering children through dialogue and discussion. *Educational Leadership 77*(7), 14–20.

Parlay. (2018). Facilitating more inclusive engagement in K–12 class discussions (Efficacy Report). *Parlay.* https://parlayideas.com/wp-content/uploads/2018/12/Parlay-Efficacy-Report.pdf.

Pear Deck. (2020). What is active learning? *Pear Deck.* Retrieved from https://www.peardeck.com/active-learning.

Petrick, E. (2011). *Bulb digital portfolios* [Mobile app]. Retrieved from https://www.bulbapp.com/h/newsroom/.

Plump, C.M. & LaRosa, J. (2017). Using Kahoot! in the classroom to create engagement and active learning: A game-based technology solution for elearning novices. *Management Teaching Review, 2*(2). Doi: 10.1177/23792981/6689783.

Puentedura, R. (2006). *Transformation, technology, and education* [Blog post]. Retrieved from http://hippasus.com/resources/tte/.

Quinn, J. (2011). *Smart Seat app* [Mobile app]. Retrieved from http://www.cornsoftapps.com/smartseat/.

Quizizz. (2015). About. *Quizizz.* https://quizizz.com/about.

Rhine-o-Enterprises LLC. (2016). *Team Shake app* [Mobile app]. Retrieved from https://www.rhine-o.com/www/iphone-apps/press-releases/.

Riden, B. S. (2019). Creating positive classroom environments with electronic behavior management programs. *Journal of Special Education Technology, 34*(2), 133–41. doi:10.1177/0162643418801815.

SchoolMint (2018). Our story. *SchoolMint.* https://schoolmint.com/our-story/.

Shaw, C. M. (2017). Using Facebook as an educational resource in the classroom. *Oxford Research Studies Encyclopedia, International Studies*. DOI:10.1093/acrefore/9780190846626.013.114.

Showalter, A., Sweeney, D., Eynon-Lynch, M., & Eynon-Lynch, R. (2014). *Pear Deck*. Retrieved from https://www.crunchbase.com/organization/pear-deck#section-overview.

Simkovskyi, S. (n.d.). *Best Sand Timer* [Mobile app]. Retrieved from https://apps.apple.com/us/app/best-sand-timer/id501940934.

Singer, N. (2017, May 13). How Google took over the classroom. *New York Times*. Retrieved from https://www.nytimes.com/2017/05/13/technology/google-education-chromebooks-schools.html.

Socrative (2010). About us. *Socrative*. https://www.socrative.com/about-us/.

Strikingly (2012). Strikingly. https://www.strikingly.com/.

Sutherland, A. (2005). About. *Quizlet*. Retrieved from https://quizlet.com/mission.

Systrom, K., & Krieger, M. (2012). About us. *Instagram*. https://www.instagram.com/about/us/.

VandenBos, G. R. (Ed.). (2007). *APA dictionary of psychology*. American Psychological Association.

Versvik, M., Brand, J., & Brooker, J. (2012). *Kahoot!* Retrieved from https://kahoot.com/company/.

Vydunda, J., & Gessler, B. (2010). *Poll Everywhere*. Retrieved from https://www.polleverywhere.com/about.

Walsall Academy. (n.d.). *Too Noisy app* [Mobile app]. Retrieved from https://toonoisyapp.com/.

Warstrom, J. (2014). *Mentimeter*. Retrieved from https://www.mentimeter.com/the-team.

Weebly (2007). About us. *Weebly eCommerce by Square*. https://www.weebly.com/about.

Whitmer, B., & Daley, D. (2008). *Instructure Canvas*. Retrieved from https://www.instructure.com/canvas/about.

Young, S., Young, D., & Young, L. (2013). About. *Classcraft*. Retrieved from https://website-production.classcraft.com/about/.

Zhao, F. (2019). Using Quizizz to integrate fun multiplayer activity in the accounting classroom. *International Journal of Higher Education, 8*(1). Doi:10.5430/ijhe.v8n1p37.

Index

Page references for figures and tables are italicized.

ABA. *See* Applied Behavior Analysis
ABC model (emotional triggers), 109
A-B-C Recording Chart, 76, 76–78, 78
abolishing operations, 84
academic behaviors, 80
academic discourse, 20
accomplishments, performance, 48
activities of daily living, 80
adolescence, emotional development during, 104–5
advance notice, 11, 12
allies, 137
Alter, P. J., 25, 55
American Psychological Association, 138
American School Counselor Association, 50, 100
Anderson, C. M., 55
announcement tools, 160–61, 162–63
antecedents, 75, 76, 76–78, 78, 80
anxiety, 118–19
Applied Behavior Analysis (ABA): behavior, as term, 74–75; behavior, defining, 81, 81; behavior, functions of, 75; behavior,
identifying, 80, 80; classroom management, dos and don'ts, 95; classroom management, impact on, 71–72; data analysis, 82–83; data collection steps, 80–85; data collection strategies, 76, 76–78, 78; data collection types, 79, 79; described, 72–76; functional behavior assessments, 76, 95; interventions, exploring, 83–85, 84, 85; misconceptions about, 71–72; strategies for classroom, 85–94, 86, 88, 90
Ares, A., 169
asexual, defined, 139
attending behavior, 81
attention-seeking behavior, 54, 75
Australian students, 48–49
authors, diverse, 147
Axelrod, S., 72

Backchannel Chat, 167, 168
backup reinforcers, 93
Bandura, Albert, 47–48
Barry, C. T., 56
basic emotions, 102

behavior: academic, *80*; attending, *81*; attention-seeking, 54, 75; defining in Applied Behavior Analysis, 81, *81*; disruptive, *81*; emotional, *80*; emotions, response to, 102; escape, 54, 75; functions of, 54–55, 75; identifying, 80, *80*; monitoring, 27–28; praise specific to, 88–89; recording, *76*, 76–78, *78*; replacement, 73, 89–90, *90*; social, *80*; tantrum "meltdown," *81*, 105; target, 74; as term, 74–75
behavioral support domains, 72
bereavement, 116–17
Best Sand Timer, *156*, 158
bias, 126–27. *See also* gender
Bielefeld, K., 65
biological sex, 137–38
bisexual, defined, *137*
Black females, 121, 136, 139, 144–45
Black males, 136, 144
Black students, 114, 136, 142, 144–45
Black teachers, 39–40
Blöemeke, Sigrid, 3
Blogger, *161*, 164
blogs, *161*, 163–64
Bloh, C., 72
Bloomz, *160*, 163
Bockenholt, U., 56
body image, 120–22; movies and, 120; music and, 120
Bouncy Balls, *155*, 157
breathing techniques, *60*, 61
Bronfenbrenner's Ecological Systems Model, 111–12
Brown, Brené, 110
Bulb, *161*, 163
Buncee, *166*
burnout, 127, 129–30

calling out, reducing, 73
Cangelosi, J. S., 21
Canvas, *171*

Castaneda, F. J., 163
Cetin, H., 56
Cetin, I., 56
chronosystem, 112
Chung, H., 50
cisgender, defined, *137*, 139, 141
cisnormative, defined, *137*
Classcraft, *157*, 160, 169
class differences, 37
ClassDojo, 56, *57*, 64, *65*, *157*, 159, *161*, 162
Classroom Circles (activity), *53*
classroom environment: inclusive, 146; name/team selection tools, *156*, 158–59; noise monitoring tools, *155*, 157; positive, 51–52, 145–47, *148*, 149, 155; reward systems tools, *157*, 159–60; safe, *60*, 62; seating arrangement tools, *156*, 159; technology, *155*–57, 157–60; timing tools, *156*, 158; transition tools, *156*, 158
classroom layout, 83
classroom management: Applied Behavior Analysis, impact of, 71–72; dos and don'ts, *95*; technology, 154–55
Classroom Q, *167*, 169
Classroom Traffic Light, *156*, 158
ClassTag, *161*, 162
class-wide token economy, 93
classwork, 17–18
collaboration skills, 20
collective efficacy, 50
Collins, P. H., 139
Common Sense Education, 160, 171–72
communication: empathic, 110; functional communication training, 94; picture exchange, 94; positivity, promoting, 147; skills, 20; student–teacher, 108–10; trauma-responsive, 108–9

conditioning, 72
consequences: extrinsic, 31–33, 34; intrinsic, 34, 35; manipulations, *80*; natural, 33–34, 35; negative, 34, 35; recording, *76,* 76–78, *78*; variables, 75
consistency, 90–91
constructive stage (moral development), 33–34, 35
Consuegra, E., 37
Cooper, J., 73, 77
cooperative stage (moral development), 33–34, 35
co-regulation, 59
Cornell Research Program on Self-Injury and Recovery, 107
counselors, school, 100
COVID-19 pandemic, 129
Cross the Line (activity), *53*
culturally responsive pedagogy, 38–40
culture: about, 110–11; Bronfenbrenner's Ecological Systems Model, 111–12; defined, 111; emotions and, 110–14; power, privilege, and oppression within, 112–13; school-to-prison pipeline, 114
cyberbullying, 119–20

daily living activities, *80*
dangles, 12–13
data in Applied Behavior Analysis: A-B-C Recording Chart, *76,* 76–78, *78*; behavior, defining, 81, *81*; behavior, identifying, 80, *80*; data, analyzing, 82–83; interventions, exploring, 83–85, *84, 85*; types, 79
de-escalation strategies, 59, *60,* 61–62
deficit mindset, 147
depression, 115–16
Desautels, L., 59

Diagnostic and Statistical Manual, 5th edition *(DSM-5),* 107, 121, 122–23
differential reinforcement, 90
digital citizenship skills, 172
Dillon, M. B. M., 56
direct instruction, 18–19
discipline, 36, 49, 142, 144
discrimination, 126–27. *See also* gender
discussions: as potentially disruptive situation, 19–20; tools for, *166–67, 168–69*
disordered eating, 121, 122
disruptive behaviors, *81*
disruptive situations, potentially: classwork and, 17–18; direct instruction and, 18–19; examples, 9; group work/discussions and, 19–20; during instructional approaches, 16–20; permission, obtaining, 14–16; start-ups, 10; timing, 11; transitions, 10, 12–14, *14*
distress tolerance, 106, 110
Djigic, G., 30
Doing-What-You-Are-Told, 65, *65*
doorbells, wireless, *156,* 158
DSM-5. See Diagnostic and Statistical Manual, 5th edition *(DSM-5)*
duration data, 79

early childhood, emotional development in, 104
eating disorders, 121–22
EATS (escape, attention, tangible gains, and sensory needs), 54, 75
Eberhardt, J. A., 39
Ecological Systems Model, 111–12
Edmodo, *171*
EdPuzzle, *166,* 168
EduBlogs, *161,* 164
Elias, M., 50
Ellis, Albert, 109
Emmer, E. T., 22, 24
emotional behaviors, *80*

emotional catharsis, 127–28
emotional development, 104–5
emotional intelligence, 106
emotional regulation, 106
Emotional Thermometer, 63, *63*
emotions: about, 99–100; anxiety, 118–19; awareness of, 60, 61; basic, 102; body image and, 120–22; classroom and, 105–6; COVID-19 pandemic and, 129; culture and, 110–14; emotional catharsis, 127–28; emotional development, 104–5; fear, 118; helping professionals and, 100–101; identifying, 63, *63,* 106, 109; loss, grief, and bereavement, 116–17; managing, 106–8; manifestation of, 101–2; minimizing, 109–10, 116; needs, 125–27; negative, 109–10; normalizing, 129; onset of, 102–4; positive, promoting, 60, 62; sadness and depression, 114–16; self-care and, 127–28, 129–30; self-efficacy and, 48; social media and, 119–21; state, 102–3; student identity and, 110–14; students, talking to about, 128; student–teacher communication and, 108–10; substance use and, 122–25; trait, 103; triggers, 109, 128
empathic communication, 110
Engels, N., 36, 37
environmental adjustments, 82–83
Equity Maps, *167,* 168–69
escape behaviors, 54, 75
establishing operations, 84
ethnic differences, 36
Evans, E. D., 50
Evertson, C. M., 22, 24
exosystem, 112
expectations, teacher, 147
experience, vicarious, 48
expert teachers, 3

extrinsic consequences stage (moral development), 31–33, 34

Facebook, *162,* 165
fear, 118
feedback, 60, 147
feelings. *See* emotions
Find Someone Like You (activity), *53*
Fisher, D., 51, 53, 58
flip-flops, 13
Flipgrid, *166,* 168
fragmentations, 13–14
Freeman, S., 165–66, 168
frequency data, 79
FreshGrade, *161,* 163
Frey, N., 51, 53, 58
friend-in-need system, 61
Froyen, L., 13
functional behavior assessments, 76, 95
functional communication training, 94

games, *167,* 169–70
Gardner, H., 165
gay, defined, *137*
Gay, G., 38
gender: bias and stereotyping in schools, 142–45; defined, *137*; discipline and, 36; positivity, promoting, 145–47, *148,* 149; race and, 136, 139, 142, 144–45; sex versus, 137–38; as social construct, 137–39; stereotyping by, 140–42; teacher–student interactions and, 36–37; terminology, *137*
gender expression, *137,* 140–41
gender fluid individuals, *137,* 138, 146
gender identity, *137,* 140
gender non-conforming individuals, *137,* 138
gender typing, *137,* 138, 140
gestural prompts, 86
Gimkit, *167,* 168

Glickman, C. D., 28–29
Gonzalez, Jennifer, 172
Google Classroom, 170–71, *171*
Google Sites, *161,* 164
Gray, Carol, 93, 94
The Great Behavior Game, *57*
greetings, 51–52, *52*
grief, 116–17
group work, 19–20

hair, 121
Hancock, D. R., 29
handshakes, 52
Happy Kids Timer, *156,* 158
Haydon, T., 25, 55
Heath, S. B., 37
Heggert, K., 171
helping professionals, 100–101
HeroK12, *157,* 159
Heron, T. E., 73, 77
heteronormativity, *137,* 139
heterosexual, defined, 139, 141
Heward, W. L., 73, 77
hierarchy of needs, 125–27
high-probability requests, 91–92
Hilton, D. J., 56
home–school connection: about, 160; messaging tools, *160–61,* 162–63; portfolios, *161,* 163; social media, *162,* 164–65; websites and blogs, *161,* 163–64
homosexual, defined, 139
Howe, C., 37

ideas, diverse, 146–47
inclusive classroom environment, 146
Instagram, 120–21, *162,* 164–65
instruction, direct, 18–19
instructional tools, student–centered: discussions, *166–67,* 168–69; games, *167,* 169–70; interactive presentations, *166,* 167–68
intentionally inviting teachers, 49, *49*

intentionally uninviting teachers, 49, *49*
interactionist teachers, 29–30
interactive modeling, 25
interactive presentations, *166,* 167–68
interest, boosting, 11
International Society for Technology in Education (ISTE), 153–54
interval recording data sheets, 79, *79*
intervention: in Applied Behavior Analysis, 83–85, *84, 85*; co-regulation, 59; deciding about, 54–56, *57*; de-escalation strategies, 59, *60,* 61–62; self-calming skills, *63, 63*–64; teacher types and, 28–31; techniques, 59–66; technology for, 64–66, *65*; timing of, 58
interventionist teachers, 29, 30–31
intrinsic consequences stage (moral development), 34, 35
ISTE. *See* International Society for Technology in Education (ISTE)

Jones, L., 25
Jones, V., 25

Kahoot!, *167,* 169
Kerr, M. M., 55
KidBlog, *161,* 164
Kilgore, K. K., 39
Kohlberg, L., 31
Kohn, Alfie, 2
Kounin, J., 12

Ladson-Billings, Gloria, 38
LaRosa, J., 169
Latinx teachers, 39–40
Learning Management Systems (LMS), 170–71, *171*
lesbians, defined, *137*
Lewis, R., 48–49
lights, volume, *155,* 157
Live School, *157,* 159

loss, 116–17

macrosystem, 112
Marzano, R. J., 23
Maslow's hierarchy of needs. *See* hierarchy of needs
McCray, A. D., 39
media, 120–21, 140, 141–42
medications, psychotropic, 124–25
Mega Seating Plan, *156,* 159
"meltdowns," *81,* 105
mental illness, 107–8
Mentimeter, *166,* 168
mesosystem, 111
messaging tools, *160–61,* 162–63
microsystem, 111
middle childhood, emotional development in, 104
Mildner, C., 50
Minahan, J., 63
mindsets, 49, 147
modeling: emotions, managing, 106–7; interactive, 25; as prompt, *86*; as self-efficacy source, 48; self-regulation, *60,* 62
monitoring behavior, 27–28
Montgomery, G. P., 50
moral development: adapting to students', 34–36; extrinsic consequences stage, 31–33, 34; intrinsic consequences stage, 34, 35; natural consequences stage, 33–34, 35
moral realism stage (moral development), 31–33, 34

name selection technology, *156,* 158–59
National Center for Education Statistics, 142
natural consequences stage (moral development), 33–34, 35
Neal, L. I., 39

Nearpod, *166,* 166
needs: attention, 54, 75; escape, 54, 75; hierarchy of, 125–27; meeting, *60, 62*; physiological, 125–26; psychological, 125–26; safety, 125; sensory, 54, 75; tangible gains, 54, 75; trust and, *60, 62*
negative consequences, 34, 35
negative emotions, 109–10
Nelson, C. M., 55
Niehoff, M., 164
Nisbet, K., 162–63
noise monitoring technology, *155,* 157
nonbinary individuals, *137,* 138
nonconforming individuals, *137,* 138
noninterventionist teachers, 29, 30
nonsuicidal self-injury, 107
novice teachers, 3

Okonofua, J. A., 39, 49
on-task, staying, 64–65, *65*
operations, abolishing *versus* establishing, 84
Opp, A., 162–63
oppression, 112–13

Parlay, *166,* 168, 169
Paunesku, D., 49
Pavlov, Ivan, 72
Pear Deck, *166,* 167, 168
peers, 65, *65,* 107
performance accomplishments, 48
permission, obtaining, 14–16
persuasion, social, 48
physical prompts, *86*
physiological needs, 125–26
physiological reactions to emotions, 101–2
physiological states, 48
Piaget, J., 31
picture exchange communication, 94
Plump, C. M., 169
Poll Everywhere, *166,* 168

Popsicle Sticks app, *156,* 158
portfolios, *161,* 163
positive classroom environment, 51–52, 145–47, *148,* 149, 155
positive emotions, *60,* 62
positive feedback, *60*
positive regard, 110
positive reinforcement, 84, *84*
power, 112–13
practice, 25–26, 61–62, 64
praise, behavior-specific, 88–89
preschoolers, moral development of, 32
presentations, interactive, *166,* 167–68
primary-grade children, moral development of, 33
privacy concerns, 120
privilege, 112–13
proactive strategies: application activities, 40–41; class differences, 37; Culturally Responsive Pedagogy, 38–40; intervening with and without consequences, 28–31; monitoring behavior, 27–28; moral development, 31–36; potentially disruptive situations, 10–16, *14;* potentially disruptive situations during instructional approaches, 16–20; racial, ethnic, gender, and class differences, 36–37; rules, 21–27
procedures, 16, 55
prompting, 86, *86*
pronoun use, 146
psychological needs, 125–26
psychological responses to emotions, 102
psychologists, school, 100–101
psychotropic medications, 124–25
punishment, 34, 35, 85, *85*
Purkey, W. W., 49, *49*

queer, defined, *137*
question-and-answer periods, 19

Quizizz, *167,* 168–69
Quizlet, *167,* 168

race: gender and, 136, 139, 142, 144–45; proactive strategies, 36; stereotyping, 141–42
Radley, K. C., 56
Rappaport, N., 63
reciprocal stage (moral development), 33–34, 35
reflection, *60,* 62
reflexivity, 145–46
refocusing, *60,* 62
regard, positive, 110
reinforcement: backup, 93; defined, 84; differential, 90; positive, 84, *84;* punishment *versus,* 85, *85*
relationship-building activities, 52, *53*
Remind, *160,* 162–63
replacement behaviors, 73, 89–90, *90*
requests, high-probability, 91–92
respect for teachers, 49
restorative justice, 51, 58
reward systems, *157,* 159–60
Ritter, J. T., 29
Roche, J., 48–49
Romi, S., 48–49
routines, automatic, 12
rules: effective, 22; enforcing, 27; establishing, responsibility for, 23–24; establishing, timing of, 24–25; intervention and, 55; necessary, 21–22; number of, 23; observable, 22–23; positively stated, 23; purpose of, 21; reasonable, 22–23; schoolwide, 24, 26–27; teaching, 25–26

sadness and depression, 114–16
safe classroom environment, *60,* 62
safety needs, 125
SAMR model, 154
school counselors, 100
Schoology/PowerSchool, *171*

school psychologists, 100–101
School Social Work Association of America, 100
school social workers, 100
school-to-prison pipeline, 114
schoolwide rules, 24, 26–27
Scott, T. M., 55
seating, 82, 83, *156*, 159
security concerns, 120
Seesaw, *161*, 163, *171*
self-calming skills, *63*, 63–64
self-care, 127–28, 129–30
self-efficacy: about, 47–48; collective efficacy, 50; defined, 47; sources of, 48; student, 50; teacher, 48–49, *49*
self-injury, nonsuicidal, 107
self-monitoring, 55–56, *57*
self-regulation, *60*, 62
sensory needs, 54, 75
sensory stimulation, 83
Serbian teachers, 29–30
Sesame, *161*
sexual orientation terms, *137*, 139
sex *versus* gender, 137–38
Shaw, C. M., 165
Shin, R. Q., 50
Silent Interview (activity), *53*
Sindelar, P. T., 39
Smart Seat, *156*, 159
Smith, D., 51, 53, 58
social behaviors, *80*
social class, 37
social media, 119–21, *162*, 164–65
social persuasion, 48
social self-efficacy, 50
Social Stories, 93–94
social workers, school, 100
socioeconomic status, 37
Socrative, *166*, 168
Speight, S. L., 50
Stahnke, Rebekka, 3
Stainback, S., 13
Stainback, W., 13

Stanley, P. H., 49, *49*
start-ups, 10
state emotions, 102–3
Stereotype Content Model, 141
stereotype threat, 143–44
stereotyping: gendered, 140–45; race, 141–42
stimulus, adding/removing, 85, *85*
Stojiljkovic, S., 30
Stop Go!, *57*
Strikingly, *161*, 164
Struyven, K., 37
student-centered learning: about, 165–66; discussion tools, *166–67*, 168–69; games, *167*, 169–70; interactive presentation tools, *166*, 167–68
student identity: about, 110–11; Bronfenbrenner's Ecological Systems Model, 111–12; culture, defined, 111; power, privilege, and oppression within culture, 112–13; school-to-prison pipeline, 114
students: attention, gaining, 19–20; Australian, 48–49; Black, 114, 136, 142, 144–45; emotions, talking to about, 128; getting to know, 146; participation by, 19; peers and, 65, *65*, 107; rules, establishing, 23; self-efficacy, 50; teachers, communication with, 108–10; teachers, interactions with, 36–37; teachers, relationship with, 51; teachers, respect for, 49
study skills, *80*
Substance Abuse and Mental Health Services Administration, 123
substance use, 122–25
suicide, 107
suspension, 142, 144

tangible gains, behavior for acquiring, 54, 75
tantrums, *81*, 105

target behavior, 74
Teacher Kit, *156*, 159
teachers: Black, 39–40; expectations, 147; expert, 3; intentionally inviting, 49, *49*; intentionally uninviting, 49, *49*; interactionist, 29–30; interventionist, 29, 30–31; Latinx, 39–40; non-interventionist, 29, 30; novice, 3; rules, establishing, 23–24; self-care, 127–28, 129–30; self-efficacy, 48–49, *49*; Serbian, 29–30; stresses on, 53–54; students, communication with, 108–10; students, interactions with, 36–37; students, relationship with, 51; students' respect for, 49; unintentionally inviting, 49, *49*; unintentionally uninviting, 49, *49*
Teacher's Assistant, 57
The Teacher's Guide to Tech (Gonzalez), 172
Teaching Tolerance, 54
Team Maker, *156*, 158–59
team selection technology, *156*, 158–59
Team Shake, *156*, 158–59
technology: classroom environment, *155–57*, 157–60; classroom management, 154–55; discussions, *166–67*, 168–69; for elementary *versus* secondary students, 154–55; games, *167*, 169–70; home–school connection, 160, *160–62*, 162–65; interactive presentations, *166*, 167–68; Learning Management Systems, 170–71, *171*; messaging, *160–61*, 162–63; name/team selection, *156*, 158–59; noise monitoring, *155*, 157; on-task, staying, 64–65, *65*; peer interaction, positive, 65, *65*; portfolios, *161*, 163; positive student behavior, promoting, 64–66, *65*; reward systems, *157*, 159–60; seating arrangements, *156*, 159; social media, *162*, 164–65; standards-based approach to, 153–54; student–centered instructional tools, 165–66, *166–67*, 167–70; theoretical frameworks, 154; timing, *156*, 158; transitions, *156*, 158; websites and blogs, *161*, 163–64; work completion, 65, *65*
television shows, 140, 141–42
temper tantrums, *81*, 105
thoughts: awareness of, *60*, 61; positive, *60*, 62; redirecting, *60*, 62
thrusts, 12
time out, 29
timers, 11, *65*, *156*, 158
timing, 11, 90–91, *156*, 158
Tingstrom, D. H., 56
toddlers, moral development of, 32
token economies, 92–93
Too Loud, *155*, 157
Too Noisy, 57, *155*, 157
TPACK model, 154
traffic pattern, 12–13
trait emotions, 103
transgender, defined, *137*, 138–39
transitions: dangles, 12–13; flip-flops, 13; fragmentations, 13–14; management techniques, effective *versus* ineffective, *14*; mistakes, 12–14; as potentially disruptive situations, 10; preparation for, 87, *88*; technology for, *156*, 158; thrusts, 12
trauma-responsive communication, 108–9
Tribble, M., 50
triggers, emotional, 109, 128
Triple E framework, 154
trust, *60*, 62
Twitter, *162*, 164

unintentionally inviting teachers, 49, *49*
unintentionally uninviting teachers, 49, *49*

validation, 61
Vera, E. M., 50
verbal preparation strategies, 87
verbal prompts, *86*
vicarious experience, 48
video, 65, *65*
visual preparation strategies, 87, *88*
visual prompts, *86*
visual stimulation, 83
Vollrath, D., 58, 61–62
volume lights, *155*, 157

Wallace, B., 56
Walton, G. M., 49
Weber, E. U., 56
websites, *161*, 163–64
Weebly, *161*, 164
Whitaker, K., 24
Whitaker, T., 24
Who could it be? (activity), *53*
wireless doorbells, *156*, 158
Wolfgang, C. H., 28–29
WordPress, 164
work completion, 65, *65*

Yoo, J., 171
YouTube timer, *156*

Zhao, F., 170

About the Authors

Joanna Alcruz, PhD, is associate professor in the School of Education and Human Services at Molloy University and teaches in the Educational Leadership Doctoral Program for Diverse Communities. Her educational background includes educational psychology from Fordham University, and measurement and evaluation from New York University. Dr. Alcruz's expertise is in cognition and learning, quantitative research, assessment, and research methods. Prior to becoming a faculty member, she served as an accreditation coordinator for the School of Education at Molloy University. Her research focus is on self-regulated learning, motivation, academic procrastination, and divergent thinking. She has presented her studies at local and national educational conferences and teacher professional development sessions, offered workshops and webinars on how to navigate learning, and written several professional publications. She is a co-founder and co-director of the Cognition and Learning Lab at Molloy University.

Maggie Blair, MA, received her degree in special education from New York University and a professional diploma in district administration. She has spent almost fifty years in the field of special education, serving as a teacher, a staff developer, and an administrator in New York City and then as the district administrator in several school districts on Long Island. During her tenure in school districts, Maggie developed and initiated successful co-teaching models, which supported classified students as they returned to general education settings. Her models were replicated by several districts. She joined the faculty at Molloy University in a newly established master's program in special education in 2003 and served there until 2020. Prior to her retirement and following her life-long goal to ensure that all students have the opportunity to access rich educational experiences, Maggie and a small group of passionate colleagues successfully designed, developed, and initiated an academic-based, employment-bound, and fully immersive college experience transition program, The MOST Program (Molloy Opportunity for Successful Transition) on the campus of Molloy University in September 2019.

Donna Cempa-Danziger, MS, EdD, is assistant professor of anatomy and physiology at Nassau Community College. She has taught pre-healthcare courses at the college level for the last eighteen years. She completed master's degrees in biology as well as in secondary education and is currently completing her doctoral studies in the Educational Leadership for Diverse Learning Communities EdD program at Molloy University in Rockville Centre, New York. Her dissertation study focuses on female instructors of STEM in higher education. She has offered professional development presentations on the topic of gender, women, and higher education. She is currently a member of Nassau Community College Federation of Teachers Diversity Committee, which works towards promoting equity on the college campus.

Audra Cerruto, PhD, is associate dean and director of Graduate Education Programs in the School of Education and Human Services at Molloy University in Rockville Centre, New York. She began her career as a school psychologist with a specialization in deaf education. After spending much time in the classroom applying information gleaned from psychoeducational assessment tools with teachers, she pursued a special education teaching certificate. While Audra enjoys teaching both undergraduate and graduate education courses, her passion lies in creating authentic teaching and learning experiences for teachers-in-training. Along with her colleagues at Molloy University, she has co-developed tutoring and enrichment programs for local communities. These programs utilize authentic children's literature with social-emotional themes to address academic, social-emotional, and higher-order thinking skills. The enrichment programs provide opportunities for mentorship with teacher candidates and faculty while providing a valued academic and social-emotional experience for students in the community. Her professional interests include critical issues in special education, social-emotional learning, development of partnerships with school districts and communities, and advocacy for diverse learners.

Madeline Craig, EdD, is associate professor and the dual degree coordinator in the School of Education and Human Services at Molloy University in New York. She has taught all levels of learners including adults, undergraduate and graduate students, as well as elementary and secondary students during her twenty-five years working in the field of learning and development. She frequently presents at conferences on the use of technology as a sound pedagogical tool and has made numerous contributions to the field by serving as conference chair, advisory board member, presenter, and author. Her work also involves the mentoring of both faculty and teacher candidates on the integration of technology into curricula. Madeline's research interests include the use of technology to improve students' learning and writing, strategies for student engagement including project-based learning, and techniques to enhance the online classroom. Madeline lives in Floral Park, New York, with her husband, three children, and two dachshunds.

Candice R. Crawford, PhD, is assistant professor in the Clinical Mental Health Counseling Program at Molloy University. Dr. Crawford is also a licensed mental health counselor (LMHC) in the state of New York and has worked in various capacities as a bilingual counselor working with children, adolescents, and their families. Also, she has served as a clinical supervisor and program director in outpatient substance abuse facilities. Currently, she owns a private practice in the Bronx where she works with women of color who have endured trauma. Her research interests include multicultural competence in counseling and supervision, cross-racial supervision, and social justice advocacy. She is involved in numerous research projects and has presented research findings at regional and national conferences. She has mentored students exploring the relationship between self-esteem and bilingualism. Additionally, she is active in numerous counseling associations including the counseling honor society, Chi Sigma Iota (CSI), where she was elected chapter president at Montclair State and was also chosen as one of CSI's international leadership fellows. Recently, she was elected secretary-elect for the North Atlantic Region Association for Counselor Education and Supervision (NARACES). Lastly, she is involved in several school and college-wide committees at Molloy University that promote interdisciplinary learning and collaboration, as well as promoting mentoring for faculty.

Sarah Farsijany, MS, is adjunct instructor in the School of Education and Human Services at Molloy University in Rockville Centre, New

York. She has been in the field of education for the past decade, working with students with developmental disabilities from elementary education through post-secondary education throughout her career. Upon obtaining her master of science in general and special education with a focus in autism, she has continued her research and works one-to-one with students using ABA therapy to address problem behaviors and increase productivity. Currently, she is co-teaching an inclusive postsecondary program at Molloy University and is pursuing her doctorate in interdisciplinary educational studies, with her research focusing on conditions that affect a positive co-teaching model using a grounded theory approach.

David Julius Ford, Jr., PhD, holds a BA in psychology and an MA in clinical mental health counseling, both from Wake Forest University. In May 2014, he earned his PhD in counselor education and supervision at Old Dominion University. Dr. Ford is a licensed clinical mental health counselor (LCMHC) in North Carolina and a licensed professional counselor (LPC) in Virginia and New Jersey. He is a national certified counselor (NCC) and approved clinical supervisor (ACS). His background includes five years' experience in residence life where he provided career and academic planning for his residents. As a PhD student, he provided career and academic planning for undergraduate human services majors. He has taught career counseling at two universities, face-to-face and online. Dr. Ford taught four years at James Madison University and is now in his third year as an assistant professor in the Department of Professional Counseling at Monmouth University. Dr. Ford's professional interests are Black Greek life, multicultural issues, college students, African American men in higher education, career counseling, addictions counseling, supervision, group work, qualitative research, queer persons of color, and persons living with HIV/AIDS. Dr. Ford is the president of the New Jersey Counseling Association. He is a 2013 recipient of the NBCC Doctoral Minority Fellowship, the 2020 recipient of the Samuel H. Johnson AMCD Distinguished Service Award, and the 2020 ACES Outstanding Counselor Education and Supervision Article Award.

Vicky Giouroukakis, EdD, is professor of education in the School of Education and Human Services at Molloy University in Rockville Centre, New York, where she teaches undergraduate and graduate courses in methods of teaching, in general, as well as in the areas of English, literacy, and TESOL. She started her career teaching English at a public high school in Queens, New York, and English as a second language to adolescents and adults. Vicky has co-authored four books on best practices, one of which became a best seller. Her passion lies in the areas of teacher education, curriculum and instruction, and cultural/linguistic diversity. Her work has been featured in numerous books and scholarly journals, and she frequently presents at regional, national, and international conferences. Vicky was the recipient of the Educator of Excellence Award by the New York State English Council as well as the Research Achievement Award and Distinguished Medal of Service by Molloy University. She lives in Manhasset, New York, with her husband and three children.

Linda Kraemer, EdD, is associate dean and director of Undergraduate Education Programs at Molloy University in Rockville Centre, New York. She began her career in elementary education in New York City public and private schools with a specialization in literacy instruction. Linda enjoys teaching both undergraduate and graduate education courses, but her passion lies in the mentoring of students and faculty. Her professional interests include instructional technology, online teaching, lifelong literacy habits, and critical issues in education.

Tricia M. Kress, PhD, is professor in the Educational Leadership for Diverse Learning Communities EdD program at Molloy University in Rockville Centre, New York. Her research uses critical pedagogy, cultural sociology, and auto/ethnography to rethink teaching, learning, and research in urban schools in the United States. She is co-editor of the book series *Imagination and Praxis: Criticality and Creativity in Education and Educational Research* and *Transformative Imaginings*. She has published in numerous academic journals and is the author or editor of several books including *Critical Praxis Research: Breathing New Life into Research Methods for Teachers* and *Paulo Freire's Intellectual Roots: Toward Historicity in Praxis* (edited with Robert Lake), which received the Society of Professors of Education 2014 Book Award.

Tyce Nadrich, PhD, is assistant professor of clinical mental health counseling at Molloy University. He is a licensed mental health counselor in the state of New York, board-certified counselor (NCC), and approved clinical supervisor (ACS). His research interests include the experiences of and mental health considerations for racially ambiguous people of color, the experiences of people of color in academia, and the intersection of mental health and infertility. He also operates a private practice where he provides counseling services to predominantly adolescents and adults of color. He earned a PhD in counseling from Montclair State University and a MSEd in clinical mental health counseling from St. John's University.

Rickey Moroney, MS, is adjunct instructor in the School of Education and Human Services in Rockville Centre, New York. She has worked at Molloy University since 2002 and has collaborated on many projects, working with colleagues to develop a tutoring program for students with special needs which has successfully integrated technology and social-emotional learning to help students succeed academically in school and beyond. Rickey currently co-teaches a course for teacher candidates incorporating supervised, hands-on experience based on social-emotional learning along with children's literature, enriching elementary students in a local school district, which has become a model for clinical practice in the field. Her specialty is in teaching courses which integrate technology into education for graduate students. Rickey has worked for over thirty years in Catholic education as an art teacher, computer teacher, and the technology coordinator at St. Agnes Cathedral School in Rockville Centre. She continues to collaborate with administrators, students, staff, and faculty members to integrate technology into courses for students with special needs and young learners in the School of Education and Human Services. Rickey is also a faculty mentor for remote learning at Molloy University.

Kathleen Quinn is adjunct instructor in the School of Education and Human Services at Molloy University in Rockville Centre, New York. She is a board-certified behavior analyst (BCBA) and NYS licensed behavior analyst (LBA). She provides technical assistance and training to families, adult service agencies, and school districts, as they include individuals with developmental disabilities within their communities. She has developed post-secondary educational programs for individuals with developmental disabilities. Kathleen is currently completing her doctoral studies in the Educational Leadership for Diverse Learning Communities EdD Program at Molloy University in Rockville Centre, New York. Her dissertation research focus includes expanding the practice of inclusion from early intervention through adulthood. As the founder of a not-for-profit foundation, she presents best practices and research-based evidence on applied behavior analysis with the focus on inclusion.

Heather C. Robertson, PhD, is associate professor of counselor education at St. John's University. She is the program coordinator for the Clinical Mental Health Counseling Program in the School of Education.

She is a licensed professional counselor (LPC, CT), licensed mental health counselor (LMHC, NY), nationally certified counselor (NCC), certified rehabilitation counselor (CRC), credentialed alcoholism and substance abuse counselor (CASAC, NY), approved clinical supervisor (ACS), global career development facilitator (GCDF), and board-certified telemental health provider (BC-TMH). Her research and advocacy efforts include substance abuse, military and veterans, career transition, telemental health counseling/training/supervision, and reducing the stigma of mental illness and addiction. She earned a PhD in counselor education and supervision from Virginia Tech, and an MS in counseling and guidance from Texas A & M University at Corpus Christi. Dr. Robertson served as the past-president of the American Counseling Association of New York (ACA-NY) and of the New York State Career Development Association.

Jill Snyder, MSEd, BCBA, LBA, has taught special education at the Manhasset Union Free School District on Long Island, New York, for seven years and, prior to that, worked in a private school for children with autism. She received her undergraduate degree in education from Long Island University, postmaster's of elementary education from Molloy University, and an advanced degree in applied behavior analysis from Hofstra University.

Matina Barbara Stergiopoulos, EdD, began her teaching career in a New York City Department of Education Title I high school in 2005. She holds an EdD in entrepreneurial leadership in education from the Johns Hopkins University, an MEd in secondary education curriculum and instruction from The George Washington University, a postmaster's certificate in educational leadership from SUNY Stony Brook, and a BA in English from Fordham University. Matina has served in various capacities as an educator, working domestically in public, New York State schools, and internationally, at the American Community Schools of Athens, Greece. Dr. Stergiopoulos is a Big Apple Awards finalist, a Teachers of Tomorrow grant recipient, and one of the Greek America Foundation's Forty Under Forty honorees. Currently, she serves as assistant principal in the Plainview-Old Bethpage School District on Long Island. She lives in Kings Point, New York, with her husband, Dr. Sotirios G. Stergiopoulos, and two sons, Georgios and Argyrios.

Maureen T. Walsh, EdD, is dean emerita and professor who served as director of Undergraduate Education Programs from 2000–2006 and as dean of the Division of Education at Molloy University in Rockville

Centre, New York, from 2006–2018. She taught courses in second language acquisition in Molloy's TESOL Master's Program and content methodology courses in Molloy's Undergraduate Education Program. She is a member of the editorial board of the *Journal for Leadership and Instruction*, an international, peer-reviewed research journal for education professionals, whose purpose is to serve as a resource for school curriculum and planning.

Amy Weinstock is a third-year counselor-in-training at Molloy University. Amy is practicing as a clinician under a licensed mental health counselor at the Mental Health and Wellness Center at Molloy University, and under the supervision of a licensed clinical social worker with the Family and Children's Association of Long Island. Amy practices through a humanistic and existential lens and incorporates an integration of gestalt therapy and cognitive behavioral therapy techniques in her counseling space. Amy approaches counseling with a present-based focus, encouraging her clients to process their lived experiences in the here and now. Amy strives to create a safe counseling space that embraces diversity, adheres to her professional and personal ethical codes, and welcomes change.

Francine Wisnewski, EdD, holds a doctorate in education from Hofstra University, New York. She has taught various grade levels and content areas during her nearly thirty years of teaching in Catholic, public, and private schools. Drawing on her experiences teaching in the field, Francine now teaches undergraduate and graduate education courses in the School of Education and Human Services at Molloy University in Rockville Centre, New York. Francine's passion lies in teaching mathematics as well as mathematics methods courses. She enjoys teaching basic instructional strategies courses, too. She is coauthor of *Back to the Basics of Teaching: Best Practices for Diverse Learners*. Francine presents at many conferences and schools on a variety of topics including strategies for teaching mathematics and differentiation of instruction. She is the recipient of the Thomas J. Reid Excellence in Teaching Award, the G. Robert Gage Award for Excellence in Teaching, and the Molloy University Faculty Recognition Award. Francine lives in New Hyde Park, New York, with her husband and three children.

www.ingramcontent.com/pod-product-compliance
Lightning Source LLC
Chambersburg PA
CBHW022012300426
44117CB00005B/149